Dedication

To my family and those with interest in
the African intellectual heritage

About the Series

The African Humanities Series is a partnership between the African Humanities Program (AHP) of the American Council of Learned Societies and academic publishers NISC (Pty) Ltd*. The Series covers topics in African histories, languages, literatures, philosophies, politics and cultures. Submissions are solicited from Fellows of the AHP, which is administered by the American Council of Learned Societies and financially supported by the Carnegie Corporation of New York.

The purpose of the AHP is to encourage and enable the production of new knowledge by Africans in the five countries designated by the Carnegie Corporation: Ghana, Nigeria, South Africa, Tanzania, and Uganda. AHP fellowships support one year's work free from teaching and other responsibilities to allow the Fellow to complete the project proposed. Eligibility for the fellowship in the five countries is by domicile, not nationality.

Book proposals are submitted to the AHP editorial board which manages the peer review process and selects manuscripts for publication by NISC. In some cases, the AHP board will commission a manuscript mentor to undertake substantive editing and to work with the author on refining the final manuscript.

The African Humanities Series aims to publish works of the highest quality that will foreground the best research being done by emerging scholars in the five Carnegie designated countries. The rigorous selection process before the fellowship award, as well as AHP editorial vetting of manuscripts, assures attention to quality. Books in the series are intended to speak to scholars in Africa as well as in other areas of the world.

The AHP is also committed to providing a copy of each publication in the series to university libraries in Africa.

*early titles in the series was published by Unisa Press, but the publishing rights to the entire series are now vested in NISC

AHP Editorial Board Members as at January 2019

AHP Series Editors:
Professor Adigun Agbaje*, University of Ibadan, Nigeria
Professor Emeritus Fred Hendricks, Rhodes University, South Africa

Consultant:
Professor Emeritus Sandra Barnes, University of Pennsylvania, USA (Anthropology)

Board Members:
1. Professor Akosua Adomako Ampofo, Institute of African Studies, Ghana (Gender Studies & Advocacy) (Vice President, African Studies Association of Africa)
2. Professor Kofi Anyidoho, University of Ghana, Ghana (African Studies & Literature) (Director, Codesria African Humanities Institute Program)
3. Professor Ibrahim Bello-Kano, Bayero University, Nigeria (Dept of English and French Studies)
4. Professor Sati Fwatshak, University of Jos, Nigeria (Dept of History & International Studies)
5. Professor Patricia Hayes, University of the Western Cape, South Africa (African History, Gender Studies and Visuality) (SARChI Chair in Visual History and Theory)
6. Associate Professor Wilfred Lajul, College of Humanities & Social Sciences, Makerere University, Uganda (Dept of Philosophy)
7. Professor Yusufu Lawi, University of Dar-es-Salaam, Tanzania (Dept of History)
8. Professor Bertram Mapunda, University of Dar es Salaam, Tanzania (Dept of Archaeology & Heritage Studies)
9. Professor Innocent Pikirayi, University of Pretoria, South Africa (Chair & Head, Dept of Anthropology & Archaeology)
10. Professor Josephat Rugemalira, University of Dar-es-Salaam, Tanzania (Dept of Foreign Languages & Linguistics)
11. Professor Idayat Bola Udegbe, University of Ibadan, Nigeria (Dept of Psychology)

*replaced Professor Kwesi Yankah, Cental Univerity College, Ghana, co-editor from 2013–2016

Published in this series

Dominica Dipio, *Gender terrains in African cinema*, 2014
Ayo Adeduntan, *What the forest told me: Yoruba hunter, culture and narrative performance*, 2014
Sule E. Egya, *Nation, power and dissidence in third-generation Nigerian poetry in English*, 2014
Irikidzayi Manase, *White narratives: The depiction of post-2000 land invasions in Zimbabwe*, 2016
Pascah Mungwini, *Indigenous Shona Philosophy: Reconstructive insights*, 2017
Sylvia Bruinders, *Parading Respectability: The Cultural and Moral Aesthetics of the Christmas Bands Movement in the Western Cape, South Africa*, 2017
Michael Andindilile, *The Anglophone literary-linguistic continuum: English and indigenous languages in African literary discourse*, 2018
Jeremiah Arowosegbe, *Claude E Ake: the making of an organic intellectual*, 2018
Romanus Aboh, *Language and the construction of multiple identities in the Nigerian novel*, 2018
Bernard Matolino, *Consensus as Democracy in Africa*, 2018
Babajide Ololajulo, *Unshared Identity: Posthumous paternity in a contemporary Yoruba community*, 2018

Indigenous Shona Philosophy
Reconstructive Insights

PASCAH MUNGWINI

Originally published in 2017 by Unisa Press, South Africa
under ISBN: 978-1-86888-841-2

This edition published in South Africa on behalf of the African Humanities Program by NISC (Pty) Ltd, PO Box 377, Grahamstown, 6140, South Africa
www.nisc.co.za

NISC first edition, first impression 2019

Publication © African Humanities Program 2017, 2019
Text © Irikidzayi Manase 2017, 2019
All rights reserved. No part of this publication may be reproduced or transmitted in any form or by any means, electronic or mechanical, including photocopying, recording, or any information storage or retrieval system, without prior permission in writing from the publisher.

ISBN: 978-1-920033-50-7 (print)
ISBN: 978-1-920033-51-4 (PDF)
ISBN: 978-1-920033-52-1 (ePub)

Book Designer: Thea Bester-Swanepoel
Project Editor: Tshegofatso Sehlodimela
Copyeditor: Shakira Hoosain
Typesetting: Andri Steyn, Nozipho Noble

The author and the publisher have made every effort to obtain permission for and acknowledge the use of copyright material. Should an inadvertent infringement of copyright have occurred, please contact the publisher and we will rectify omissions or errors in any subsequent reprint or edition.

Contents

Acknowledgements		xi
Preface		xiii
1	**Introduction: Philosophy and its realities**	1
2	**Indigenous Shona philosophy**	8
	The quest for indigenous Shona philosophy	8
	The question of method	12
	The universal and the particular	23
	The African intellectual heritage	27
	Questioning the scriptocentric fallacy	33
	Proverbs and Shona philosophy	38
3	**Who are the Shona?**	48
	Concerning the Shona past	48
	Who are the Shona?	50
	The politics of naming	56
	The 'invention' of tradition	59

Contents

4	**Indigenous Shona metaphysical thought**	**68**
	The question of metaphysics	68
	The question of appropriation	74
	The concept of Mwari	78
	Spirits and traditional leadership	82
	The concept of *chivanhu*	86
	Causality among the Shona	91
	Causality in Shona life: An example	93
	Death and immortality	95
	The concept of person	95
	Death and cremation	99
	Belief in witchcraft and occult forces	100
	Other metaphysical concepts	108
5	**Knowledge among the indigenous Shona**	**112**
	The question of knowledge	112
	African epistemology	116
	Shona epistemology	120
	Revealed and esoteric knowledge	124
	The place of secrecy	125
	Divination and knowledge	127
	The question of efficacy	129
	Proverbs and knowledge	133
6	**Indigenous Shona morality**	**138**
	The nature of African morality	138
	Morality among the Shona	143
	Kuva munhu muvanhu	144
	Shame cultures and the panoptic effect	147
	The morality of relations	150
	Proverbs and Shona morality	154
	Shona ethics of nature	157
	From the past to the future	160

7	**Indigenous Shona aesthetics**	**164**
	Aesthetics and African culture	164
	Art and philosophy	166
	Beauty among the Shona	172
	Metaphysical dimensions of Shona art	174
	The soapstone birds of Great Zimbabwe	176
8	**Conclusion**	**184**
References		**187**
Index		**206**

Acknowledgements

The manuscript for this publication was prepared with the support of an African Humanities Fellowship, established by the American Council of Learned Societies and supported financially by the Carnegie Corporation of New York.

By its very nature, the process of writing this book has left me indebted to so many individuals most of whom I cannot mention by name. These include many friends and colleagues with whom I have discussed some of the ideas in this book. However, I shall specifically single out Prof MB Ramose who took his time to go through my very first draft and gave me some eye-opening suggestions. I should also mention my friend and fellow philosopher, Dr Kudzai Matereke, with whom I often debate philosophical issues on Africa.

Special acknowledgement goes to the African Humanities Program (AHP) for awarding me the fellowship and to its editorial team and secretariat for their dedication and support to AHP fellows. I also wish to thank Unisa Press – publishers of the Africa Humanities Series – and the anonymous reviewers who provided valuable commentary on my

Acknowledgements

draft manuscript. My special thanks also go to Dr David Kaulem, the development editor appointed by the AHP editorial team to guide me through the revision of the draft manuscript. His critical insights and suggestions helped me to clarify my thoughts on a number of philosophical issues. I of course, remain entirely responsible for all the mistakes and/or errors.

Finally, I wish to thank my family for all the support they have given me throughout my life and in my career as an academic.

Preface

African philosophers and theorists have pointed to the existence of an epistemic dimension to Africa's problems in that intellectual traditions from other cultures are given priority at the expense of the indigenous ones. Philosophy occupies a crucial position in being able not only to react to this historical nemesis which has afflicted the continent but also in laying the ground for creating a world free from epistemic hegemony through intercultural dialogue. The story of civilisation needs to be revisited in order to create a platform on which the different peoples of the world are able to isolate and pronounce their historical place in the development of humanity. To be able to leave a significant mark on the world, Africans must come to appreciate the ontological significance of the classical dictum 'African know thyself'. It is in response to the parameters set by this dictum that Africans will be able to reassert their identity as a people of 'equal ontological density to the rest of humanity and second to none'.

Part of that process entails creating a body of literature both classical and contemporary from which inspiration to transform the continent and its peoples can be derived. The traditions of thought, indigenous philosophical ideas and political ideals should be re-appropriated in the context of the present in order to help define who we are as a people. The African intellectual heritage should be conferred with the immortality that other classical ideas enjoy across the world, by making it possible for future generations not only to dialogue with this heritage but to innovate it as well. That metaphorical dialogue with the past can only be maintained into the future if such traditions have been rendered perpetually present and thus immortal through reconstructive writing. This is the whole point of this work.

As an exploratory text on the thinking of the indigenous Shona, this book forms part of the process of continuous self-understanding so necessary in postcolonial Africa. It is a project on the recovery and reconstruction of indigenous African philosophical traditions. Such reconstruction is not only meant to salvage indigenous ideas and thought systems facing the threat of oblivion, but it is more importantly a significant initiative to lay down the foundations upon which dialogue among civilisations can be possible. The future of humanity lies in dialogue, that is, in the reciprocal elucidation of meaning in search of truth, knowledge and justice. This book not only lays the foundation for future generations to dialogue with their African past but it also provides a platform for other cultures to collaboratively interrogate the philosophical basis of thinking and acting in some of Africa's cultures.

Unless ongoing space explorations spring us a surprise by identifying another planet in which human beings can thrive, we are now and for the foreseeable future, bound together on this earth. The logic of co-existence demands that we understand and appreciate each other's traditions including the underlying assumptions that drive our different modes of thinking and being. In this book, I have laid out crucial insights into the thinking of one of Africa's indigenous cultures, although I should also remind the reader that there are indeed 'deep affinities of both thought and feeling across the entirety of Africa'. In historical terms, 'the culture now classified as "Shona" originated from Bantu settlements on the high fertile plateau between the Limpopo and Zambezi rivers, bounded in the East by the drop towards the coast and in the West by the Kalahari desert' (Bourdillon 1987:6). The Shona are the founders of the ancient Great Zimbabwe civilisation and the builders of the Great Zimbabwe UNESCO world heritage monument. This is the group whose philosophical thoughts are laid out in this book.

Pascah Mungwini
Pretoria

Introduction
Philosophy and its realities

> Even when many 'others' become convinced that a certain mode of doing Philosophy is interesting and useful, that does not make this way of practicing Philosophy a universal standard. Philosophy is always there in the plural. (Van Hensbroek 2013:32; caps original)

I consider the above submission not only axiomatic but a precise articulation of the position that informs my thinking in this work. The belief that a particular 'mode of doing philosophy is interesting and useful' should not be allowed to translate into a dogma that is detrimental to the realities of philosophy. The specific problem of contemporary philosophy arises out of a situation where one of the cultural settings of the past has been more successful than others in establishing itself on a global scale as a non-traditional and scientific enterprise (Wimmer 2010). While this crucial fact correctly captures the dilemma of the present the main concern should be how to transform this situation in order to create a platform on which philosophical traditions in their diversity could be celebrated. But the question for many is how to reach such a transcultural and universalist dream. Perhaps there is something that philosophy can learn from space science in that what was unthinkable half a century ago has become today's reality. As the famous physicist and pioneer rocket engineer Robert Goddard (1882–1945) famously stated: 'it is difficult to say what is impossible, for the dream of yesterday is the hope of today and the reality of tomorrow'.[1] Given its history of having been complicit in the rationalisation of all sorts of iniquities, philosophy owes humanity an indelible debt. It must play its part in dismantling the grounding metaphysics for the injustices still prevalent in this world including those on the epistemic front through dialogue. This is where the potential of philosophy lies. At this point, as Okere (2003) urges, I distinguish the reality of philosophy from the promise of philosophy, that is, the history of philosophy as we know it, and the promise it holds, the great hope it imbues, and the as yet unachieved potential of philosophy. To realise a world without epistemic hegemony, philosophy must reconstruct its own ideology and lay down the basis of dialogue and reciprocal elucidation in search of knowledge and justice across cultures. That in itself requires paying significant attention to reconstructing indigenous philosophies across the world. I relate my work to that of organisations such as the Council for Research in Values and Philosophy (RVP) in Washington D.C. which have over the years promoted research and publication on various traditions of thought across the world in a bid to 'respond to the new awareness of the cultural grounds of human life and the newly global character of their interaction'. Its aim, among others, has been to promote research on cultural heritage and contemporary change by urging 'understanding and appreciation of one's own culture and values that shape aspirations and actions'. As part of its mission it has also emphasised the importance of understanding other cultures and 'to develop a positive and yet critical appreciation' of those traditions.[2] For me that in itself should constitute the hallmark of contemporary philosophy anywhere which is one of the reasons why I wrote this book.

Throughout this book I engage in dialogue with the work of philosophers from different traditions and continents in an effort to make better sense of the ideas at the heart of traditional Shona thought. From its inception as an academic discipline, philosophy in Africa has been implicated in historical circumstances of an intercultural nature. At the centre of this work is an attempt to contribute to the disssemination of the thoughts of those cultures whose ideas have not always been suffiently disseminated or documented but have influenced and continue to influence the lives of people throughout history. Being a narrative centred in human experiences, philosophy in Africa must acknowledge its history and find its way from that history to help define the future of humanity (Mungwini 2015). As such my focus in this work is not so much on the 'destructive criticism of hegemonic philosophical thought' but on making visible another mode of thinking and philosophical framework that has been historically marginalised. As the Unesco constitution clearly declares, 'ignorance of each other's ways and lives has been a common cause, throughout the history of mankind, of that suspicion and mistrust between the peoples of the world through which their differences have all too often broken into war'. To make available a written text on the philosophy of the indigenous Shona is not only to make a significant contribution to world philosophy, but more importantly, it is to declare war on ignorance concerning each other's traditions. Adequate knowledge of each other's traditions is a crucial aspect which the discipline of philosophy has historically negated by circumscribing the circle of reason.

This book is basically an introductory text to the philosophy of the indigenous Shona – that group credited with the founding of the ancient Great Zimbabwe State and for building the famous Great Zimbabwe monuments. Despite the existence of sterling works from historians, archaeologists, linguists and anthropologists, it seems no comprehensive text exists on the philosophy of the Shona. The Shona have been selected for analysis in this study for their role in the establishment of a widely celebrated ancient civilisation and culture which has endured until today and for the simple reason that they are the group that the writer is most familiar with by virtue of belonging to the same ethnic group. In epistemic terms the book comes at a time when interest in ancient civilisations such as research into the Mapungubwe – Great Zimbabwe transfrontier civilisations, interest in epistemologies of the South, and the African intellectual heritage is regaining momentum. For a long time in my philosophy career, I have felt the need for such a text in order to provide students of philosophy and other disciplines with a book on the thoughts of the indigenous Shona people. I have, however, written this book not only with students of philosophy and philosophers in mind, but with other readers from such fields as African studies, culture studies, politics, African religion, art and heritage studies in mind. This book is also a culmination of my own interest in understanding the intellectual heritage of the African people. For the new generation of philosophers to be innovators of our intellectual traditions they require access to resources that speak to this classical heritage. It should be remembered that, 'what informed Diop's focus on ancient Egypt was the knowledge that any civilisation constructs for itself a classical period as an archive which influences both the present and the future' (Amadiume 1997:5). It is also true that the spirit of intellectual inquiry and hence progress anywhere can be hampered by the unavailability of such an archive for reference and inspiration. Even development experts and modernists have now come to acknowledge that indigenous ideas and traditions are integral to any programmes of social transformation.

Chapter 1

Perhaps I should also mention that by writing on the philosophy of the indigenous Shona I am also responding to the tendency, itself widespread, to perceive ideas from the African past as dead and of little or no relevance to the present. My attempt is therefore to keep those ideas alive by ensuring not only that this philosophical knowledge is available but that debate on the validity and efficacy of such ideas continue. What the Indian scholar Chakrabarty (2000) bemoans about the intellectual heritage in the Asian world is equally true of Africa. Chakrabarty observes:

> Sad as it is, one result of European colonial rule in South Asia is that the intellectual traditions once unbroken and alive in Sanskrit or Persian or Arabic are now only matters for historical research for most – perhaps all – modern social scientists in the region. They treat these traditions as truly dead, as history... And yet past European thinkers and their categories are never quite dead for us in the same way. South Asian(ists) social scientists would argue passionately with a Marx or a Weber without feeling any need to place them in their European intellectual contexts. Sometimes – though this is rather rare – they would even argue with the ancient or medieval or early-modern predecessors of these European theorists. (Chakrabarty 2000:5–6)

The point by Chakrabarty that European theorists and ancient philosophers are never 'dead' in the same way their Asian and, I would include, African counterparts are, is philosophically telling. While such a development has largely to do with the politics of knowledge it does indicate the existence of a serious problem in these other cultures. While of course nobody can deny the fact that scholars from Europe have made sacrifices to make their intellectual heritage available for posterity and thus rendering their thinkers perpetually present and therefore 'immortal', it is a question of how the fossilisation of the once vibrant traditions were precipitated and why it continues to find local accomplices which requires attention. It is at this point that the question of attitude towards the indigenous intellectual heritage by Africans themselves becomes important. More often than not we have African students of philosophy who are so enmeshed in the Western tradition of philosophy including some of its most ancient philosophers but hardly know anything about Nkrumah, for example, and his philosophy – thanks to us, their teachers. Part of the problem is that

> for too long the teaching of ... philosophy in Africa was decontextualised precisely because both the inspiration and questions it attempted to

answer were not necessarily based upon the living experience of being-an-African in Africa. (Ramose 1999:35)

Furthermore, there seems to be a disturbing tendency to treat African theorists like Nkrumah and company together with their philosophical ideas as being ancient and dated compared to those of Western classical thinkers. Some of our own philosophers express dismay at those who butress their arguments on the 'antiquated' ideas of say Nyerere or Nkrumah but surprisingly these same critics go on to draw from the 'evergreen' Plato. This is an issue which philosophers in Africa and those enstrusted with teaching philosophy in Africa must address. Both traditions of thought are important and valuable, though we should not forget 'that philosophy always functions in the context of a given culture, receiving from it impulse and direction' (Gracia 1992:160). Different traditions of philosophy enrich rather than impoverish humanity. Again, we should take serious consideration of the Unesco Paris Declaration of Philosophy which proposes that

> knowledge of philosophical insight in different cultures, comparison of what each has to offer, analyses of what brings them closer together and what separates them, should be pursued and supported by research and teaching institutions.[3]

This book is thus an attempt to add to the available written traditions of thought in Africa. As Wiredu (1992:9) states: 'a volume in Ghanaian philosophy [that is, on the thoughts and ideas of its ethnic peoples] is a volume in African philosophy'. Talk of a communal philosophy does not necessarily imply unanimity in thought. It only means that 'anybody thoughtfully knowledgeable about the culture will know that such conceptions are customary in the culture' (Wiredu 1998:25). And the same logic applies with equal significance to this work on the indigenous Shona.

This work is divided into seven chapters respecting to some degree the traditional divisions of philosophy. The first chapter is an introduction. The second chapter deals with some of the perennial questions in African philosophy such as (a) the question of method, (b) the link between philosophy and culture, (c) the question of language and philosophy, (d) the issue of writing and (e) the question of proverbs as sources of philosophy. The chapter makes use of an extensive analysis of these issues to argue the legitimacy of an indigenous body of knowledge called Shona philosophy. It draws from established philosophical traditions to assist in laying down an appropriate conceptual framework within which the indigenous philosophy of the Shona can be articulated. The point of departure for this chapter and the entire text is that while the critique of Eurocentrism as an integral step towards the rehabilitation of Africa remains crucial in African philosophy, several years after independence; the best way to deal with the colonial misfortune and its painful reality, is not to dwell on its ills and to stay there, but to use philosophy to re-affirm indigenous epistemologies through the critical reconstruction and re-appropriation of African traditions. Chapter three proceeds to look at the question of identity with reference to both the group of people called the Shona and the nature of their tradition. It draws on historical, archaeological, and anthropological sources to shed light on the history of the Shona peoples and the origins of the name Shona. The chapter also examines the question of the colonial invention of tradition. This is done in order to address questions concerning the historical context within which the Shona past is to be understood.

Chapter four draws from the speculative propensity in humans concerning the nature of reality to enter into the discussion on Shona metaphysics. What emerges is that human thought everywhere including that of the Shona is incomplete without metaphysical speculation. An understanding of Shona metaphysics provides an important window through which we can make sense of many other aspects of their philosophy. There is a long tradition of metaphysical speculation among the Shona which has helped to shape the society into what it is today. Chapter five articulates what I describe as a Shona ethnoepistemology. What motivates my argument is the position that all human beings from time immemorial have sought knowledge both for practical purposes and in order to satisfy their curiosity. It is on this basis that an attempt is made to outline aspects of indigenous Shona knowledge. Chapter six, which examines indigenous Shona morality, proceeds from the premise that no society can exist without a set of rules to guide its conduct or the behaviour of its members no matter how rudimentary. Morality is universal to human culture. From their indigenous wisdom, the Shona articulated an 'art of living' including morality, on whose basis social relationships were defined. The final chapter, which is chapter seven, deals with the question of indigenous Shona aesthetics. Art, like philosophy, is a conscious creation which invariably reflects the cultural horizon out of which it comes. As they 'roam into the imaginative world of art', Shona artists rely on the traditions, mythology, religious beliefs and customs of their community to inform the themes of what they depict in their works.

From an analysis of the works of art and other forms of artistic expression, it is possible to capture the philosophy that lies embedded in those artistic creations.

Notes

1. This quotation is available at the Goddard Space Flight Centre website: http://www.nasa.gov/centers/goddard/about/history/dr_goddard.html (Accessed 18 November 2015).

2. I have summarised the mission statement of the Council for Research in Values and Philosophy as articulated on its website. I strongly believe that its mission should inform much of our philosophical practice particularly in this age which is marked by growing global interconnectedness and the search for identity and meaning. For more detail see http://www.crvp.org/crvp/rvp-mission.htm (Accessed 18 November 2015).

3. See the Unesco, Paris Declaration for Philosophy, http://www.unesco.org (Accessed 12 November 2015).

Indigenous Shona philosophy

The quest for indigenous Shona philosophy

> During the abortive Geneva Constitutional Talks, I (Mr. Samkange) found myself one day talking to some very opinionated London-based perennial 'O'-Level students ... When I said I am a 'Hunhuist' the sneers and smiles of derision that carved their faces could have turned fresh milk sour. 'What is that?' they scornfully asked ... 'Whose fault is it', I asked, 'if no one knows about the philosophy of your grandfather and mine? Is it not your fault and mine?' We are the intellectuals of Zimbabwe. It is our business to distil this philosophy and set it out for the whole world to see. (Samkange and Samkange 1980:9)

The submission above serves as a reminder to African philosophers on the nature of the task that needs to be undertaken. Not many African philosophers have articulated philosophies embedded in their communities in a way that answers to the passionate call being made by Samkange above. The call is part of the reason why this effort to reconstruct an indigenous philosophy of the Shona peoples constitutes a worthwhile undertaking. It is the duty of philosophers to put together written accounts of the philosophical traditions of their communities. There is no doubt that this challenge extends with equal significance to a large number of philosophers in Africa. Although there are some who have already responded to this call from within their various localities across Africa, much still remains to be done if we are not to lose the intellectual heritage of those various communities in Africa. I do acknowledge that a good amount of philosophical work has been done on some communities by some of Africa's own eminent scholars such as Wiredu and Gyekye on Akan thought in Ghana, the works of famous Nigerian philosophers on the Ibgo and Yoruba cultures, Claude Sumner's philosophy of the Oromo in Ethiopia, Oruka's Sage philosophy project in Kenya, and the *Ubuntu* philosophy and tradition so extensively dealt with from Southern Africa. These listed achievements are by no means the only ones but they do indicate that the task I seek to embark on is indeed a continuation of the journey that African philosophers have been travelling from their different corners united by the same objective, that is, to reaffirm the philosophies of their various communities. I view this project as part of the work that has always remained to be undertaken, because to my knowledge there is no comprehensive text devoted to Shona philosophy to provide upcoming philosophers and students with a head start on the thinking of this community who are descendants and inheritors of the Great Zimbabwe civilisation so famously documented in works of history and archaeology. This work coincides with a period of great significance in the reconstruction of ancient civilisations by historians, linguists, and archaeologists from Southern Africa who have taken renewed interest in understanding the Mapungubwe – Great Zimbabwe transfrontier civilisations. I agree with Samkange that if no one knows about the philosophy of our fore-parents, we have no-one else to blame except ourselves.

This work is an endeavour to provide a written text on Shona philosophy. Retrieving and indeed re-affirming the African intellectual heritage remains a crucial defining element of the African philosophical agenda. As a result of colonialism, African philosophy has emerged and carved its mission starting with the critique of Eurocentrism as an integral step towards the rehabilitation of Africa. While this goal remains crucial and important to the whole thrust of African philosophy, this work argues that, several years after independence, the best way to deal with colonialism and its painful reality and still maintain a critical attitude towards it, is not to dwell on its ills and to stay there, but to use African philosophy to reaffirm indigenous epistemologies through a conscious reconstruction and critical re-appropriation of African traditions. This critical reconstruction and re-appropriation is important, not only in order to salvage and revitalise African forms of knowing and traditions threatened with extinction, but also as a way of providing for posterity a history of African philosophical thought. It is time for scholars to identify and analyse the basic African epistemic frameworks and principles in a manner that will make African traditions useful to the world. There exists a misnomer in that unlike other cultures and civilisations, the African intellectual heritage, comprised of the social, cultural, philosophical and spiritual contribution of its indigenous cultures, is not finding its way into the future easily. Of course part of this problem is historical in that 'Africa's indigenous cultures were, in both principle and fact, disqualified from occupying a place in the philosophical arena' (Hallen 2002:3). Such false and deeply offensive typing of the cognitive significance of the African civilisation extended to other indigenous peoples of the world. In order to be able to enter into dialogue with other philosophical traditions around the world and take part in the reciprocal elucidation of our beliefs and traditions, it is important for African philosophers to pay significant attention to reconstructing their indigenous philosophies.

In their attempt to respond to the Western typing of their civilisation and therefore demonstrate the existence of African philosophy beyond any shadow of doubt, African philosophers have engaged in intense debate concerning the nature of their discipline. This attempt to map out the nature of their discipline has been anything but unanimous, starting from the definition of philosophy itself and the approaches they thought could best yield African philosophy. However, such divergence of opinion, which is itself the hallmark of philosophy, has been of immense value to the discipline as scholars have been occasionally forced to substantiate their views. One does not need to go very far to get a sense of the polemics. For example, as a rejoinder to what he felt was a misplaced attack on him from those who disagreed with his position on ethnophilosophy, Hountondji wrote:

> Allow me to make a few remarks, in a most direct manner, a clarification of meaning, scope and aim of my criticism of ethnophilosophy. I am forced here to go through an exercise which I do not like; to respond point by point (or 'fist by fist', in line with a joke of a friend of mine whom I cannot mention here) to criticisms which sometimes just look like personal attacks. But I do it with much pleasure, because, beyond these 'ad hominem' criticisms, founded on a strong will not to understand, there are fortunately many others, which do justice to the problems presented and have the additional merit of pointing out real theoretical problems and, from time to time, at inaccuracies and other loopholes in my formulations. (Hountondji 1989:3)

The analogical significance of 'fist by fist' and the subsequent cringe that follows, though dramatic, captures in part the heated nature of the debate that has always characterised African philosophy from its early age. Of course it was only natural that Hountondji, and on behalf of his fellow anti-ethnophilosophers, had to react in this way since they had been labelled a bunch of elitist and 'neocolonialist devils preventing people from affirming their otherness' as Africans by unashamedly continuing to pander to Western perspectives under the pretence of scientism[1] (see Mudimbe 1988:162). In any work on African philosophy it is therefore impossible to turn one's back on the theoretical and methodological controversies that have defined the discipline over the last five or so decades. Part of it had to do with the meaning of the term philosophy itself. Contributing to the debate on the nature of African philosophy, Keita (1991) observes that the term philosophy has witnessed important shifts in meaning throughout the history of philosophy. Keita argues:

> Philosophy in the sense of Aristotle is not 'philosophy' in the sense of Quine. Newton thought he was doing philosophy in his *Philosophiae naturalis principia mathematica* (1687) and was also regarded as a natural philosopher, whereas Einstein was seen as a natural scientist. (Keita 1991:198)

It is also equally important to note that:

> until the eighteenth century the word 'science' (*scientia*, from *scio*, to know) was commonly used to refer to philosophy as well as to what today we refer to as the *natural sciences*, and the word 'philosophy' was used to refer to the natural sciences as well as to philosophy. (Gracia 1992:3)

These alternate usages of the terms 'science' and 'philosophy' go back through the medieval to ancient Greek period. Within the European tradition itself, there seems to be no consensus even on the method of investigation that is proper to philosophy. Keita (1991) draws our attention to the dispute between continental philosophy and its Anglo-American analytic counterpart concerning the question of what ought to be genuine philosophy. According to Keita:

> philosophical research in the Anglo-American world holds that continental philosophy is not genuine philosophy, and those whose main interests are in that area of philosophy hold a similar disregard for Anglo-American analytic philosophy. (Keita 1991:198)

The point I wish to underscore is that despite the supposed controversies and lack of consensus concerning philosophy and the method considered most appropriate to inform its practice in the West, philosophy has thrived for centuries and we as Africans must draw valuable lessons from that.

The question of method

My approach in this work is informed by a set of correlative assumptions about the nature and purpose of African philosophy in particular and its historical moorings. It is my conviction that African philosophy has a historic responsibility to the peoples of Africa in terms of not only restoring the honour that the continent has lost as a result of its colonial nemesis, but in helping Africans engage with the rest of the world in the universal quest for truth and knowledge. African philosophy has been characterised by its own debates on method and Oruka's classification of approaches in African philosophy has been seminal in shaping discussion on this matter. I will now say something about the trends in African philosophy. The reason why I chose to examine the question of trends in African philosophy despite the fact that so much has been written about them is to provide the reader with my own conceptualisation of the nature of African philosophy which will in turn inform this work. A critical reading of the historical circumstances out of which African philosophy emerges will reveal that, rather than being incompatible or unreservedly antagonistic, the different trends that Oruka identified – ethnophilosophy, philosophical sagacity, nationalistic ideological philosophy and professional philosophy – could fit together to constitute complementary units aimed at constructing an African philosophy conscious of its own environment. I will restrict my analysis to these four even though I am aware of other approaches that have been suggested since the publication of Oruka's work. I am convinced that African philosophers can draw valuable insights from each and every one of these trends in their effort to further the discipline. I should also point out, right from the onset, that my interest in the philosophies of Africa's indigenous cultures is not an attempt to take Africa backwards, but to provide an important intellectual heritage necessary for understanding contemporary society. Humanity is the only species with interest in recording and studying its past (Mazrui and Ajayi 1993). Therefore the Africans' quest for the intellectual heritage of the past, like everyone else's, is at heart, an expression of the natural inclination to affirm their humanity.

Since a great deal of energy has been expended on articulating what has been called the different approaches or trends in African philosophy not much space will be devoted to them here other than drawing attention to a few points which inform this discussion. I agree with Deacon (2002:98)'s observation that Oruka's classification of the trends in African philosophy has seemingly been adopted, by the majority of African philosophers as being a true rendition of the structures of African philosophy. At the heart of the suggestion by Oruka is an implicit conclusion that the discourse of African philosophy has progressed in a linear fashion through distinct stages 'from the substandard ethnophilosophy through to the more sophisticated professional trend' (Deacon 2002:99). This popular but unfortunate picture has had both positive and negative effects on the development of African philosophy. Positive in that it has tended to encourage African philosophers to concentrate on those issues seen as universal core problems of philosophy dealt with in other philosophical discourses around the world. Even the yearning to belong to the category of professional philosopher and to be classified as such or to so classify oneself, has had a huge effect on the choice of topics researched and published on by most contemporary African philosophers. However, despite this positivity, I think the classification itself and the picture it has unfortunately painted about the discourse, has had more negative effects on the discipline than advantages particularly given the history of Africa. African philosophy has a huge historic responsibility to the people of Africa not only because it is the foundational discipline upon which success in other domains depends, but because it is the ability to think and to philosophise that defines what it means to be human. That responsibility involves taking initiatives aimed at reconstructing the missing history of philosophy in Africa seriously. It would be of great significance both to philosophy itself and to humanity in particular if the African philosophical heritage could be recorded following in the footsteps of the UNESCO General History of Africa in which a wonderful attempt has been made to provide a complete picture of Africa's own history beginning from its ancient civilisations.

Another drawback that I want to point out has to do with the selection of names to identify these trends. Serious implications can be drawn particularly in relation to the two often regarded as paradigmatic representatives on the weighing scale of African philosophy, that is, ethnophilosophy and professional philosophy. First and foremost the picture created places at the apex of African philosophical discourse that which passes for professional philosophy and, in the same breath, depreciates that which is designated as ethnophilosophy. This is because of what has come to be a close association between the term 'professional' and the idea of 'excellence'. And yet, as we all know, it is these very same professional philosophers who produce work on various ethnicities such as the Akan concept of ..., the Yoruba concept of ..., the Shona concept ..., the Gikuyu belief in ...; subject matter which is correctly known as philosophy but which seems to fit very well with what has been termed ethnophilosophy. The names used in these classifications had their distinction compounded further by carefully selected and overly ambitious descriptors coined by those who arrogated unto themselves the right at that particular point in history to denigrate what they disagreed with for various reasons. The question that we should ask ourselves is: is it really true that the so-called best examples of ethnophilosophy – the works of Tempels, Mbiti and Kagame – are basically a collection of beliefs and myths about Africa devoid of any reflection? I do not seem to think so. These works may have their shortcomings, but so are the works of those who call themselves representatives of the professional school. Deacon (2002) is convinced that a critical reading of the historical circumstances out of which these works were born would reveal their philosophical significance. For this reason, Deacon (2002) argues that in order to fully appreciate the work of ethnophilosophy it is important to understand the person of Tempels not only as a missionary and therefore an appendage of the colonial mission, but his transformation as a person through his being in the world on earth with the African in Africa. Just as contemporary Western philosophical discourse is a product of its own history, which explains why its many styles and problems hang together in the way they do, the historical circumstances in Africa cannot but be reflected in its philosophy. The various trends are not symptomatic of any failure to make headway in African philosophy nor should they be pitted against each other with the misleading insinuation that some trends are superior to others. Instead, these different trends are in themselves complementary efforts each driven by the quest to respond to specific aspects of the colonial history out of which its discourse takes its form in order to deal with the purported lacunae voiced at that particular point in history.

    Over the last few decades debate concerning these different trends has created an unfortunate hostility towards ethnophilosophy, in the process dismissing it and its particular concerns as trivial. Who on earth would be prepared to put up with the label or title of ethnophilosopher given the negativity surrounding this epithet? But just switch the name to cultural philosophy and you will witness how large in number the adherents are. My point is that the choice of the name ethnophilosophy, and the characterisation that was consciously selected to go with it, is largely responsible for its subsequent placement on the lower ranks of the hierarchy of philosophical discourse in Africa. And I place the blame for this squarely on those who 'invented' and popularised the term.[2] Why did they not call it classical or ancient philosophy just like it is called in other cultures? In a recent publication, Mangena, a philosopher at the University of Zimbabwe vehemently disagrees with Hountondji and Appiah's characterisation of ethnophilosophy as a collection of shared beliefs and worldviews that are not rational. I am referring here to his article 'Ethnophilosophy is rational: A reply to two famous critics' published in *Thought and Practice: A Journal of the Philosophical Association of Kenya* in 2014. Mangena convincingly argues that ethnophilosophy is not a mere collection of shared beliefs and worldviews and neither is it devoid of reason. Since I see this problem as something created by coining a particular name and definition, the question that I have is whether this penchant for coining derogatory names that in effect have the consequence of debasing the entire edifice of traditional African thought is itself not reminiscent of colonial practice and its attitude towards African traditions. Have we not succumbed to the very same practice that we strongly condemn in others? Could it be that the sheepdog by virtue of the time it spends among sheep from its tender age inevitably grows to think that it is protecting its own when it guards the sheep? This is the kind of attitude that one seems to sense from those who outrightly condemn ethnophilosophy since they think they are doing African philosophy a favour when in actual fact they are stifling its varied manifestations as a philosophy fertilised by different, but of course, overlapping ideologies. The point that I wish to underline is that it would be unfortunate if African philosophers were to congregate around so-called trends and fail to realise the most important fact which is that irrespective of where one is located along the African philosophical plain there is a fundamental mission for philosophy in Africa: to reassert the African identity.

I shall now proceed to demonstrate how all these different trends are invariably united and not necessarily antagonistic in their pursuit of this historic quest. At this point I return to Deacon's important observation (which I strongly agree with) in which she argues:

> I cannot accept a linear approach to the development of African philosophy. The various trends have commenced at various, and sometimes diverging times, while the influences, challenges, and contexts forcing them into

> being should not be ignored. Each trend has a distinct interpretation as to the nature of African philosophy. The context of the origination of each of these trends should be readily understood in order to render full comprehension of their roles in the entire field of philosophy in Africa. (Deacon 2002:99)

What this means is that none of the trends should be seen as unimportant. For me, behind these seemingly distinct interpretations of the nature of philosophy is a shared historical mandate. For the purposes of this discussion I will adopt the following classification of trends in African philosophy: a) the cultural school, b) the ideological school and c) the critical school. This analytic classification subsumes the four trends of Oruka and I prefer it for the basic reason that it dispenses with the name ethnophilosophy which I do not like for reasons already outlined; although I should also say I have a similar problem with the name 'critical school' accorded to the third trend. This again unfortunately attempts to create the impression that other schools are not critical when in fact they all are as befitting schools of philosophy to which different professional philosophers continue to contribute. Names and systems of naming developed through another language to define processes in a foreign cultural context will always remain problematic. I hope the lead taken by a group of renowned African philosophers to publish an anthology on African philosophy in African languages will trigger a process to assist us develop and describe these trends in terms that are amenable to what we intend to convey. I am here thinking of the book edited by Chike (2013), called Listening to Ourselves: A Multilingual Anthology of African Philosophy. Let me now examine each the three schools outlined above.

The cultural school (ethnophilosophy) is characterised by Osuagwu as

> an African negation of European negation of Africanity. This dialectic is essentially meant to be contradictory to but also corrective of European prejudices which deny Africans of rationality, culturality, morality, religiosity, historicity, scientificity, etc. [It] investigates, reconstitutes, rectifies and elaborates the existence of a traditional African philosophy. (Osuagwu 1999:129)

Affirming this point Ramose argues:

> Alexis Kagame's exposition of the Rwandese philosophy of be-ing is a classic in African philosophy. The exposition is much more than a

conversation with Aristotle's *Categoriae* and the *De interpretatione*... One of the major aims of Kagame is to challenge this fallacy [that Africans are not rational] and reaffirm the fact that the Bantu peoples – and by extension the Africans – were capable of abstract reasoning from time immemorial. (Ramose 2006:53,57)

I will return to comment on this but at this point let me briefly outline the essential traits of the other two remaining schools first, that is, the ideological school and the critical school. The ideological school is political and is concerned with those ideas and theories articulated by African political leaders and champions of the anticolonial struggle. Its main thrust is the work of specific individuals such as Kwame Nkrumah, Julius Nyerere, Kenneth Kaunda, Mnandi Azikiwe, and Franz Fanon among others who regard African philosophy as particularly concerned with the liberation of Africa. They believe African political philosophy, like a chameleon, must take cognisance of its environment and respond accordingly. It must find its weapons in the peculiar African locus (Osuagwu 1999:166) and from that locus annunciate its own vision and mission. I shall draw mostly from Nkrumah for illustrative purposes. In his book *Consciencism*, Nkrumah notes the following about philosophy, society and ideology:

> Social milieu affects the content of philosophy, and the content of philosophy seeks to affect social milieu, either by confirming it or by opposing it. In either case, philosophy implies something of the nature of an ideology. In the case where the philosophy confirms the social milieu, it implies something of the ideology of that society. In the other case in which philosophy opposes a social milieu, it implies something of the ideology of a revolution against that social milieu. Philosophy in its social aspect can therefore be regarded as pointing up an ideology. (Nkrumah 1964:56)

Highlighting the centrality of philosophy to social revolution, Nkrumah continued:

> Our philosophy must find its weapons in the environment and living conditions of the African people. It is from those conditions that the intellectual content of our philosophy must be created. The emancipation of the African continent is the emancipation of man. (Nkrumah 1964:78)

These views of Nkrumah are an acute reflection of the ideological school and its views on the role of philosophy in Africa. African political philosophy arises in response to colonialism and the colonial ideology. It is the colonial ideology that prompted an African response as a counter ideology, more specifically as an African decolonial ideology (Osuagwu 1999:169).

Let me now turn to the 'critical school' or the professional trend in African philosophy. I will capture this school by making reference to one of the most outstanding postcolonial African philosophers, Eze who writes concerning contemporary African philosophy:

> In order to find our way, then, I suggest that for the moment we allow ourselves to return to, and be guided by, the concept of the '(post)colonial' of the title of this volume. Admittedly, the concept of the '(post)colonial'[3] also quickly embroils us in the question of its cousins: the 'colonial' and the 'precolonial,' and it is a legitimate gesture to ask, in protest: Why should colonialism be accorded the status and role of a singular and dominant prism through which the nature and boundaries of African/a philosophy ought to be thematised and articulated? This, surely, is a credible and, in some cases an appropriate objection. However, when the question concerns the professional field of African philosophy, the strength of this objection nearly evaporates, or at least is significantly attenuated. This is simply because *the single most important factor that drives the field and the contemporary practice of African/a Philosophy has to do with the brutal encounter of the African world with European modernity* – an encounter epitomised in the colonial phenomena. (Eze 1997:4; italics original)

This to me captures, to a greater degree, the nature of postcolonial philosophy and how it approaches African philosophy.

Having briefly captured each of these schools of African philosophy let me then proceed to juxtapose them in order to underline the point that discourses in African philosophy in their diversity are in pursuit of the task among others to redeem Africa and to define who we are – no matter where they begin. The cultural school, the ideological school and their professional or critical counterpart are all involved in defending the place of Africa on the epistemic front by either setting the record straight concerning the precolonial picture of Africa or rearticulating those precolonial ideas as a counter ideology or by literally returning to the precolonial as resources upon which to articulate a postcolonial African philosophy. In all cases the single most determinant factor to the nature and course which the different approaches in African philosophy take is the 'brutal encounter of the African world with European modernity', that is, the colonial encounter. There is a common thread running through the different trends in African philosophy which gives African philosophy its identity. That thread inheres in culture and the existential circumstances of the African which are linked to the colonial experience. It is because of the colonial experience that the precolonial has become so important and it is again because of colonialism that ideologies for a social revolution became a necessity, and without this precolonial and colonial history, postcolonial African philosophy would be difficult to comprehend. In fact the very name 'postcolonial African philosophy' is only rendered meaningful and legitimate because of the existence of a precolonial and colonial encounter. From the cultural school, the ideological school or the critical school – whatever the approach – the agenda seems to be at all levels to redeem Africa and to place it where it belongs – alongside other nations on the philosophical table. This is the liberative agenda inherent in all instances of African philosophy as a philosophy born out of the rage and humiliating experiences that our history is so familiar with.

The decolonial drive and its liberative ideals are key to understanding much of what happens across the field of African philosophy irrespective of the approach. Decoloniality refers both to the analytic task of unveiling the logic of coloniality and the prospective task of contributing to build a world in which many worlds will coexist (Mignolo 2011:54). I identify decolonial theorising as being at the centre of all the trends in African philosophy for the simple reason that the philosophy as practised and written by various academics and professionals today has to contend with the problem of coloniality specifically at the ontological and epistemic levels. Coloniality refers to long-standing patterns of power that emerged as a result of colonialism and which continue to define culture, labour, intersubjective relations, and knowledge production well beyond the strict limits of colonial administrations. As Maldonaldo-Torres confirms:

> [coloniality] is maintained alive in books, in the criteria for academic performance, in cultural patterns, in common sense, in the self-image of peoples, in aspirations of self, and so many other aspects of our modern experience. (Maldonaldo-Torres 2007:243)

This is the condition that created and continues to fuel epistemicide in Africa and the perpetuation of what Fricker (2007) terms 'epistemic injustice'. Briefly put, epistemic injustice which can be experienced in various forms includes the injustice suffered when one is refused credibility as a knower because of prejudice, and when powerless groups in society are excluded from contributing to the epistemic practices that shape collective understanding through systematic marginalisation (Fricker 2007:154). Latin American theorists of the decolonial school remind us that modernity created coloniality as its darker side and since conquest the third world has been mired in problems constitutive of coloniality including the coloniality of being, power and knowledge (see Maldonaldo-Torress 2007, Mignolo 2011, Grosfoguel 2011, and also Ndlovu-Gatsheni 2013 who writes the same about Africa). As described by Mignolo,

> modernity is a complex narrative whose point of origination was Europe; a narrative that builds Western civilisation by celebrating its achievements while hiding at the same time its darker side, coloniality. (Mignolo 2011:2)

It is within the context of coloniality, both as a condition of African existence and an extension of the colonial hold on power and knowledge beyond the colonial era that the nature of most African philosophical discourse must be understood. There is that common drive to reassert the historicity of African forms of knowing and existence.

In order to appreciate the unending quest which unites all the different trends in African philosophy as articulated above, one has to seriously consider the historical picture and reaction thereof to the story of human civilisation articulated by Mignolo in the following extract:

> Before 1500 the world order was polycentric and non-capitalist. After 1500 the world order entered into a process in which polycentrism began to be displaced by an emerging monocentric civilisation. Western civilisation emerged not just as another civilisation in the planetary concert, but as a civilisation destined to lead and save the rest of the world from [the] Devil, from barbarism and primitivism, from underdevelopment, from despotism, and to turn unhappiness into happiness for all and forever. (Mignolo 2011:28)

Of course nobody can dispute that Western civilisation has changed the world but whether it has delivered happiness for all and forever remains contestable given the turmoil in the world today reminiscent of Huntington's (1993) prophetic essay 'The clash of civilisations'. Without losing sight of the reason I drew from Mignolo, the point I wish to make is that as one goes through the works of philosophers from Tempels (as the most acclaimed representative of the ethnophilosophy trend) to all professional philosophers today, whether in the domain of metaphysics, ethics, epistemology, or axiology in African philosophy, the common thread in much of the discourse is to react to the problem created by the meteoric rise of one civilisation and its subsequent installation as the only dominant mode of knowing at the expense of the rest. This is what fundamentally marks off African philosophy from other discourses such as Western philosophy. In the entire edifice of African philosophy there is never an attempt to merely return to the past as some detractors may want us to think, but instead there is the expressed desire 'to reinscribe the past in the present toward the future'. As succinctly captured by Mignolo:

> when those who have been the target of colonial and imperial subjugation and made 'others' and 'barbarians' assert themselves in fullness, their claim is not to be integrated into western proclaimed 'humanity of the same' but to delink and assert 'humanity in difference. (Mignolo 2011:49)

African philosophy is not inherently anti-Western, it simply wants to celebrate its own contribution to philosophy and humanity. The intellectual content of our philosophy must be created out of Africa's conditions and its historic cultures. This is why revisiting the African past in order to distil out of it indigenous systems of knowing across the breadth and length of Africa has to be encouraged, after all as Wiredu (1992) acknowledges any volume on the thoughts of Africa's ethnic peoples is a volume in African philosophy.

In this work I strongly endorse the position of Mudimbe (1983) and Outlaw (1996) that the term 'ethnophilosophy' should be understood simply as the 'ethnos-philosophia or weltanschauung of a community'. The two philosophers elaborate on the importance of understanding ethnophilosophy not in the pejorative sense in which it is used by most of its critics, of course led by Hountondji (1983), and urge us to employ the term in its etymological sense. Mudimbe argues:

> Towa and Hountondji have popularised the term 'ethnophilosophy' which, in a negative manner, designates works that are philosophical in a wide sense ... I am using the term in its etymological value: ethnos-philosophia or weltanschauung of a community. (Mudimbe 1983:149)

This etymological meaning is more preferable for it represents the original meaning of the concept outside that which it has been made to assume by scholars critical of certain forms of doing philosophy. There is great value in adopting this understanding as it avoids the danger of always trying to look at African products with European eyes, a practice that although done without any malicious intent inevitably fuels invidious comparisons with unfortunate consequences on the part of indigenous peoples. In settling for this etymological meaning I consider it important as a point of emphasis to quote at length from Outlaw on the reasons why he shares Mudimbe's opinion that the term ethnophilosophy be understood simply as *ethnos-philosophia*. According to Outlaw:

> The term 'ethno-philosophy' is problematic. It is used by some to classify a group of works that, it is argued, mistakenly attribute achievements in Philosophy to 'traditional' Africa ... Hountondji was at one point a leading proponent of this view .... I, like Mudimbe, differ with Hountondji and others who use 'ethnophilosophy' as a term of derision, or at least as a characterization that denies 'traditional' Africans the capacity for and/ or achievement of self-reflection of a kind that can appropriately be identified as philosophizing. [At the heart of Hountondji criticism is a privileging of philosophizing as Philosophy, as, in his words, *science*, a privileging of writing as a necessity for the practice of Philosophy, and the equally erroneously privileging of 'critical self-reflection' as something not yet achieved by 'traditional' Africans.] *No* people who do not involve themselves in and succeed at reflecting on the nature and conditions of their life and, as a result, identifying rules, principles, values, etc., for the conduct of that life, which they then mediate to succeeding generations, will last for more than one generation. Obviously, African peoples have been successful in this regard. And a great deal of ethnological literature provides ample evidence of the results of this kind of reflexive praxis among African peoples. Why, then, is it proper to deny of these peoples the recognition that they were participants in activities *we* now call 'philosophy'? At the very least, Odera Oruka is on a more correct path with his category of 'philosophic sagacity'. Finally, *any* attempt to recount (ie, reconstruct) a (as opposed to *the*) history of philosophy will be to reconstruct a history of philosophy *as practiced by particular individuals who are part of particular cultural life-worlds*. (Outlaw 1996:213; italics original)

Following Mudimbe's lead, Outlaw makes a fundamental point concerning the way concepts can be (mis)applied with adverse consequences for the very issues we seek to confront. In other words, by resorting to this

Houtondjian understanding of ethnophilosophy which, as already shown, goes beyond the simple and etymological value of ethnos-philosophy as a concept, Africans invariably confirm the colonial mantra of primitivity and the absence of philosophical acumen in 'traditional' Africa.[4]

The universal and the particular

The question of whether the philosophical enterprise in Africa and its resultant product will command the respect and recognition of the same nature as that of its erstwhile centre is an issue that is now captured in the controversy between universalism and particularism. Universalists look to science to provide the model for philosophy and as a measure of rationality. But the major problem is that:

> in identifying the logico-scientific reasoning as the definitive measure of cultural rationality, the other cultures could not fail to emerge as deficient in point of rationality, given that, by definition, these cultures do not define their rationality in those terms. (Healy 2000:63)

The point is there must not be blind conformity to a set standard, that is, unwavering allegiance to the dictates of logical positivism. The evaluation of cultural beliefs and their claims to knowledge must not be blind to the context out of which such ideas arise. Reason must be able to read different realities differently in terms of how cultural ideas are to be assessed for their efficacy. There is no point in subordinating philosophy everywhere to what Feyerabend (2011) has branded as the 'tyranny of science'[5]. By 'tyranny of science', Feyerabend refers to the story about the rise of Western rationalism and the entrenchment of a mythical, and yet oppressive, scientific worldview (Oberheim 2011:vii). Of significant importance are the terms 'mythical' and 'oppressive' that have been used to characterise science for these must forever remind us of the 'personality of science' – or science as some kind of bully since its rise to prominence. According to Oberheim, in his work Feyerabend does well to remind us that

> while unanimity of opinion may be fitting for a church, for frightened victims of some (ancient, or modern) myth, for the weak and willing followers of some tyrant; variety of opinion is a feature necessary for objective knowledge; and a method that encourages variety is also the

only method that is compatible with a humanitarian outlook. (Oberheim 2011:x)

This is the spirit with which African philosophers must approach their discipline. Philosophical traditions from across the diverse peoples have no reason to subordinate themselves to the standard of rationality as defined by Western philosophy. To be convinced that one perspective delivers the truth is to be blinded to the truths offered by other cultures. 'There is no idea, however ancient or absurd, that is incapable of contributing to the improvement of knowledge' (Oberheim 2011:x). In almost all areas of life including the academy, diversity and not unanimity is what is real. If at the end of the day there are still disagreements and philosophical battles rage on about disparate approaches, such developments should not be taken as detrimental to philosophy. Rather, what is detrimental to philosophy is the attempt to subject everybody to the same rule in search of the so-called harmony in the discipline which in reality is a form of tyranny.

Feyerabend traces an important historical development in philosophy which is of crucial importance here as we continue to examine the nature of African philosophy. For Feyerabend

> like scientists, artists and religious reformers, philosophers have by now accumulated a rather disorganised heap of opinions and approaches. There are Kantians, Hegelians, Heideggerians; there are Kuhnians, Popperians, Wittgensteinians; there are followers of Foucault, Derrida, Ricoeur; there are neoaristotelians, neo-thomists …. Most of these philosophies started as attempts to put an end to the battle of the schools. The attempts soon became schools themselves and joined the battle …. So, disconnection is the rule and harmony not just the exception – it simply does not exist. (Feyerabend 2011:8–9)

The lesson is that philosophy flourishes in spite of the multiplicity of schools and approaches. If philosophers in the West had waited to agree on a single method, or even put their tools down to listen to critics it is probably true that those tools would have remained permanently down. But the reality is they did not, hence the prevalence of diverse schools of philosophy today and the same lesson must be extended to Africa. Let those who pursue sage philosophy, nationalistic ideological philosophy, analytic African philosophy, African philosophical hermeneutics, ethnos–philosophia, postcolonial African philosophy, African feminist philosophy, among others, embark on such endeavours with the blessing of the diversity of schools and approaches that the history of philosophy has taught us. In other words, African philosophers need not be blinded by the seemingly irresolvable problem of its two broad schools of thought, that is, universalism and particularism in the same way philosophy in the West has not been hampered in terms of its progress by the seemingly irresolvable differences between the analytic tradition and its continental counterpart.

Rather than being bogged down in the controversies over universalism versus particularism it is important to just respect each of them as representing important philosophical positions that will forever provide the framework within which philosophical work can proceed. Crucial to the debate is the question whether traditional African thought could also count as philosophy. The response that is given to this question is important because the refutation of the colonial denigration of Africa depends on a clear answer to the question. The other significant question that should be at the back of our minds in dealing with these methodological controversies is whether an understanding of Africa free from Eurocentric biases is possible and of the approaches at hand which one promises such a possibility? In Africa's 'struggle for reason' real and radical criticism only begins at that stage when the West is no longer viewed as the only model of philosophy against which Africa has to be measured because there are other traditions of philosophy outside the West (Kebede 2004). There is always the danger of using Western philosophy, a philosophy specifically designed to promote the hegemony of the West, to measure the potential of Africa. In other words, once an attempt is made to resort to the standards of the West in order to judge that which that very model was designed to denigrate then it is impossible to escape Eurocentrism and its disparaging perspectives on indigenous African thought systems. This is part of the major problem facing the professional school in African philosophy, which accedes to the Eurocentric canons of philosophy and its so-called universality. African philosophers belonging to the professional school seem to have been so mesmerised by science and its rationality that they almost forgot to remind themselves that there could be other ways of assessing the substance of other traditions such as those of Africa whose traditions did not distinguish between rationalism, mysticism and empiricism in their approach to knowledge (see Kebede 2004).

Since the question of African philosophy has always been a moral and political issue, the fundamental concern comes down to the issue of what is it that can liberate Africa from the suffocating tutorship of the West. Those so-called collective and uncritical beliefs designated disparagingly as ethnophilosophy by some did not just originate by themselves but owe their existence to individual thinkers who initiated them. It is for this reason that some philosophers hold that even collective thinking be considered as philosophy in its own right for the simple reason that those beliefs originated in the brains of specific individuals before being adopted by the community. The particularist school which feeds both from ethnophilosophy (read as ethnos-philosophia) and the postmodernist rejection of universality and the affirmation of plurality, remains an enticing position to a number of African scholars particularly those concerned with the mental and conceptual decolonisation of Africa. Postmodernism liberates those people marginalised because of colonialism and Western hegemony to call on their own particulars. As pointed out by Kebede (2004:115) 'particularism remains a fact as long as there are traits particular to Africans'. Once Western universality is removed, a pluralist view of philosophy is inevitable. In other words, possibilities are created for a different definition and understanding of philosophy from that of the West, which takes cognisance of the geography and historical circumstances out of which those philosophies are born. Those who defend this position are convinced that there is no timeless essence or essential unity that characterises all philosophising since there can certainly be no single style of inquiry. The classical philosophies of the Sophists, some of which are a collection of pithy sayings, are not similar in style to modern philosophy in the West or the analytic and continental traditions of philosophy. It would be remiss of Africans if they failed to realise that the model of philosophy championed by the West with its obsession with rationality and science was the reason why in the first place Africans were denied not only philosophy but their humanity. To accede to that model is tantamount to enslaving Africans to Western ideals. As Kebede (2004:149) rightly points out: 'since the purpose of colonial discourse is to paint Africa as an insolvent debtor, nothing could be more damaging than Africans acquiescing to the discourse of viewing themselves as merely borrowers'. Philosophy everywhere, even within the West itself, is plural.

Even if we were to keep the definition of philosophy as inherited from the established tradition of philosophy, as Africans the need to establish veritable philosophical texts of our own will inevitably direct our focus onto the particular. Advocating for what he calls strategic particularism, Wiredu (1998:28) reminds us that for the time being, we in Africa have no option but to include in our projects, as a matter of urgency, a decolonising program of pursuing the universal by way of the particular in the form of particularistic studies of traditional African philosophies.

The African intellectual heritage

> [We must never forget] the quasi-miraculous fact that once on this earth… walked other men and women, as actual as we are today, thinking their own thoughts, swayed by their own passions, but now all gone, one generation vanishing after another, gone as utterly as we shall shortly be gone as ghost at cock crow. This is the most familiar and certain fact about life, but it is also the most poetic. (Trevelyan 1949:13)

Perhaps this is the reason why every generation owes it to those who have gone before it to tell the story of their achievements and to preserve it for those still to come. Such is the purpose of this work, for there is no doubt that the Africans, and in this case the Shona who have gone before us, have left something for us to cherish. The image of indigenous African systems of thought as uncritical, unreflective, unscientific, closed, and of no philosophical substance represents one of the enduring misconceptions about African thought and culture. In this work I maintain that a critical and systematic analysis and interpretation of the traditions often taken for granted that encompass imaginative oral narratives, myths, folktales, songs, proverbs, riddles, idioms, art works, ritual practices and beliefs, and wise sayings can yield a Shona philosophy. It should be possible to salvage an indigenous and African intellectual heritage under threat from dominant epistemologies and put together a book on the indigenous philosophy of the Shona people of Southern Africa. The question of how to retrieve the tradition of philosophy from the indigenous cultures of Africa, despite the absence of a proper means of documentation within those cultures, is among some of the polemical issues in postcolonial African philosophy (Gyekye 1987; Hallen and Sodipo 1997; Awolabi 2001). It is important at this stage to note that the question of written records is itself another contentious issue. That is what we identify in this work as the scriptocentric fallacy, an issue that will be dealt with in coming sections. The installation of a tradition versus modern ideology within Africa is traceable to what Eze (1997:4) characterised as 'the brutal encounter of the African world with Western modernity'. It initiated a dualism in both modes of thought and existence which has greatly affected Africa's relationship to its traditions. Binary opposites such as tradition versus modernity, primitive versus civilised, magical versus scientific, oral versus written, among many others which have come to define African existence, have had, in general, a debilitating effect on the epistemic significance and validity of indigenous African thought.

For some time now African philosophers have been engaged in a debate of their own trying to close what seems to be a yawning gap in their discipline and to help establish a clear and continuous record of philosophical discourse that links postcolonial African philosophy to its pre-colonial cousin. Without a record of pre-colonial African philosophy, the history of African philosophy would be anything but complete. The question of how to get this silenced part of the African pre-colonial past speak to postcolonial Africa and the rest of the world is one that has been undertaken by a few notable scholars who stand out as champions of historical reconstruction. Notable among these are the works of Parker, *The African Origin of Grecian civilization*; James's *Stolen Legacy*; Obenga's *Egypt: Ancient History of African Philosophy*; Diop's *The African Origin of Civilisation: Myth or Reality*; and Bernal's ground-breaking work *Black Athena: The Afroasiatic roots of Classical civilization*, to select but a few. That these works touched a raw nerve is reflected in the overwhelming responses they generated ranging from those who were relieved that at last the truth was beginning to be told to those who thought this kind of 'heresy' had no place in scholarship and therefore felt the urge to stop it forthwith. For this reason these scholars have been celebrated and vilified at the same time. As Parker confirms:

> to claim an African origin of the Grecian civilisation is hardly in keeping with the historical tradition inherited from our school days. It savours of a sort of heresy and passes far beyond the limits of popular opinion. (Parker 1917:334)

As for Bernal (1987), his choice of title alone – Black Athena – is an open call to revisit the entire story of Western civilisation. Athena was apparently the most ostentatiously Hellenic of ancient Greek deities (van Binsbergen 2011:20). Bernal's book was seen not only as an affront to scholarship but also as an attack on the society that prided itself in this 'stolen' history. The exposé was indeed intolerable as it threatened to subvert the 'universal truth' and to reduce Western history to another racialist myth. In his *Black Athena Comes of Age*, Van Binsbergen offers some insight into the nature of Bernal's project and how it unfolded. Van Binsbergen writes:

> Wreaking havoc on the Western identitary and cultural self-image; addressing issues that directly relate to the main trends of contemporary history and sociology (racism, exclusion, cultural domination, White and Western/North Atlantic hegemony), and the latter's challenge by representatives of other continents and other cultures; and combining an inveterate tendency to champion theories outside the specialist mainstream with passion for ad hominem arguments derived from his personal sociology of knowledge – Bernal blazed a trail of polemics and conflicts throughout a considerable number of international scholar fields, conferences, and learned journals. (Van Binsbergen 2011:5–6)

Despite their courage, people like Bernal and those who share similar views about the story of human civilisation continue to be victims of disparagement by those in the dominant tradition. For example, soon after the publication of his book, a collection of twenty essays by leading scholars from a broad range of disciplines under the title *Black Athena Revisited* was published to confront what was perceived as Bernal's radical reinterpretation of the roots of classical civilisation. He was accused of putting forward unjustified claims and making gross exaggerations. Through the eyes of African philosophy these responses are reminiscent of the reactions that Tempels' text *Bantu Philosophy* provoked from the colonials when he proclaimed the existence of African philosophy. It is probably not coincidental that the qualifier in the title *Black Athena Comes of Age: Towards a Constructive Re-assessment* by Van Binsbergen is an attempt to set the tone of his own book apart from most of the responses that Bernal's work has received and possibly to define a new and constructive path for engaging with Bernal's historical arguments. A look at the works of the five scholars of historical reconstruction identified above reveals that all of them are united by the need to reveal what they perceived as the suppressed truth regarding Africa's contribution to world civilisation and to reclaim the position of Africa among other civilisations. There is consensus among them that classical civilisation has its roots in Afroasiatic cultures, but such influences have been deliberately and systematically suppressed since the 18th century for racist reasons. For these scholars the project of historical reconstruction is necessary as a precursor to the rehabilitation of proper relations among the world's peoples. In order to achieve their task and correct the so-called conventional history, these scholars have put forward historical, archaeological, and linguistic evidence to demonstrate the indebtedness of classical Western civilisation to Africa. For Bernal (1987:2) it was 'necessary not only to rethink the fundamental bases of "Western civilization" but also to recognise the penetration of racism and "continental chauvinism" into all historiography, or philosophy of history'. Their argument is that historians who have championed the Aryan model in the origin of civilisation have permitted their prejudice to cloud their judgment of the facts by making sure that no credit is given to other civilisations outside their own or anyone that falls within the pale of their prejudice. Asante (2003:37) correctly argues that 'African cultural interests have been consistently undermined by a determined Eurocentric intellectual conspiracy that began in the 15th century'. Not only has the West denied history to the African but they have also attempted to plant their race at every significant symbol of civilisation even in pre-colonial Africa. We are here reminded of colonial theories about the construction of the Great Zimbabwe monuments together with the sustained efforts to sever and disinherit ancient Egyptian civilisation from the rest of Africa. The attitude of most Western scholars towards scholarship that seeks to challenge the prevailing hegemony of the West in world civilisation remains largely dismissive. However, in the circles of Afrocentric scholars the arguments put forward by these champions of historical reconstruction represent an important step in the effort to revisit the whole global politics of knowledge, its production, dissemination and consumption. Efforts to close that knowledge gap created by conquest and subsequent years and years of subordination are critical among the indigenous peoples who suffered colonialism.

Philosophers in postcolonial Africa have not only benefited, but also furthered the efforts of historical reconstruction. In African philosophy this great intellectual history is now speaking to the contemporary reconstruction of African philosophy. A closer look at recent developments in African philosophy reveals various efforts at retrieving and reconstructing its history. Perhaps one of the outstanding efforts to try and preserve the African intellectual heritage has been the Sage philosophy project propounded by the famous Kenyan philosopher Henry Odera Oruka. Philosophical sagacity was an attempt to locate wise old men and women in the community who were not yet 'contaminated' by Western influence and interview them in order to rebuild a tradition of individualised philosophical activity in pre-colonial Africa. But one insurmountable hurdle to the continued application of that approach is the reality of cultural 'contamination' that has occurred and continues to occur across communities in the world. In other words, it is no longer possible to find traditional epistemic authorities who have not yet been influenced or 'contaminated' by outside cultures. However, despite this amount of influence from outside, traditional and indigenous forms of knowledge continue to exist and to inform life in most rural communities of Africa in their oral form. Indigenous systems of knowing and traditions can be salvaged through a deliberate process of engaging these sages and by going through the oral sources of information and narratives that still constitute an integral part of most rural communities in Africa. The question often posed is: how can the oral and often taken for granted myths, sayings and this whole gamut of African traditions be transformed into a critical and systematised collection of knowledge to constitute African philosophy? It is in dealing with this question that the significance of ordinary language philosophy and other interpretive methodologies like hermeneutics becomes apparent. This appears to be the only means by which an endeavour to seek out the philosophical traces of the past, make sense of them, and then fashion them into a coherent and logical account can be achieved. However, like in all the other social sciences any work which is interpretive and reconstructive cannot constitute the final word on the matter. But as Gardner (2010:24) rightfully notes, 'to accept that we cannot achieve a 100 per cent standard of truth in our knowledge of the past implies no contingent requirement to accept a direct inversion of the standard to the level of zero per cent'. Contestation and debate on the interpretation of texts and their meanings is indeed part and parcel of what defines philosophy as a discipline.

To reconstruct a philosophical record of traditional Shona philosophy this work also draws on the method of hermeneutics. Since its objective is understanding and its approach is interpretation, hermeneutics constitutes a method which encompasses elements of human communication, language and discourse at its centre. These are also elements that define traditional African thought in its predominantly oral character. The application of the hermeneutical method in our endeavour is ideal because language, in its nature and in its use, is complex and capable of supporting many different meanings; 'it is polysemic through and through'. Given the basic and multiple functions of language it is not difficult to see that language has to be interpreted because the words used carry different meanings in different contexts and this affects the message they in turn seek to convey. Okere (1983:15) locates African philosophy within the whole interpretative framework of hermeneutics by taking hermeneutics as an epistemological tool, a method of mediation, for making the passage between culture as lived and culture as reflected.

The term hermeneutics is etymologically linked to the Greek words *hermeneuein* and *hermeneia* which point back to the Greek messenger-god, Hermes. As the messenger-god, Hermes was associated with the function of transmitting what was beyond human understanding into a form that human intelligence could grasp. The Greeks credited Hermes with the discovery of language and writing, the very tools which human understanding employs to grasp meaning and to convey it to others (Palmer 1969:13). According to Okere (1983:19), the term 'hermeneutics' means either to express, to explain, to translate, or to interpret. Hermeneutics originally meant the investigation of the nature and principles of correct interpretation of realities whose meaning is not immediately evident (Okere 1983:19). The goal of interpretation is to uncover the hidden meaning, to bring to light, to decipher and to understand. Ricoeur (1974) submits that interpretation is the work of thought which consists of deciphering the hidden meaning in the apparent meaning and of unfolding the levels of meaning implied in the apparent meaning. For Okere, it is only within the context of hermeneutics that African culture can give birth to African philosophy. Dilthey (1986) on the other hand saw in hermeneutics the core discipline which could serve as the foundation of all the disciplines concerned with understanding humanity and its art, actions and writings. Within the context of trying to reconstruct indigenous philosophies, hermeneutics can therefore be taken as the system of interpretation; 'both recollective and iconoclastic' employed to reach the meaning behind the text in its broader sense and which is here understood as encompassing myths, symbols of society and traditions. It is a process of deciphering that goes from the manifest content and meaning to latent or hidden meaning (Palmer 1969:44). In representing the past to the present, the task of hermeneutics is to uncover the meaning of the texts that remain to us, within the context that makes their comprehension possible. Hermeneutics takes seriously the historicity of a people, given that culture provides the horizon of philosophical reflection. Hermeneutical philosophers are therefore open and respectful of the cultural heritage of Africa (Kebede 2004). Documents and monuments are expressions of life and through interpretation they enable us to relive and recapture a reading of the hidden meaning in the text of an apparent meaning. In this work, hermeneutics will be employed as an interpretive tool to examine the language, proverbs, sayings, myths, symbols, narratives and worldviews of the Shona which can shed light on the various facets of their life, which when put together can yield their philosophy. It is important to emphasise that the reconstruction of the indigenous Shona philosophy will rely on both the written traces of their traditions as well as oral accounts that constitute part of the everyday discourse and experiences in the community.

Questioning the scriptocentric fallacy

> 'Illiteracy' is a 'scriptocentric' term – it presupposes writing as the norm, and the absence of writing as a flaw. (Miller 1990:68)

According to Miller (1990:68), the term 'illiteracy' imposes a negative judgement and prevents one from thinking in positive or at least neutral terms of orality that is, concerning those non-literate verbal arts and forms of expression that sustained cultures for centuries before modern forms of writing came along. Kadiatu (1998:19) observed that 'the diagnosis of illiteracy upon another society points directly towards a "scriptocentric" world view which marks a state of "orality" as a state of nature'. The ascription of illiteracy was often politically motivated as it located those communities designated as such as occupying a blank and negative space outside history. It was appropriate and politically expedient for the anthropologist, as a colonial agent, to postulate the absence of 'text' in traditional Africa. In this way the absence of text became indicative of the absence of self-consciousness or even of self-knowledge with which the ethnographer is then able to create and donate to the subjects of her analysis in order for them to make sense of themselves. The invention of the savage by the colonial anthropologist and ethnographer is therefore at the root of the whole scriptocentric fallacy that has sought to deny epistemology to traditional Africa. It is this invented myth which needs to be deconstructed in order to allow African traditions to make their contribution to the global knowledge landscape. As correctly noted by Keita:

> From a strictly historical point of view the notion of an oral Africa and literate Europe is clearly forced. Literacy is a recent phenomenon in Europe – of course a very small minority of Greeks, and much later on, a small number of West Europeans learned to read and write Latin, but the vast majority of the inhabitants of feudal and industrial Europe were illiterate. Individuals learned to read and write during the recent advent of mass education. On the other hand some Africans knew how to read and write before the colonial era. Thus the term 'oral tradition' as opposed to 'literate tradition' should be employed guardedly. General usage, however, seems to imply that in some way 'orality' is inherent to African 'essence' while 'literacy' is a 'physiological' trait of Europeans. (Keita 1984:74)

This in itself demonstrates why a proper understanding of Africa is necessarily deconstructive in order to correct this harshly stereotyped and negated African past.

> Mudimbe's invention of Africa is a brilliant general survey of how Western construction of 'primitive' and 'savage' images of Africa, particularly in historical and anthropological studies, has influenced the rise of alienated discourse and self-identity among Africans themselves. (Masolo 1994:178)

This is what Africans have to consistently and consciously struggle against. Niane cited in Miller (1990:96) argues that 'our knowledge will remain incomplete so long as we have not extracted from the traditionalists the secrets they hold'. The need to document and communicate ideas among indigenous communities across the world including of course the Shona is something that cannot be ignored. Language is central to philosophy because philosophy without language would become a solitary task available only to the single individual.

Weighing in on the debate on the nature of African philosophy and in an effort to demonstrate the value of oral narratives as sources of philosophy, Richard Bell draws our attention to the village palaver in the African traditional setting as an indispensable point of call to see philosophy at work in its very Socratic form. The point he makes is crucial to the discussion of the Shona as one example of a community to which his observation applies with utmost relevance. According to Bell:

> If we search for what kinds of narrative situations force critical dialogue in the African context we need not look far. The very nature of village life yields many such critical dialogues. A property dispute is brought before the elders and debated – why? So justice can be served. When concern for illness or a community crisis arises, we might ask why a diviner or healer is called or a council convened? The village model in Africa is a model of free discourse for the purpose of making good judgments and for doing justice for individuals and the community. These narrative situations force dialogue and give rise to human reflection, and they are far from uncritical. Each dialogical situation has earmarks of the Socratic enterprise; each is formative of the values characteristic of that community; each reflects the existential texture of human life; each dialectically serves to move a community from injustice to justice, from wrong to right, from brokenness to wholeness, from ignorance to truth.

> As each community 'revaluates' its life in terms of new external factors, it can critically evolve its traditions to meet modernity. (Bell, 1989:373)

Unlike the written text which is literally fixed and without change, oral discourses are 'alive' and subject to collective refashioning; they occupy the temporal space of the moment and are in that sense securely connected to the immediacy of the present and open to the creativity of change. Many believe that it was not because Socrates could not write that he did not put his philosophy in writing but it was simply because of his dislike for writing. Socrates believed that writing weakened the power of the mind and memory, and that writing was a process of killing words as it hinders the back-to-forth exchange or movement of words typical of conversations. Africa's oral narratives just like Socrates' oral classes engage participants, enabling them to respond in a critical dialogical manner.

That the philosophical discourse does not require writing as a prerequisite for its existence is a point which has been forcefully made in African philosophy debates and elsewhere. In other words, while nobody can doubt the importance of writing to the philosophical enterprise, the power of the oral and what Bell (1989) calls 'narrative in philosophy' cannot be underestimated. Socrates, who is the father of Western philosophy, gave philosophy its oral identity and presents us with an oral master class in philosophy. For this reason it is ideal that we also extend the same validity to oral dialogue and narrative in traditional Africa as authentic sources of philosophy. As Bell (1989) argues, focusing on the oral and the narrative is of great significance to contemporary African philosophy because it allows us not only to reclaim part of the rich oral heritage from our past but also, by taking the oral and the written alongside each other in African thought, we are able to reaffirm that continuity between the non-literate and literate communities which still coexist in the African context. Bell argues that 'there is no greater divide between critical and literate contexts and narrative and non-literate contexts in African culture' (Bell 1989:376) and that is an idea I also subscribe to, particularly as I seek to reconstruct a philosophy from the Shona's traditional past which was also devoid of modern forms of writing. Prejudice against oral sources as forms of knowledge is one of the serious problems that Africa has had to deal with for ideas from its pre-colonial past to constitute an integral part of the postcolonial knowledge landscape.

In his *Of Grammatology*, Derrida (1967) put forward an argument to address the problem of binaries of speech versus written, presence versus absence, written versus oral. He redefined and broadened the concept of writing dealing a blow to the purported distinction between literate and oral cultures. His definition of writing goes beyond writing as ordinarily understood and in its restricted graphematic sense to include speech (Norris). According to him we cannot conceive of spoken language without structure, without system, conventions, parts of speech, grammar, tenses, codes, systems of relationships and difference. According to Norris, what Derrida meant was that writing is therefore in some sense prior to speech, not in the historical, chronological or diachronic sense, but prior in the sense that spoken language presupposes the possibility of writing.[6] In other words, 'the potential of writing, along with many of its structural characteristics, is built into the very nature of spoken language from the outset' (Norris). Derrida gave the concept of writing 'a far broader and more general sense to the point where writing – as arche-ecriture or a kind of proto-writing – becomes almost co-existent with every culture' (Norris). Even in the so-called primitive societies, territorial markers or signs of ownership, like a path across the middle of a field to demarcate two separate pieces of property, are forms of proto-writing, of arche-ecriture; they are visible inscriptions which signify a certain legally enforced order of property relations. The dualism of oral versus written, among other binary opposites such as primitive versus civilised, logical versus illogical, magical versus scientific, forms a set of thinking about the other that has been used by the West to denigrate and suppress other forms of knowing and existence. Derrida provides a framework within which orality may not be looked at as a condition defining and characterised by 'absence' of literacy, but instead a potential and fertile ground oozing with writing possibilities. What, then, does it mean to say that a seemingly oral culture 'has' writing? Unlike the popular and most famously held position that speech precedes writing, Derrida held that writing precedes speech by giving writing a different interpretation. Derrida's notion of writing as that which conditions the possibility of speech is linked to the recognition that the discernment of signs, especially words, presumes the perception of spaces or intervals, such that one word can be separated out from another upon hearing and reading (Derrida 1967:39). The prior existence of writing in all cultures implies that writing as ordinarily understood does not have a uniform source and history. Cultures developed various methods of expressing their thoughts and of communicating the message to each other. Senner (1989) argued:

> Some 20th century linguists and historians of writing see the earliest precursors of writing in the innumerable cave drawings and carvings of the upper Paleolithic. Scattered throughout the world from the famous caves at Lascaux, France, to the rock shelters of central India and the far reaches of Southern Zimbabwe, these durable products of imagination of prehistoric man seem to lend credence to the theory that the human need to communicate is too universal and diversified to admit of a single source. (Senner 1989:2)

Although scholars such as Diringer (1978) would want to convince us that rock paintings are 'isolated, arbitrary and unsystematic' and a form of 'embryo-writing' which must be distinguished from 'conscious writing', I tend to agree with the views of those scholars like Baron (1981) and Senner (1989) who argue that rock paintings do not depict meaningless doodles or scratches but they are stratified representations that are pregnant with meaning (see Senner 1989:2–4). In certain cases they even demonstrate a degree of productive combination, a major criterion of syntactic writing. Gracia (1992:169) argued that linguistic signs, put down and codified, have meaning and significance only insofar as there is a community of individuals that understands the concepts for which the signs stand, and insofar as that community takes what principles and rules the signs reveal into consideration in its behaviour. Pictography is indeed a form of writing and in and of itself rock art was a sophisticated form of writing, a practice of fixing ideas and laying them down for posterity. Writing about prehistoric art in Africa, Ki-Zerbo made the following important point concerning rock art:

> The term 'petroglyph' has been coined for rock pictures. More than any other in fact, this kind of art is a sign language, that is, a bridge between reality and idea. It is a set of graphic symbols and to read it one needs a key. (Ki-Zerbo 1981:667)

The symbols on caves were in this case forms of writing and on that basis there seems to be no reason why one should regard pre-colonial Africans as illiterate and hence devoid of any knowledge. Equally significant is Wa Thiong'o's analysis of the relation between the tongue and the pen in which he stresses the primacy of the spoken word by asserting 'the pen imitates the tongue. The pen is clerk to the tongue. It draws pictures of the spoken. The pen speaks the already spoken' (Wa Thiong'o 2013:159). For Wa Thiong'o, if we are to develop knowledge, philosophy, and all the other arts in Africa and through African languages then we have to listen to the

African tongues and what they are saying. My intention is not to enter into the debate on orality and writing but to illustrate that within philosophy there are arguments that have been put forward that in essence debunk the myth of emptiness premised on the assumed absence of written discourse. From the oral heritage it is therefore possible to develop an autochthonous philosophical heritage that does not owe anything to outside or Western traditions of thought. This philosophical tradition is important in order to establish that thread of philosophical thought from the pre-colonial past to the African present – a continuity almost completely severed by colonial conquest. Those obsessed with writing as it is ordinarily understood should therefore rethink the implications of what they say when they deny a tradition of philosophical thinking to traditional Africa on the basis of the absence of writing. Different cultures have created different epistemologies to understand, predict, and manage their environment. These organised bodies of knowledge which provide meaning, direction and coherence to life are carried in language giving rise to different forms of knowledge. It is imperative for African philosophers to learn from the traditions, tales, myths and proverbs of their people, so as to draw from them the concepts of a true African philosophy and to bring out the specific categories of African thought. Philosophers are both effects and causes of their social circumstances, politics, institutions and beliefs of their time. African philosophers within the analytic tradition such as Wiredu (1980), Gyekye (1987), Hallen and Sodipo (1997), and Hallen (2006) are convinced that through a careful analysis and interpretation of indigenous African languages it is possible to formulate a philosophical system that meets the rigor of philosophy while avoiding the problems of simple narration or description. The readily available sources of an oral philosophical tradition are communal proverbs, maxims, tales, lyrics, poetry, art, and myths among others. It is to proverbs that I now turn the focus of my attention.

Proverbs and Shona philosophy

> The genius, wit, and spirit of a nation are discovered in its proverbs. In them is to be found an inexhaustible source of precious documents in regard of the interior history, the manners, the opinions, the beliefs, the customs of the people among whom they had their course. (Sir Francis Bacon, 1561–1626)

The above quotation is consciously selected to serve two specific purposes. First, it serves as a response to those scholars who are sceptical about the philosophical import of proverbs, and secondly, to affirm the basis upon which proverbs are taken as important resources from which philosophical ideas can be distilled. Wimmer submits that the collection of sayings and proverbs, of tales and myths, and analysis of linguistic patterns and structures hardly provide any arguments on philosophical matters. He argued:

> Can we ever expect to get arguments in favour or against, say, Kantian concepts of time (or moral duties) by reading Grimm's tales? It sounds no less absurd to me when I hear that Kant's theory of the categorical imperative is proved to be invalid by some Gikuyu sayings. What we do not learn from Gikuyu or Tyrolian, Chinese, or any other sayings is the one thing which we ought to know: what exactly are the criteria, the methods, the proofs and where can they be found, which could entitle us to say that a proposition is true or false, that a norm is valid or not? Proverbs have taught us to be cautious, they do not teach us the way to obtain knowledge. A proverb never 'refutes' any (philosophical or other) argumentation. (Wimmer 2002:20)

As a response to Wimmer one wonders whether he could argue the same about the pithy sayings of such ancient philosophers like Heraclitus that to this day constitute an integral part of the history of Western philosophy famously designated as classical philosophy. Wimmer's position appears to be ill-conceived as it attempts to perpetuate the very myths that other postmodern approaches to philosophy have sought to dispel or fight against. There are diverse views and methods of conceiving of philosophy across cultures and modern Western philosophy should not constitute the yardstick against which all other traditions should be measured. Why does it sound absurd for him that one African saying from a specific African culture can refute Kant's categorical imperative? Is it because the logic contained in the Gikuyu saying cannot match that contained in Kant's categorical imperative or is it a question of failing to deal with the old categories of thinking manifesting themselves rather implicitly in every view that pits African and Western against each other? While individuals may hold different opinions, typical of the philosophical enterprise, there is greater consensus regarding the philosophical import of proverbs and other traditional sayings and narratives. Scholars such as Gyekye (1987), Wanjohi (2008) and Kimmerle (1997a; 1997b) among others all agree that these varieties of traditions constitute the philosophical substratum of the thinking of African peoples. Proverbs can be conceived as philosophical sayings and as sources of philosophy. Within this vein, it is therefore legitimate to regard proverbs as repositories of philosophy contrary to the opinion of Wimmer who in my eyes has failed to see clearly through the age old prejudices perennially directed against African traditions. D'Israeli reminds us that:[7]

> the interest we may derive from the study of proverbs is not confined to their universal truths, nor to their poignant pleasantry; a philosophical mind will discover in proverbs a great variety of the most curious knowledge. The manners of a people are painted after life in their domestic proverbs; and it would not be advancing too much to assert, that the genius of the age might be often in those proverbs.

It is the variety of curious knowledge as alluded to in the above position that I set myself out to discuss. Proverbs provide us with a window to enter into the minds of our forebears and their experiences as expressed in this wisdom. Wisdom can be identified as the first and most significant quality of a proverb and is defined simply as 'moral advice based on experience' (Taylor 1981:4). There is no doubt about the fact that proverbs are a subject of speculative curiosity to most of the philosophers in Africa. These vestiges and memorials of thought which in themselves represent, undoubtedly, a collection of successive knowledge over the years must be an integral part of our present together with the truths they propound concerning life and existence. We cannot allow prejudice against this reservoir of insight into facets of life to rob African philosophy of one of its most basic and primary texts of reflection. There is no doubt in my mind that Africa's own philosophical identity must be linked to its cultural heritage, and proverbs are one such cultural heritage out of which critical philosophical ideas inherent in indigenous Africa can be fashioned. These treasures of wisdom and jewels of thought are in themselves a condensed oral text of experience and knowledge about existence transmitted through generations for posterity. It is probably not coincidental that Taylor (1981) chose the following telling title to his article on proverbs – 'The wisdom of many and the wit of one' – to emphasise the fact that proverbs are ingenious ideas invented by individuals, but accepted by the community because of their moral and practical utility as life lessons based on shared experience.

The opening quotation at the beginning of the section which comes from the famous British philosopher and statesman, Francis Bacon, captures in a fundamental way the spirit and conviction that drives me to focus on Shona proverbs as sources from which an indigenous Shona philosophy can be reconstructed. I regard proverbs as forms of condensed wisdom or assertions that captivate and capture the attention of any curious mind. To regard proverbs as repositories of philosophy is in turn to acknowledge their force as sources of creative practical knowledge that allow society to negotiate the pitfalls and contradictions of life. In themselves they are basically summaries of the whole life experiences of a people; experiences built over centuries of interacting with each other and the environment. As repositories of wisdom for living, proverbs derive from the experiences of the wise men and women of society, affirming either clearly or metaphorically, popular indisputable truths about life in general. As Kudadjie (in Saayman) submits:

> the ultimate purpose of proverbs is to impart wisdom, teach good moral and social values, warn against foolish acts, provide a guide to good conduct, influence people's conduct, and help them to succeed in life. (Kudadjie 1997:179)

Since their content and symbolism is basically cultural in origin and orientation, proverbs constitute the basic text from which the Shona people's great thoughts on life can be located, systematised and analysed. Within the African context, proverbs can be regarded as the book of life; the reference text of existence and of living well with others in community. The originators of these proverbs, who are the elders, are the equivalent in today's academic terminology of the professors or experts in knowledge. Proverbs contain wisdom that can still be applied in dealing with problems of our contemporary society. As highlighted by Gyekye (1987:21), proverbs represent wise sayings of individuals with acute speculative intellects. They draw special interest from philosophers because they touch on fundamental truths about human beliefs, their picture of reality and experience. Philosophy is basically an enterprise defined on the basis of its pursuit of wisdom and since proverbs are in a sense the fountain of a culture's wisdom, they inevitably and appropriately constitute the subject of philosophical interest and must be subjected to interpretation.

Any mention of proverbs within the Shona culture automatically draws one's attention to the conventional prefix which normally precedes the use or application of a proverb to any circumstance. These are the phrases *vakuru vakati* (the elders said) and its other variant *hanzi nevakuru* (and so the elders said). These two will constitute the starting point of my reflection on Shona proverbs. The two phrases highlighted above have an important bearing on the Shona conception of knowledge and their communal ontology. The word *vakuru* means 'the elders'. These are the sages, both living and dead, accredited with the authorship of this wisdom and for their unparalleled generosity in bequeathing this important wisdom at no cost to posterity. The *vakuru* are therefore individuals who deserve respect and are accordingly acknowledged all the time, in all circumstances, before one can appeal to a proverb. The honour is what this phrase (*vakuru vakati*), which prefixes the application of a proverb, is meant to fulfill. The appeal to *vakuru* also serves another important purpose: besides being a means of locating oneself within the line of cultural experts and a way to honour and respect the elders, the phrase also serves to evoke the value, shared consensus, and timelessness attached to the wisdom of the elders as contained in the proverbs. As one uses a proverb one is in actual fact appealing to the authority of the elders; to their accumulated wisdom which has provided counsel and direction from time immemorial. Given that the Shona believe that the origin of humanity cannot be measured in time but goes back to infinity and it is only *Musikavanhu* (God) who is privileged to know the real beginning of humanity, they equally imply by the same token that the wisdom contained in the proverbs is wisdom that dates back to time immemorial and the ideas they contain have been refined to a sufficient level where they almost now pass as expressions of indubitable truths about life and living with others. Because of the Shona cosmic vision, the *vakuru* are not just ordinary persons, they are those who have seen it all, those who, through experience as elders, were being drawn closer and closer to the truth about life; they are those who have literally read the book of life, that is, those who have accumulated valuable lessons of life through experience. From their detailed observation of the behaviour of human beings and meticulous attention to detail as they interacted with their environment, which includes fellow human beings and all natural phenomena, and being influenced by their picture of the world and knowledge of be-ing, they have been able to put together short but powerful guides to practical living in the form of proverbs within their cultures. This is precisely the reason why Sumner (1999:22) argues that tradition is re-actualised each time a proverb is uttered in the sense that the image of the ideal society and the authority of tradition find themselves being brought to the fore in the course of the dialogue.

Another equally important function of the phrase *vakuru vakati* is connected to the need to protect the one passing a comment or offering counsel from any ad hominem attack of any kind from the one to whom comment is directed. It is thus a way of claiming immunity to attack by forestalling any angry responses from the person being given counsel or being reprimanded. By recourse to the famous prefix *vakuru vakati* the person is basically claiming that he/she is only a messenger, so please do not shoot the messenger. This is because most proverbs reveal painful truths. The *vakuru* as the equivalent of professors in today's society can be called professors whose area of specialty is 'living with others' in society and whose distilled wit and wisdom expressed in countless proverbs is the equivalent to today's refereed publications. In summary, therefore, the phrase *vakuru vakati* and its variant *hanzi nevakuru*, are phrases that seek to, among other things, acknowledge the value of this important and immemorial wisdom; recognise and pay due respect to the originators of the wisdom; act as an appeal to the authority of tradition, or a veiled call for attention, and a means to create a platform from which to give/launch attack, criticism or counsel. In the language of scholarship it can be taken as an acknowledgement of a source of literature just as modern scholarship would say 'according to this or that author'. The phrase plays the role of a footnote that acknowledges the originators and authors of the ideas in the entire discourse of proverbs. The fact that knowledge is communally owned coupled with the absence of an individualistic approach to claiming firm and genius, together with the overriding ontology of the Africans, has culminated in the situation that no individuals claim authorship of those proverbs.

Among the many features of Shona proverbs there is one that stands out and which may deserve brief analysis – this is their apparent contradiction. Some scholars have attempted to dismiss the value of proverbs on the basis of their apparent tendency to contradict each other, where one proverb recommends this while the other advocates something to the contrary. However, as Kriel (1971) observed, two proverbs that appear to contradict can both be understood within the quest for moderation as a virtue among communitarian Africans. The two proverbs should be taken as addressing two excesses in behaviour whose middle point defines appropriate behaviour. For example '*mwana asingachemi anofira mumbereko*' (a baby that does not cry can die in the baby carrier) versus '*mugoti unopiwa anyerere*' (it is the quiet individuals and not those too demanding and pestering that often get favours). Kriel argued:

> proverbs are not rallying calls which spur people on to seek what is highest and noblest in life, but rather checks to those who have deviated either to the left or the right of the golden mean. The more proverbs are

> grouped into classes which form contradictory pairs, the more their users appear as people who put a premium on moderation. (Kriel 1971:15)

Appealing to the Aristotelian doctrine of moderation proposed by Kriel (1971), it would make sense to view the two proverbs above as imploring people to seek the mean between unbridled attention seeking and not seeking attention at all. A middle position would be much more appropriate where individuals are encouraged to seek attention without becoming a nuisance particularly to others within the community. Of the two proverbs above, the second proverb is meant, on one hand, to encourage those who are so outspoken to the extent of overshadowing the demands of all others to exercise some restraint and take note of others, while on the other hand the first one calls on those who are conspicuously quiet to speak out when they do require assistance because people should not be left to guess as to whether or not the individual requires assistance. In a way the two proverbs advocate what may be called a diplomatic approach where one is able to strike a balance between being too assertive and not making any demands at all. Having a character or behaviour that somehow fits in this middle ground is what the elders sought to encourage as marking appropriate behaviour.

Other scholars who have considered the apparent opposition in African proverbs have explained it away as an indication of the power and strength of language among the different African societies. They regard this as an ability by the elders to demonstrate their technique to resolve problems and offer educative counsel by playing with words and turning ideas around to respond to specific situations. As Mutsvairo (1978:169) submits, 'in the hands of an experienced linguist, they (proverbs) can be utilised most beneficially to warn, admonish, instruct, teach, and even enrich the point under discussion'. In his article entitled 'Do proverbs contradict?' Yankah (1984:2) argues that the claim that there is contradiction in proverbs is an illusion which is in part created by a superficial understanding of the dynamics that govern proverb usage. For him it is inappropriate to talk about contradiction between proverbs because their meanings are situational or contextual. The real meaning of a proverb is only revealed when it has been contextualised and that is why the application of proverbs is varied and flexible. Mieder, elaborating on the position of Yankah, submits that:

> today it has almost become a cliché to point out that proverbs must be studied in context. Proverbs in normal discourse are not contradictory at

all, and they usually make perfect sense to the speaker and the listener. After all people do not speak in proverbs pairs unless they are dueling with proverbs as verbal contests. (Mieder 2004:134)

It is important to remember that the annunciation of a proverb is contingent and coloured by circumstances (Sumner 1999:30). For those who may not be convinced with context and insist that indeed proverbs contradict, a different explanation may suffice. To account for the contradiction one may argue that probably, conscious of avoiding the fallacy of accident, which is committed by applying a general rule to all situations including a situation whose circumstances render the rule inapplicable, the elders developed these seemingly contradictory proverbs not to apply them in similar circumstances, but to make them work and offer advice in situations whose circumstances render the application of one of the other proverbs inappropriate. To an abnormally quiet person they would use one proverb to prompt them to speak their mind and how they feel about issues while to the extremely demanding and pestering individual they would use its opposite to encourage them to be patient. In both cases the aim of each proverb would be to correct inappropriate behaviour lying at both extremes.

In concluding this discussion on the philosophy of proverbs it may be important to quote from D'Israeli's succinct submission in which he writes:[8]

> PROVERBS embrace the wide sphere of human existence, they take all the colours of life, they are often exquisite strokes of genius, they delight by their airy sarcasm or their caustic satire, the luxuriance of their humour, the playfulness of their turn, and even by the elegance of their imagery, and the tenderness of their sentiment. They give a deep insight into domestic life, and open for us the heart of man, in all various states which he may occupy – a frequent review of PROVERBS should enter into our readings; and although they are no longer the ornaments of conversation, they have not ceased to be the treasures of Thought! [All caps are original].

It would be folly if we as African philosophers fail to tap into this corpus, a source of verbalised knowledge, and an indisputably genuine treasure of thoughts located in our midst. It is no wonder that Hamutyinei and Plangger (1974) dedicated their book which is a collection of Shona proverbs in honour of '*kumadzibaba vedu vari kunyakadzimu. Imi matsime nezvisipiti matinochera mvura youngwaru hwenyu hwamakasiyira isu vanhasi*' translated as 'our forefathers – the hidden authors of this book of wisdom'. In this way they sought to pay tribute to those who originated this wisdom and to acknowledge how useful it is still today. In the chapters that follow proverbs will constitute one of the important sources out of which aspects of indigenous Shona philosophy encompassing their ontology, epistemology, ethics and aesthetics will be articulated. It is because of the centrality of proverbs as sources of traditional wisdom that I saw it appropriate to devote a section of this nature to their analysis. Other oral sources of philosophy and their contributions will be assessed in various sections dealing with the different branches of indigenous Shona philosophy in the chapters to come.

Notes

1. In his article entitled 'Theory and practice in African philosophy: the poverty of speculative philosophy' Yai (1977) devotes an entire discussion to expose shortcomings in the critique of African traditional philosophy by those he calls the 'speculative philosophers' represented by people like Hountondji. These are the philosophers, according to Yai, who find all discussions on African philosophy prior to their own, nothing but mythologies, cosmogonies or at best 'ethnophilosophies' and who place greater emphasis on meta-language and on abstract-speculative constructions than on reality. For Yai, even their criticism of ethnophilosophy is vacuous because it does not rest on an analysis of African societies but derives from a prejudiced definition of philosophy representing European standards. Yai castigates these speculative African philosophers for being an elite of the elite who invoke science in order to justify their speculations instead of getting down to understand the thoughts or philosophies of the masses/people in their existential contexts. For him 'the elitism, philosophism and scientism of our abstract-speculative philosophers aims also at sparing them the test of coming into touch with facts, although this contact would have shown them that philosophy, both in Africa and elsewhere, is not above men or class, rather it is permeated by class struggle'(16). Philosophy in Africa should not be divorced from the politics and lived experiences of its people.

2. It may be important to mention that at the 23rd World Congress of Philosophy of 2013 held in Athens, Greece, which I also attended, the same issue was raised by one famous Nigerian philosopher in his presentation in the African Philosophy session that was chaired by none other than Hountondji himself.

3. Eze proposes that the post of 'postcolonial' African philosophy be written with special markers or under erasure to signify the unfulfilled dreams of the independence in Africa. His suggestion is an apt description of what some of us who subscribe to decolonial thinking and its liberative ideals think about the conditions in Africa.

4. In light of this, what I wish to emphasise is the fact that the label or prefix 'ethno' should not be seen as unique to philosophy. It appears in ethno-medicine, ethno-musicology, ethno-botany, ethno-science, ethno-mathematics, ethno-epistemology, where the 'ethno' is understood to be a designation of the native originativeness of whatever is under consideration. It is arguably within the context of philosophy that this term has been emphasised pejoratively and in the process earned itself a bad name. However, what is crucial and important to realise is that the 'ethno' of ethno-philosophy in its proper sense is no different from the 'ethno' in ethno-science or ethno-botany in that it seeks to highlight the cultural embeddedness of the ideas being articulated. This is the way I wish to employ the term in this work. Let me also take this opportunity to make the point that because of the fact that the term ethnophilosophy is widely used in African philosophical discourse I shall continue to use it in order to avert confusion, but I do so under protest because of my misgivings about the appropriateness of the term as outlined.

5. I am referring here to the work by Feyerabend with the same title see Feyerabend, P. 2011. *The Tyranny of Science*. Cambridge: Polity Press.

6. I am referring here to the work Christopher Norris, 'Derrida and Oralcy: Grammatology revisited', Available at: http://www2.lingue.unibo.it/acume/acumedvd/zone/research/essays/norris.htm (Accessed 21 October 2013).

7. Isaac D'Israeli (1766–1848) Curiosities of Literature. The Philosophy of proverbs. Available at: http://www.spamula.net/col/archives/2006/02/the_philosophy.html. (Accessed 13 May 2014).

8. Isaac D'Israeli (1766–1848) Curiosities of Literature. The Philosophy of proverbs. Available at: http://www.spamula.net/col/archives/2006/02/the_philosophy.html. (Accessed 13 May 2014).

3

Who are the Shona?

Concerning the Shona past

> By appealing to the praxis and wisdom of our African foreparents, we do not mean to repeat them, but we mean to make use of this praxis and wisdom as interpretive tools to enlighten present generations of Africans. (Makang 1997:336)

This submission is carefully selected not only for what it explicitly spells out but for what it implies as well. The statement is as much an elucidation of the importance of tradition as it is a silencing of misguided critics. This heritage which the elders, as great thinkers, bequeathed to present generations constitutes an indispensable body of literature that deserves careful consideration and analysis. We must be prepared to sift through this legacy, retaining that which is alive, casting off that which is lethargic, and critically appropriating what is valuable from the past with modern scientific conceptions. That is what will help us define the future. It is correct to claim that every culture produces a philosophy and that there is a philosophical component to every cultural thought system. Philosophy in Africa is rooted in an indigenous African cultural base from which it draws its problematic and presuppositions (Pearce 1992:441). As Serequeberhan (1994:17) reminds us 'philosophical discourse itself originates from and is organically linked to the concrete conditions-of-existence and life-practices of the horizon within and out of which it is formulated'. My argument for a Shona philosophy is driven by the particularistic conviction that philosophy is a product of culture, and that different assumptions and models of experiencing reality lead to different philosophical doctrines.

That knowledge not only originates from, but is also constituted by its social, linguistic or cultural context. What is distinctively African about African philosophy in general lies in its traditions from the past. And that is why the Shona past matters in this context. It is true that philosophical endeavours begin with the everyday, the familiar, which is part of the indigenous, and are embedded in the locutions that bridge our relations with the external world around us. This is a claim long established in the ordinary language philosophy movement (Masolo 2003:28). The language of the Shona people constitutes a valuable index to their philosophy since language serves both as an incubator and an agent of philosophical thought for language is 'the home of being'. Shona language is full of figurative, metaphorical and idiomatic expressions all of which paint valuable insights into the thinking and experiences of the Shona.

For Gyekye (1987:33) philosophers have to realise that language as a vehicle of concepts, not only embodies a philosophical point of view, but also influences philosophical thought. Highlighting the indebtedness of philosophy to language, Gyekye (1987:34) reminds us that even Western philosophy itself was brewed in a cultural soup whose ingredients were the mentalities, experiences, and folk thought and folkways of Western peoples. Philosophy proceeds from the facts of experience and it must be distilled from the comprehensive thought of the community through elaboration, clarification, and interpretation. The restoration of the Shona and by extension all of Africa's pre-colonial philosophical thinking and cultural references is not only necessary for the purposes of reasserting the waning African identity, but it also allows the indigenous societies to interpret and organise the world from their own standpoint. It entails assessing that intellectual heritage on the basis of what it meant for the indigenous peoples rather than how it compares to the modern scientific modes of rationality. This is precisely the point that Wiredu (1984) attempts to drive home in his article with the telling title 'How not to compare African thought with Western thought'. Doing justice to African traditions involves reading them within the context of their history. In this work I seek to interpret and translate the Shona past into conceptual categories that can be intelligible and useful to the present. Deprived of the African experience as a key aspect of the story of human civilisation, philosophy will remain incomplete and unrepresentative of the true reality. At this point it is important that I turn my attention on the Shona in terms of defining who they are as a people.

Who are the Shona?

The question concerning the identity and origin of the Shona peoples is one that has been dealt with extensively by historians (Garlake 1973; Beach 1980;1984; Nelson 1983; Chigwedere 1985; and Mudenge 1988), among others. There is general consensus among historians that the Shona are part of the Bantu people that came to settle in the central plateau of present day Zimbabwe and are credited with building the Great Zimbabwe stone structure which served as their political headquarters. As Nelson pointed out,

> the early history of the landlocked territory between the Limpopo and Zambezi rivers, found in oral chronicles dating back to the sixteenth century, is one of prosperous tribal confederations whose political and cultural development was centered at Great Zimbabwe. (Nelson 1983:3)

Although effort was made to deny the Shona the honour of having constructed one of the wonders of the world in the form of the magnificent Great Zimbabwe stone structure on the basis of the racist notion that they could not have done so on account of their colour, however,

> in 1906, British archaeologist David Randall-MacIver silenced skeptics when he published the findings of his systematic excavations, establishing that the stone structure at Great Zimbabwe was unquestionably African in every detail. (Nelson 1983:6)

In present day Zimbabwe, the Shona are an ethnic group that constitutes three quarters of the country's population. It is important to begin the discussion of the name Shona by drawing the reader's attention to the views of at least five scholars who have traced the historical origins of this name from different perspectives. My concern is to highlight the ways in which the different scholars have explained how the people called the Shona today came to acquire this umbrella identity. My exposition will somehow confirm Appiah's observation that throughout the world identities continue to flourish despite their roots in myths and falsehoods.

According to Appiah,

> every human identity is constructed, historical; every one has its share of false presuppositions, of the errors and inaccuracies that courtesy calls 'myths', religion 'heresy,' and science 'magic'. Invented histories, invented biologies, invented cultural affinities come with every identity;

each is a kind of role that has to be scripted, structured by conventions of narrative to which the world never quite manages to conform. (Appiah 1992:174)

Identity narratives in Africa have to a large extent been influenced by major historical processes that unfolded in the continent including of course colonialism. As such one cannot ignore the historical reality that 'the African identity is, in part, a product of the European gaze' (Appiah 1992:81). However, due to the familiarity engendered by time and habit, the controversial circumstances under which some of these identities were fashioned and eventually concretised into what they are today, is often forgotten and taken for granted. Let me now present a seriatim examination of the five submissions.

According to Kriel:

> It is very unlikely that a century ago anyone would have claimed to be a muShona ... The origin of this embracing term is still a matter of conjecture, but in spite of efforts to find an alternative the name still prevails, and has come to be accepted for indicating the largest language area of the country. (Kriel 1971:1)

In a note on terminology which is part of the preface to his work entitled *The Shona and Zimbabwe 900–1850*, Beach writes:

> I have used the term 'Shona' throughout, even though it came into use in the nineteenth century. The nearest historical approach to a name for the Shona-speaking people, 'Karanga' cannot be proven to have been used outside the north and east before the eighteenth century. The Shona people never had a name for the whole of the country in which they lived. Instead they used the local names of their separate territories. (Beach 1980:vi)

On the same issue Ranger argues:

> It seems to be clear that before 1890 no-one called themselves 'Manyika', 'Zezuru', 'Karanga', in the sense in which these terms are used today; it seems to me clear that before 1890 no-one called themselves 'Shona' at all ... (Ranger 1985a:4)

Chimhundu also weighs in:

> The name Shona itself became generally accepted only after Doke's Report. Previously, Karanga and Shona had been used interchangeably by the European writers, grammarians and lexicographers, virtually all of whom were missionaries. *Vanhu* was the name of the people taken collectively ... All the people were *vanhu,* and groups of *vanhu* were classified in terms of kinship and lineages, or *madzinza*. Each such group belonging to a common lineage was led by a chief, who was both the judge and the spiritual leader of this relatively small but well-defined group. It was Doke who recommended the use of the term Shona as a classificatory convenience. Doke argued: 'Both the grouping and the use of group-names are necessary for the purposes of linguistic classification. Similarly, it is essential to use a definite name as a label for the whole cluster of groups. The fact that the people themselves do not acknowledge this name is really immaterial'. (Chimhundu 1992:90–95)

And finally a submission cited in Brutt-Griffler (2002:83) goes:

> It has been widely felt that the name 'Shona' is inaccurate and unworthy, that it is not the true name of any of the peoples whom we propose to group under the term 'Shona-speaking peoples', and further, that it lies under strong suspicion of being a name given in contempt by enemies of the tribes. It is pretty certainly a foreign name, and as such is very likely to be uncomplimentary ... The idea that it is a contemptuous name is widespread ... It is true that the name 'Mashona' is not pleasing to natives, but that may simply [be] because it is a group name imposed from without, and ignoring all tribal distinctions. Certainly no people in the country claim the name Mashona as their tribal name, and each would prefer to be described by the proper name of his particular group. (citing the Southern Rhodesia report 1929:25–6)

These submissions underscore the fact that the origin of the name Shona is much more recent although in historical terms the people to whom this name was applied were already in existence sharing a common language and culture. According to Fagan (1984) there is significant evidence, both oral and archaeological, to believe that most of the later Iron Age cultures between the Zambezi and the Limpopo can be associated with Shona speakers. In fact, the significant political and economic developments epistomised by the famous Great Zimbabwe ruins that took place after the twelfth century belong to the Shona speakers. Bourdillon also confirms this point when he reminds us that 'the culture now classified as "Shona" originated from Bantu settlement of the high fertile plateau between the Limpopo and Zambezi rivers, bounded in the East by the drop towards the coast and in the West by Kalahari desert' (Bourdillon 1987:6). In historical terms this testifies to the existence of a Shona culture and language which predates the colonial encounter. Beach (1984) points to the close connection between the birth of the name Shona and the arrival of the Nguni-speakers who settled permanently in present day Zimbabwe around the 1830s. According to Beach,

> it was around this time [1830s] that the term 'Shona' first came to use, at first as a term used by the Ndebele about the Rozvi and gradually adopted by the Shona-speakers themselves. Prior to this different sections of them had called themselves Karanga, Kalanga, Zezuru etc but they seem to have had no universal name for themselves. (Beach 1984:52)

It was, however, through the colonial government and particularly through the work of its language taskforce that the name Shona came to be ascribed as the official name of all the tribes native to Zimbabwe who spoke dialects of what we now call the Shona language. Brutt-Griffler reports that having enlisted the services of the renowned linguist Clemmons Doke to create a standard grammar from the different language groups,

> the most difficult question the committee faced was what to call this new language it had created or more accurately, cobbled together. It arrived at the conclusion that the only possible name for the language was Shona. (Brutt-Griffler 2002:83)

The committee that settled for the name Shona was aware of its unpopularity and of the fact that it was an imposition, but despite all that they went ahead because they had to have a common name for the language and the imposition of names was nothing new for the colonial masters. The name was necessary for the sake of linguistic classification and, as Doke clearly argued, the fact that the people themselves did not accept or identify with the name was immaterial. This testifies to the level of arrogance that defined the colonisers and their attitude towards indigenous people. It is perhaps for the same reason that Bullock wrote:

> the word Mashona is used *faute de mieux*; nor need we look for its etymological derivation, because it has none. It is simply one of those British bowdlerization, which are borne patiently by a long-suffering world. (Bullock 1927:12)

Despite the clearly unpleasant history of the origin of the appellation,[1] it was only a matter of time before the protesting and aggrieved people accepted and internalised their new moniker thanks to the healing potential of time.

The exposition above is a historical account of how colonialism created a platform on which the name Shona as an identity was invented and concretised. It is conceivable that if a different process of consultation regarding the name had been followed we would probably have a different name to refer to these people whom we call the Shona today. As has become clear, the name Shona is a linguistic designation that describes the various groups of people in the country who all speak what are called dialects of the Shona language. Beach argued that

> whatever its derivation, the word 'Shona' is now used to name the South-central Bantu language of most of the modern Later Iron Age people of the plateau and, by extension, the people themselves, even though in many cases the grandparents of the people of today would not have used that name to describe themselves. (Beach 1980:18)

Beach's (1984) testimony that the Zimbabwean plateau was dominated, from the Late Iron Age up to the middle of the nineteenth century, by people who spoke the language we now call Shona is testimony to the long existence of the Shona language and culture. In fact, other historians like Nelson (1983:4) argue that 'recent linguistic research has attempted to demonstrate that the Shona language had developed as a distinct branch of the Bantu language family within the region before the tenth century'.

If correct this would mean that the people regarded today as the Shona are descendants of and inheritors of a language that evolved among the early Bantu-speaking inhabitants of Zimbabwe. This point is strongly expressed by the Zimbabwe historian, Mudenge, when he asserts:

> Present day Zimbabwe, therefore, is not merely a geographical expression created by imperialism during the nineteenth century. It is a reality that has existed for centuries, with language, a culture and a 'worldview' of its own, representing the inner core of the Shona historical experience. Today's Zimbabwe is, for these reasons, therefore, a successor state. As successors to all that has gone before, present Zimbabweans have both materially and culturally, much to build and not little to build on. (Mudenge 1988:364)

From the above submission it is clear that the inhabitants of the central plateau which is present day Zimbabwe not only had a similar language (today called Shona) but also shared a culture and worldview which can historically be traced to the expansion of the influence of the Karanga and their rule across the plateau. Although minor variations remained in local customs, the overriding social ontology and metaphysical belief system were basically the same. That the name Shona is a product of an acrimonious history does not in any way affect its significance and function as a collective identity for the speakers of the language in contemporary Zimbabwe. For the name to take shape and eventually establish itself, there had to be African collaboration in terms of willingness to accept and own it. After all, it came with its own political advantages. In fact, the majority is not even aware of its history and considers it as immemorial and natural. Outside those who delve into history and others interested in etymology, the name Shona designates vibrant cultural groupings of people whose philosophy I seek to layout in this work. In the same way that historians write of Shona history dating back several centuries, I shall also proceed to write of a Shona philosophy to be reconstructed from their age-old traditions and thus dating back in history.

Like its counterpart Africa, the name Shona epitomises the naming power of the coloniser and the invention of identities. Those who have looked at the name Africa and traced its etymology claim that the name Africa was not given by indigenous peoples. There are various views regarding the origin of the name and several etymological illustrations have been used, among which are submissions that it may have been derived from the Latin adjective *aprica* (sunny) or the Greek *aprike* (free from cold). Another submission claims that Africa is a Roman name for what the Greeks called 'Libya', itself perhaps a Latinisation of the name of the Berber tribe *Aourigha*, perhaps pronounced 'Afarika. For some, the term Africa is derived from the Arabic term *Ifriqiya* which most probably represents a transliteration of the word *Africa*. However, despite there being no consensus on the etymology of the name Africa, what is abundantly clear is that the name Africa was conferred from outside. The conclusion that one may reach is summarised by the following submission by Zeleza (2005):[2]

> Africa was a European construct…whose cartographic application was both gradual and contradictory in that as the name embraced the rest of the continent it increasingly came to be divorced from its original North African coding and became increasingly confined to the regions referred

to in Eurocentric and sometimes Afrocentric conceptual mapping as 'sub-Saharan Africa', seen as the pristine locus of the 'real' Africa or what the German philosopher Georg Wilhelm Friedrich Hegel (1770–1831) called 'Africa proper'.

This in itself confirms how the African identity is in part a product of the European gaze. The name Shona itself was at one point in the history of Zimbabwe questioned or contested. Chimhundu (1992) reports that soon after independence there was debate involving scholars to replace the name Shona with Mbire. The proposal was to rename the 'Shona people' the 'Mbire people'. However, this did not materialise as it was based on what Chimhundu dismissed as frivolous history championed by questionable historians. Chimhundu (1992:89) submits that after the collective name Shona was given to the people following a recommendation by Doke in 1931, it has remained the preferred name, despite attempts by non-conventional historians to lobby for the name to be changed to Mbire after the country's independence in 1980. This was in apparent reference to oral historian, Aeneas Chigwedere, and the late Shona writer and scholar Solomon Mutsvairo, who attempted to advance what Chimhundu (1992:89) termed the 'Mbire theory' soon after independence. While the name change proposition never saw the light of the day, an important point to note is that at some point in history, Shona people did debate and indeed questioned the authenticity of this name as an identity. The 'Mbire theory' could be looked at as an attempt to revisit the past and correct the distortions caused by colonialism. It is an attempt to respond to the way power was used to recreate history and identities in Africa through seemingly harmless processes of naming. Since naming constitutes the way to assert power and the means to appropriate space and peoples, it may be important to digress a little and examine, in philosophical terms, the significance of naming.

The politics of naming

> African nationalists...looked to Great Zimbabwe monuments as a source of inspiration, as evidence of a glorious pre-colonial past, and as a national shrine. People from across the political spectrum accepted the re-naming of Rhodesia as Zimbabwe, as undoubtedly it identified the country with its most distinct and dominant cultural heritage. Zimbabwe became the only country in the world named after an archaeological site and tradition. (Pikirayi 2006:756)

There is no better way to begin our reflection on the politics of naming than Zimbabwe itself. What Pikirayi (2006) captures above is of immense significance in that a close association between the past and the present is demonstrated in the very name of the country. In philosophical terms, the adoption of the name Zimbabwe or more appropriately its renaming from Rhodesia to Zimbabwe was a significant act of (re)membering in the sense of putting back together that which was dismembered through colonial conquest. The renaming meant the continuity between the past and the present, which was temporarily severed through brutal conquest, was thus restored. From the submission above, it is significant to note that Zimbabwe was not only named after the monuments but also after a tradition.

Scholarly work exists on African systems of naming, the significance, and meaning of names from a variety of perspectives – among them are Pongweni (1983), Kaphagawani (1991), Okere, (1996), Martin (2000), and Ramose (2008). These scholars concur on the point that the purpose of assigning a name is to identify, to distinguish and to classify objects of experience. The practice of naming therefore is an important step in the process of distinguishing and creating an identity. Martin (2000:101) argues that names participate in the construction of social reality since to name is also to classify, and therefore to assign a position. The individual or object named is situated in the order of the world, in the structures of meaning invested in by a particular collectivity. Naming also plays a significant role in the reproduction of power and privilege within the social world. With regard to geographical places, naming can be a way of claiming a landscape, a means of claiming ownership by appropriating the space. This is precisely the reason why Alderman, (2008:197) argues that in themselves names can be recognised as active and contestable processes of claiming and constructing the landscape around certain ideological visions about the past. In Africa colonial authorities employed naming as a tool of control and a means of inscribing and reifying or denigrating certain cultural and political ideologies. Any naming implies a relationship based on power, and to name is to confer a form of life (Martin, 2000). Ramose concurs arguing:

> By giving a name to an aspect of reality those who do so arrogate unto themselves the power to define and describe that reality. Acceptance of such definition and description often entails practical consequences and these may not always be to the benefit of the named. To challenge imposed identities is in effect to question the power of the name giver

and, ultimately to reverse the adverse negative consequences that flow from the imposed identity. (Ramose 2008:327)

The power to name, just like the power to inscribe, is in and of itself a process of creating history hence it is very important and significant. It symbolises the power to leave a mark that may continue beyond the life of the signifier. Because names are a form of symbolic capital, tools for asserting power and a significant means of writing or rewriting history, they attract public reaction and contestation. At both the national and individual level, postcolonial Africa is replete with strong sentiments about the need to rename in order to reassert lost identity or correct distorted history. Regarding this power and significance of naming on a people, Martin could not have expressed it any better when he avers that:

> the power of naming perhaps does not appear anywhere more obviously than in colonial situations where it was a question of both seizing a space, and the people occupying it, and of categorising these people in such a way that the 'differences' assigned to them legitimised and perpetuated the domination resulting from this conquest. (Martin, 2000:101)

Analysing the significance of naming, Okere (1996:147) argued that in oral societies naming was not only a privilege but also a way of perpetuating history and hence an effective way of conferring immortality to thoughts that would otherwise not outlive the breath by which they were uttered. It is no wonder then that the colonialists attempted to literally rename everything including both places and people in Africa. Because names confer immortality to thought, continued use and application of names coined by the coloniser, despite the changes in history, only helps to perpetuate the very objective for which they were initiated in the first place. To erase a memory one has to do away with the name that immortalises it. This is the reason why soon after independence most postcolonial governments embarked on projects of renaming places, particularly cities and even countries themselves. Within the context of colonialism, names served a political function and they were a means of appropriating space and history as well as an important means of throttling competing epistemologies and denying the indigenous peoples the voice of expertise. Names also served as epithets to express approval or disapproval particularly when applied in the Eurocentric and racist depiction of things African while other names did not have any meaning or significance for those named.[3]

The name Shona is part of the legacy of colonial signification and identification and today it has come to be accepted as referring to a group of people who arguably share a common language and culture and who constitute about three quarters of the population in present day Zimbabwe. But by renaming the country from Rhodesia to Zimbabwe at independence, the new leadership and everyone behind them were reclaiming their heritage and identity. If one were to use the popular, decolonial parlance championed by students in South African universities in 2015, this was probably the true beginning of the 'Rhodes Must Fall' initiative. One could also interpret this renaming as an act of the restoration of tradition, a reclaiming of the past and a deliberate gesture of authentification.

It was important to consider the question of naming and who the Shona are in order to provide a picture of our focus group in this discussion– the group whose indigenous philosophy I seek to articulate.[4] Having looked at this there is one crucial issue itself directly connected to the question of ethnic identities in postcolonial Africa. This is the question of the 'invention' of tradition. It is crucial to consider arguments behind the theory of invention in order to deal with the question of whether or not Africans and by extension the Shona are the original creators of their living cultures.

The 'invention' of tradition

> It hurts to be told by foreign scholars that, in earlier days, the ingenuity of your forebears was so constrained by 'cultural tradition' that people were condemned to repeat themselves endlessly, to be stuck in the same rut for time immemorial. This simply flows from rank incomprehension. It is no consolation to be told by others that, because there are no written sources, no past can be recovered, as if living traces of that past were not part and parcel of daily life. (Vansina 1990:xi)

This crucial submission by Vansina is a vivid representation of the feeling that has haunted most indigenous scholars. Unfortunately it has not gone away even today, given the dominance of such views and their prevalence in much of the literature that indigenous peoples continue to encounter. In Africa historians have in most cases taken the lead in trying to dispel such perceptions by championing the rewriting of African history. Philosophers too have championed the reconstruction of philosophy in Africa. Such endeavours must continue in order to provide a better appreciation of the

Chapter 3

traditions and thoughts of the indigenous peoples of the world. Now let me get back to the question of tradition. As I seek to write about the Shona and their past I am also at the same time aware of the challenge posed by theories of the 'invention of tradition' in colonial Africa. The 'invention of tradition', as a theory of understanding the social and cultural unfolding in Africa, opened up new ways of looking at the past and particularly our conception of indigenous African traditions. As one thinks particularly about indigenous African traditions the idea of 'invention' and its implications cannot be taken lightly. I have elected to say a little more about this topic as a result of concerns that one often has to deal with when attempting to revisit what I would call the 'African archive' – that is, issues that have to deal with understanding African traditions from its pre-colonial past. The most famous article on this subject on colonial Africa is Ranger's 'Invention of tradition in colonial Africa' published in 1983. In that famous article, Ranger attempts to draw attention to the fact that much of what we consider today as African traditions or customs are in fact colonial 'inventions'. The adoption of the concept 'invention' and its application to describe the cultural process in colonial Africa was itself of immense significance because of the consequences it would have on tradition and its authenticity. To those who sought to revisit the past and reconstruct the history of pre-colonial Africa and its cultures the major challenge was how it would be possible to get back to the realities behind these 'inventions'. In examining this thesis of 'invention' the first thing to do would be to examine the concept of 'invention' itself. A quick internet search for the meaning of this term reveals that to invent is 'to create, to contrive, to originate, or devise something previously unknown by use of ingenuity and imagination'. In light of this it would seem understandable to infer that if indeed tradition is 'invented' then it must be ahistorical but if that is the case then the question is what qualifies it as tradition? Is it not that the idea of invented traditions implies or signifies falsity and/or contrivance? If traditions are not historical in their origin then they may well be considered forgeries (Plant 2008). According to Zeleza (2006:14) 'invention implies a history, a social process; it denaturalises cultural artifacts and practices, stripping them of primordial authenticity and essentialism'. Since the publication of the seminal work, *'The Invention of Tradition'* by Hobsbawn and Ranger in 1983, the theory of invented traditions has been widely applied including in scholarly articulations of indigenous cultures.

While nobody can dismiss the theory of 'invention' and its attractiveness in accounting for the African past and what it obtains today, it is crucial at the same time to examine some of its implications particularly in relation to the question of agency and the historicity of African ideas and institutions. It is important to highlight that while most scholars, particularly on tradition in colonial Africa, draw from Ranger's most popular chapter 'The invention of tradition in colonial Africa' published in 1983, few seem to demonstrate a similar kind of awareness of the fact that ten years after the publication of this seminal essay, Ranger published a sequel in which he criticises his earlier analysis including the inappropriateness of the term 'invention' to capture what transpired in colonial Africa. I am referring here to Ranger's article entitled 'The invention of tradition revisited: The case of colonial Africa' published in 1993. It is in the latter that Ranger makes a candid admission that indeed despite the success of their book '*The Invention of Tradition*', 'its central argument, and its exposition in my chapter in particular could be attacked in various ways' (Ranger 1993:6). According to Thomas Spear:

> the case for colonial invention has often overstated colonial power and ability to manipulate African institutions to establish hegemony. Rather, tradition was a complex discourse in which people continually reinterpreted the lessons of the past in the context of the present. (Spear 2003:3)

Furthermore, Ranger acknowledges that the rift that is drawn between custom and 'invented' tradition, and pre-colonial and colonial African societies is open to both theoretical and factual criticism. While the division between the pre-colonial and the colonial is indeed important for historical reasons, it is crucial to realise, at the same time, that the myth that a new kind of person was installed in Africa at colonialism is not completely true as old ways of be-ing continued to influence day-to-day thinking and existence. No one can deny the fact that change indeed took place in Africa with the advent of colonialism, but it would seem that the level of agency afforded to the colonials in defining a new course for Africa and in 'inventing' a new African self and tradition feeds into the discourse of colonial racism and the putative mental differences. The main actors in the process of 'invention' are given, of course, as the colonial administrators and missionaries with some African patriarchs as mere collaborators. Thus the real and conscious actor was the colonial and his /her counterpart, the missionary, while the majority of the populace were not even part of the process save for a few patriarchal elders. One can argue, and of course and strongly so, that the so-called colonial 'invention' of tradition in Africa portrays and indeed celebrates the genius of a handful of colonialists and missionaries as the creators of a new tradition in Africa. The colonials, following in the footsteps of their forebears who invented the compass, the printing press, the gun, and the flying machine, went on to 'invent' tradition in Africa. This sounds like a familiar story does it not?

If one were to consider the term 'invent' within its scientific context from which the historians and anthropologists have appropriated it, the question that arises is to whom does this 'invented' African tradition belong? In other words, who owns the patent? At this point one realises how problematic the theory of 'invention' can be. Agency is ascribed to that one obvious group at the expense of the Other who 'invented' nothing. Ten years after publishing the work Ranger makes a candid admission that the process he had described and the analysis he had made in the colonial 'invention' of tradition in Africa simplified an otherwise complex process. At that point Ranger admits that the word 'invention' inhibits a full and more accurate historical treatment of African participation and initiative in innovating their customs. As correctly pointed out by Mazrui and Ajayi (1993:633), 'African realities are not simply a derivative of colonialism. A more powerful force in Africa than the colonial experience is African culture itself'. Could it not be possible also that the so-called reification of tradition in Africa was triggered by the conscious need to preserve and protect the cultural identity of these African groups in the face of the threat posed by colonialism? In contemporary times we have witnessed this desire to protect and safeguard identities, both religious and cultural, in response to the threat posed by globalisation manifesting itself through the rise of religious and cultural fundamentalism. The reification of tradition in response to the threat of colonialism and its foreign culture could in itself have been a natural reaction by the Africans that is not unique to Africa, but common to any group that is facing the potential threat of foreign intrusion.

To highlight what I would consider was a thoughtful shift in Ranger's thinking on tradition in colonial Africa I will draw from his article, 'The invention of tradition revisited: The case of colonial Africa' published in 1993. The significance of Ranger's autocriticism cannot be overemphasised especially within the context of this work. I shall therefore quote from this erudite scholar at length. This I do, firstly, because of the canonical status afforded the theory of the colonial 'invention' of tradition in Africa and, secondly, to appreciate the level of scholarship demonstrated by Ranger through his ability to self-re-examine despite the popularity of his initial theory and the legion of followers it may still command. Not many scholars are able to accomplish such a feat. Concerning the theory of 'invention' and its problematical nature Ranger writes:

> I have come to think that the defects of the term 'invention' compromise not only my chapter but also some of the later work on colonial custom. The idea can be a foreclosing one. It emphasises, and emphasises rightly, a contrast between pre-colonial fluidity and the reification of colonial classification, between mobile custom and static tradition ... To focus on the innovation of a tradition is certainly to approach it historically ... So the word 'invention' gets in the way of a fully historical treatment of colonial hegemony and of a fully historical treatment of African participation and initiative in innovating custom. I have come to prefer Benedict Anderson's word from his *Imagined Communities*. Some traditions in colonial Africa really were invented, by a single colonial officer for a single occasion. But customary law and ethnicity and religion were imagined by many different people and over a long time. These multiple imaginations were in tension with each other and in constant contestation to define the meaning of what had been imagined– to imagine it further. Traditions imagined by whites were re-imagined by blacks; traditions imagined by particular black interest groups were re-imagined by others. The history of modern tradition has been much more complex than we have supposed. Above all, I like the word 'imagining' because, much more than the term 'invention', it lays stress upon ideas and images and symbols. However politically convenient they were, the new traditions were, after all, essentially about identity and identity is essentially a matter of imagination. (Ranger 1993:24–25)

In the same article and in the section entitled 'Rethinking the invention of ethnicity', Ranger goes further to elaborate his new thinking:

> It seems best to begin a reconsideration of the invention of tradition in colonial Africa with a topic of ethnicity ... Over the eight years during which I have been seeking to resolve the problem of modern southern African ethnicity I have been changing my mind, away from the notion of 'invention' and towards the notion of 'imagination'. The sequence of my work on ethnicity began by placing almost all the emphasis upon imposed colonial classifications of identity ... The argument ran that colonial administrators needed comprehensible and manageable units and so invented tribes ... These ready-made common-sense 'inventions' were given greater legitimacy by the classifying (and sometimes frankly racist) tendencies of colonial science and social science. These were the 'European ideas' which Africans 'accepted'. *The emphasis was perhaps an odd one for someone as closely associated as I had been*

Chapter 3

> with arguments for 'African initiative', especially since a sense of ethnic identity could hardly be simply imposed from outside or from above. There plainly had to be more than merely African 'acceptance'. At the least there had to be African collaboration. (Ranger 1993:25–26) [italics mine]

These are, no doubt, reflections of a more mature Ranger looking back ten years later and, rightfully so, correcting some of his earlier mistaken ideas. The last three sentences beginning from the one italicised to the end of the quotation are, for me, by far, the most crucial, particularly in terms of the question of identity and tradition. His perspective on identity appears to settle the problem of most ethnic identities in Africa, including Shona identity, in that while the name may have been initially imposed from outside its installation could not have succeeded without the prior existence, however implicit, of a conscious oneness, despite the people belonging to this or that chief. This conscious oneness derived from a shared language and culture. It is critical that as he looked back at his work, Ranger personally acknowledged how foreclosing 'invention' discourses have been on Africa. The shift to imagined traditions opens up whole possibilities in terms of revisiting and reconstructing the past from those resilient aspects of tradition that have made their way to the present.

For us Africans, it is important to remember that at the core of the theory of 'invention' lies the following issue: are Africans not therefore the original creators of their living cultures? A sequel to this question would be: Can a tradition, deeply embedded in a people's language, institutions and collective consciousness, really die? My answer to the second question is negative if tradition is viewed as discourse (see Feierman 1999; Spear 2003) imbued with inbuilt dynamism and continuity. In the preface to the '*UNESCO General History of Africa volume 1*', M'bow reminds us that historically:

> there was a refusal to see Africans as the creators of original cultures which flowered and survived over centuries in patterns of their own making and which historians are unable to grasp unless they forgo their prejudices and rethink their approach. (M'bow 1981:xvii)

Historians have shown us through their most acclaimed reconstructions of the history and civilisations of the African past that Africans were, from time immemorial, historical. The issue of tradition is linked to the question of identity in Africa in the sense that the historical identity of a society or of the ethnic group rests on the continuity of the past with the present. Etymologically, the term 'tradition' comes from the Latin word *tradere*, which means to transmit, or give something to another for safekeeping. As noted by Giddens:[5]

> *tradere* was originally used in the context of Roman Law, where it referred to the laws of inheritance. Property that passed from one generation to another was supposed to be given in trust – the inheritor had obligations to protect and nurture it.

Whereas modifications are the order of the day, certain elements in a tradition persist over time throughout modifications. In his discussion on 'the identity of societies through time', Shils (1981:163) argues that in spite of ceaseless change, 'each society remains the same society. Its members do not wake up one morning and discover they are no longer living in, let us say, British society'. The identity of society owes itself to memory in that it is the connection between tradition and memory that enables societies to go on reproducing themselves while at the same time changing. Spear agrees that:

> tradition' has been one of the most contentious words in African historiography, widely condemned for conveying a timeless, unchanging past and the evil twin of modernity. But it remains critically important in understanding historical processes of social change and representation. Traditions endure for long periods of time, but only because cognitive categories are in dialogical tension with social reality, continually readjusting while simultaneously projecting an image of timeless continuity ... Traditions have their own histories, histories that can be recovered by careful excavation of their successive representations. (Spear 2003:6)

It is from these excavations that historians, anthropologists and linguists have been able to reconstruct the story and life of societies from the African past. As Gyekye rightfully points out:

> from the point of view of a deep and fundamental conception of tradition, every society in our modern world is 'traditional' inasmuch as it maintains and cherishes values, practices, outlooks, and institutions bequeathed to it by previous generations and all or much of which on normative grounds it takes pride in, boasts of, and builds on ...A tradition is any cultural product that was created or pursued by past generations and that,

> having been accepted and preserved, in whole or in part, by successive generations, has been maintained to the present. (Gyekye 1997:217)

For anything to enjoy the status of tradition, it has to be accepted as legitimate. The people in question 'must believe that it embodies an efficacy born of past experience' (see Spear 2003). Another important point to note is that 'traditions may be imposed from above but they remain impuissant as long as they do not strike a resonant chord in the community' (Spear 2003:6, citing Harries 1993). The same logic applies with equal significance to the question of identity.

As we think of identities in pre-colonial Africa there is need to reject the dubious proposition that Africans had no collective sense of themselves prior to conquest. According to Spear,

> what gives tradition, custom and ethnicity their coherence and power is the fact that they lay deep in people's popular consciousness, informing them of who they are and how they should act. Yet, as discourse, traditions, customs and ethnicities are continually reinterpreted and reconstructed as 'regulated improvisations' subject to their continued intelligibility and legitimacy. (Spear 2003:26)

As pointed out by Vansina (1990) traditions are historical phenomena which are found everywhere. Traditions 'consist of changing, inherited, collective body of cognitive and physical representations shared by their members' (Vansina 1990:259). Their cognitive representations are the core which both inform the people's understanding of the world and give meaning to changing circumstances. Among the Shona traces of the past are still part and parcel of daily life even in urban settings which are the places where tradition is expected to have lost much of its cognitive influence on the peoples. Because these living traces of that past are still part and parcel of daily life, it is possible to trace a tradition of thought from the pre-colonial to the present which can legitimately constitute the basis from which an indigenous philosophy of the Shona can be articulated. That is what I shall try to lay out in the remaining four chapters of this book.

Notes

1. In fact Hilda Kuper (1955:9) raises the same point in her examination of the nomenclature Shona. She agrees that the name Shona is

generally regarded as a derogatory name whose exact meaning is doubtful and alleges that the name was apparently applied by Ndebele conquerors to indigenous populations. She further submits that the name 'Mashona' has been extended by Europeans to cover all Bantu peoples in Southern Rhodesia who speak dialects officially recognised as Shona (Chishona).

2. See http://www.encyclopedia.com/history/dictionaries-thesauruses-pictures-and-press-releases/africa-idea (Accessed 13 July 2011).

3. On this argument see also my article entitled 'Philosophy and tradition in Africa': Critical reflections on the power and vestiges of colonial nomenclature' *Thought and Practice: A Journal of the Philosophical Association of Kenya* 3(1), 2011, 1–19.

4. I wish to state that in view of these questionable origins of the name and the reality that it was a name imposed on the people without their consent I shall continue to use the name but I do so under protest. My use of the name also hinges on the fact that, despite its questionable origins, the name has come to be widely accepted by the people and it appears in all published literature concerning this group of people. Without the collaborative acceptance of the name by the people themselves it is difficult to see how the name would have succeeded. In spite of its questionable origins the name has had its unintended benefits which the coloniser must have rued later as it helped to sustain that consciousness of unity and oneness that helped in the demise of colonialism.

5. Giddens, A. 1999. Reith Lecture 3, 'Tradition' http://news.bbc.co.uk/hi/english/static/events/reith-99 (Accessed 19 May 2014).

4

Indigenous Shona metaphysical thought

The question of metaphysics

> Metaphysics, and philosophical inquiry more generally, would perhaps not be necessary were it the case that we all shared a coherent and unproblematic notion of what the world consists in, and so never raised reflective questions about the nature of the world and of our knowledge of it, but a moment's reflection will show that this is far from being so. (O'Hear 1985:11)

This observation by Anthony O'Hear not only sums up the reasons why examining the subject of metaphysics is important but it more significantly pre-empts the basis on which any sceptic could question not just the existence of metaphysics but the prevalence of different and potentially conflicting perspectives of the world. Perhaps the philosophical importance of such diversity to humanity was poignantly put by Bernstein (1988:272) in his presidential address to the Metaphysical Society of America when he reminded them:

> We live in a radically pluralistic universe, and this affects metaphysical speculation. The plurality of metaphysical orientations and interpretations is not a cause for despair. It does however mean that we must always be willing to risk questioning our own commitments in and through the critical encounter with what is different and other. We must resist

the temptation 'to reduce the other' to a constituent part of my 'total discourse'.

I have no doubt in my mind that this observation attains added significance if it is particularly read against the backdrop of the disquiet often expressed towards so-called peripheral philosophies and their articulations. For me, both the observation by O'Hear and the insight from Bernstein, serve to flag the context out of which my view that there is a Shona metaphysics worthy examining finds its justification.

Metaphysics is a branch of philosophy that deals with questions about the ultimate nature of reality. The term metaphysics comes from the Greek word *meta ta phusika,* a title that was given to a compilation of Aristotle's work that comes after his work on physics, probably in the library at Alexandria (Hamlyn 1984:1). From the two terms (*metá*) ('beyond' or 'after') and (*physiká*) ('physics') came the name metaphysics. Questions have been raised on how from a mere library classification the idea of metaphysics as a branch of philosophy could be born and why it was given such prominence. Of course there is no doubt, as rightfully pointed out by Hamlyn (1984:1), that the correctness of the library classification would imply that there was at least a similarity of theme in those writings. Without treating a common subject it would remain difficult to see how the library classification criteria could have been determined. Metaphysics deals with issues about the ultimate nature of the cosmos as well as questions of ontology. It tries to answer questions like: What is existence or being? What types of things exist or constitute the universe? What is the true underlying nature of reality? Of central concern to metaphysics are investigations into notions of causality, space, substance, self, time, freedom and determinism, the problem of universals, being, force, appearance and reality among many concerns that try to address the question of reality and what constitutes the universe.

Cosmology and ontology are often taken as the traditional branches of metaphysics. In most literature the terms 'ontology' and 'metaphysics' are considered synonymous and therefore used interchangeably. However, some scholars have disagreed with this view and instead insist that though the distinction is very difficult to establish there is a sense in which metaphysics can be distinguished from ontology. In his famous article 'On what there is', Quine (1948) wrote a statement from which the following is taken: 'that part of metaphysics called ontology'. This submission points to the existence of a clear distinction between metaphysics and ontology where probably one feeds off the other. This is probably the reason why

Varzi went on to argue concerning the distinction between metaphysics and ontology that:

> According to a certain, familiar way of dividing up the business of philosophy, made popular by Quine, ontology is concerned with the question of *what entities exist* (a task that is often identified with that of drafting a 'complete inventory' of the universe) whereas metaphysics seeks to explain, of those entities, *what they are* (i.e., to specify the 'ultimate nature' of the items included in the inventory). (Varzi 2011:407)

While not everybody will agree with this division, the submission is particularly important in that it alludes to the existence of such a distinction while bringing out the indebtedness of metaphysics to ontology where metaphysics becomes nothing more than a philosophical attempt to theorise on what there is, in a sense creating the impression that ontology precedes metaphysics. If accepted, the distinction between ontology (that which concerns itself with what entities exist) and metaphysics (that which concerns itself with clarifying what are these entities) is taken seriously then this may have a significant effect on whether Africans 'entertain only ontology and not metaphysics', as alluded to by some scholars in African philosophy and whether the term 'African metaphysics' is really appropriate for capturing the African experience.

The positivist attack on metaphysics has led people over the years to question whether metaphysics stands for any legitimate enterprise. Logical positivists characterised metaphysics as an attempt to gain access to what transcends observation – a description which for the logical positivists was pure nonsense.

> From time to time in the history of philosophy scholars of a positivist tendency have produced criteria of meaningfulness by which metaphysics could be shown to be nonsense at one fell swoop. Hume, for example, wished to consign to the flames anything that contained, in effect, pure *a priori* reasoning, except for abstract reasoning concerning quantity and number. (Hamlyn 1984:9)

In his work entitled 'An Enquiry Concerning Human Understanding' Hume (1748) declared:

> If we take in our hand any volume; of divinity or school metaphysics, for instance; let us ask, Does it contain any abstract reasoning concerning

> quantity or number? No. Does it contain any experimental reasoning concerning matter of fact and existence? No. Commit it then to the flames, for it can contain nothing but sophistry and illusion. (Bennett 2004:86)

The accusation that metaphysics has no sense, therefore, has had a long history in the struggle for meaning and what constitutes knowledge in Western philosophy. It was indeed the logical positivists of the Vienna circle who stood out clearly for their break from metaphysics. The antagonistic attitude towards metaphysics between those who dismissed it and those who tried to save it is aptly captured by Burtt as follows:

> For two decades the debate remained for the most part on the level of pontifical repartee rather than that of constructive analysis, the primary aim of the positivists being to damn metaphysics into the Cimmerian darkness of obvious irrationality, while those in the opposite party feverishly laid about with all the weapons in their arsenal in the hope of rescuing their speculative darling from this threatened catastrophe. (Burtt 1945:533)

The reason why metaphysics received such scrutiny had partly to do with its subject matter which is often conceived as that which is beyond the ordinary senses. It is on this basis that Schlesinger is probably correct in declaring that:

> Perhaps the most glaring dissimilarity between science and metaphysics is that scientific disputes however sharp are bound to be resolved, while metaphysical controversies go on forever. Indeed, it is this feature of metaphysics that gave the major impetus to the hostile view held by some, that it is a barren discipline; that it is a discipline in which all arguments are futile, in which no problem is ever solved; that in spite of the enormous amount of mental energy invested throughout history in metaphysical thinking no real progress has been achieved. (Schlesinger 1981:233)

Of course, logical positivists and other scholars of similar persuasion were convinced that since metaphysical claims were said to be unverifiable with reference to experience and not merely logical or mathematical in content they could not be meaningful. However, to then proceed and claim that no real progress has been achieved in metaphysical thinking would be an overstatement. There is no doubt that although there may

Chapter 4

not be any consensus achieved there has been a definite contribution from the very process of seeking to clarify the nature of the universe and its entities. As one reflects on this debate it is perhaps crucial to realise, as Hamlyn (1984) points out, that the history of metaphysics, like history in general, is untidy and therefore instead of rushing to dismiss metaphysics altogether one only needs to proceed with caution. After all, being a branch of philosophy, metaphysics could not escape being shrouded in controversy which is typical of philosophy in general including even the definition of philosophy itself. As is now clear to philosophers and logical positivists alike, logical positivism itself (as represented in what is called science today) has not stayed clear of metaphysical assertions as exemplified in the ongoing debate on scientific realism, particularly with reference to the status of scientific entities. In fact, it seems that it is in science more than anywhere else that we find the highly sophisticated metaphysical assumptions so popular today in that branch of science called cosmology which, although defined as the scientific study of the universe and its properties as a whole in order to understand the origin, evolution and ultimate fate of the entire universe, sounds acutely metaphysical. The verdict on the outcome of the controversy between metaphysics and logical positivism was captured best by Bernstein as follows:

> In one fell swoop, the logical positivists sought to dismiss metaphysics by claiming that metaphysical 'propositions' are pseudo propositions. They are non-sense; they lack cognitive meaning. But the positivist program demanded a rigourous specification of criterion of cognitive meaning and its justification. But positivism not only failed to specify and justify such criterion; every one of its dogmas has been seriously challenged. Whatever judgement we make about the legacy of positivism, it failed in its attempt to rid us of metaphysics. Indeed its own unquestioned metaphysical biases have become evident. (Bernstein 1988:260)

Of crucial significance in this submission is to understand the point being made not just about logical positivism but more significantly about the endurance of metaphysics. The position which Bernstein arrives at unsurprisingly joins a long line of philosophers who have defended the value of metaphysics and the inevitability of metaphysical speculation in human lives. Perhaps this point was made centuries earlier by the philosopher Kant. In defence of metaphysics in his work entitled *Prolegomena to any Future Metaphysics*, Kant, having been woken up from his dogmatic slumber by Hume's attack on metaphysics declared:

> That the human mind will ever give up metaphysical researches is as little to be expected as that we should prefer to give up breathing altogether, to avoid inhaling impure air. There will therefore always be metaphysics in the world; nay, every one, especially every man of reflexion, will have it, and for want of a recognised standard, will shape it for himself after his own pattern. (Smith and Grene 1957:360)

The analogy between metaphysics and the futility of any attempt to stop breathing in order to avoid inhaling impure air confirms the indispensability of metaphysical speculation as long as humans live. In other words, metaphysical speculation is by its nature unavoidable in the very same way that breathing is to human beings. Human thought is incomplete without metaphysical speculation. Whether or not metaphysics is regarded as a contamination of the knowledge landscape as positivists would want us to believe, it is something that will forever remain part and parcel of the knowledge landscape. There are fundamental ontological questions that human beings upon attaining a certain level of consciousness cannot avoid addressing. To be alive is to be a speculative and thinking being and each individual as a person with capacity for reflection participates in metaphysical speculation. That is how metaphysics is unavoidable as an enterprise. Instead of paying so much attention to the positivist critique of metaphysics, my view is that we should rather draw on the prophetic insights of Kant on the inevitability of metaphysics and consign behind us all questions concerning the meaninglessness of metaphysics. Philosophical focus should instead be on the position metaphysics has occupied and continues to occupy in human lives. Probably the main concern should be to establish why metaphysical thinking remains central in the lives of different peoples even in the face of unprecedented scientific achievements. It is at this point that one is reminded of Bernstein's submission on the value of metaphysics. According to Bernstein, what Kolakowski says about philosophy is especially true of metaphysics. Metaphysics seeks to build the spirit of truth, which means

> never to let the inquisitive energy of the mind go to sleep, never to stop questioning what appears to be obvious and definitive, always to defy the seemingly intact resources of common sense, always to suspect that there might be 'another side' in what is taken for granted, and never to allow us to forget that there are questions that lie beyond the legitimate horizon of science and are nonetheless crucially important to the survival of humanity as we know it. (Bernstein 1988:257)

On this assumption it seems therefore appropriate to declare that human beings will always entertain certain metaphysical, ontological and cosmological questions and beliefs about the nature of the world, the destiny of humanity, and the forces behind life and existence. These questions deserve the attention that philosophers accord them for they have a bearing on how societies organise themselves and make sense of the world around them. Having shown that speculative thinking is integral to human life and is therefore part and parcel of what defines humanity it is appropriate that I turn to examine Shona metaphysics. But to do so I will again begin my discussion with an attempt to clarify the appropriation of this seemingly Western concept to describe African experience in order to lay the ground for the exposition of 'Shona metaphysics' which is itself subsumed under 'African metaphysics'.

The question of appropriation

In his article entitled 'African Religions from a philosophical point of view' Wiredu opens his discussion by stating:

> If there is wisdom in starting with first things first, then a philosophical discussion of African religions should start with an inquiry into the applicability of the concept of religion to African life and thought. (Wiredu 2010:34)

I would like to proceed on the same logic in my analysis of the term metaphysics and its applicability to African experience and thought. The point of my conceptual analysis is that since metaphysics is a Western concept that Africans have appropriated to define a certain category of their thoughts, it is only philosophically appropriate to examine whether there is a resemblance between what it describes in its original Western usage and what it designates in the African context. This I will do at two levels. Firstly, I think there is need to establish whether there is a connection between the works of Aristotle classified as metaphysics, and what is referred to as 'African metaphysics'. The objective is to establish whether there is a relationship in point of the subject matter treated in both instances. I have decided to use the term 'African metaphysics' with special markers or quotational reservations at this point to highlight the fact that it is a concept for which clarity is being sought. There appears to be consensus among scholars that the work of Aristotle that is classified as metaphysics dealt with a subject beyond matter or beyond what can be experienced through the senses. The logical consequence is that a clear distinction was therefore established between two realities one natural (physics) and another beyond the natural (metaphysics). To proceed to talk of 'African metaphysics' in this first sense would out of necessity presuppose that Africans are at ease with the assumed worldview which has 'nature' versus 'supernature' as its two distinct realities. This is an issue that I will return to in a short while.

Secondly, I could also choose to capitalise on the distinction between ontology and metaphysics, briefly outlined above, where ontology concerns itself basically with an inventory on what there is, while metaphysics becomes a reflection at a more abstract level on the nature of what there is. The significance is that making this distinction may allow me to clearly claim not only that there is indeed an African ontology without any doubt because Africans have an inventory of what there is, but also that Africans have a metaphysics because they indeed reflect theoretically on the nature of those entities found in their inventory of the world. In this second sense, in my opinion, there appears to be no difficulty at all in extending the term metaphysics to capture African experiences. It is universally acclaimed that philosophy begins in wonder and the universe is humanity's basic text of wonder. Africans have indeed wondered about the universe as evidenced in numerous mythological accounts about the origins of the universe and some of its elements such as the sun, the moon, the stars, day and night, and even the different seasons. So at this second level of understanding there is, without any doubt, an African metaphysics.

Let me therefore return to the first position stated above where what becomes crucial in terms of establishing the appropriateness of the concept to define African experiences is to see whether there are explanatory and conceptual affinities between metaphysics as conceived in the West compared to its African referent. It is at this level that significant philosophical differences begin to emerge. Whereas both traditions, the Western and the African, would within the domain of metaphysics, consider non-physical entities like spirits and spiritual beings, there is a clear distinction on how these realities are conceived between these two traditions. In the Western tradition a clear distinction in terms of existence is established between the world of material beings and that of spiritual beings. In other words, the realm of the spiritual and the physical are two different realities best expressed in the language of the natural world versus the supernatural world. For most African philosophers such a distinction is not so clear cut among the Africans. They strongly argue that it may in actual fact be non-existent. To illustrate this point allow me to quote the following passage from Wiredu (2010) which provides a lucid articulation of the problem. According to Wiredu, for Africans:

> It makes scant sense to divide the world order into two, calling one nature and the other supernature ... The world order operates in every detail according to laws, some commonplace, others more recondite; but the latter do not contradict or abrogate the former, and interactions between the realms predominantly governed by these kinds of laws are perfectly regular in a cosmological sense. Accordingly, explanations of some puzzling phenomena in common experience in terms of the activities of 'spirits', for example, do not generate the sense of 'going out of this world' which the ascent, in another worldview, from the natural to the supernatural would seem to suggest. Certainly, 'spirits' are regarded as being out of the ordinary, but they are not felt to be out of this world. Moreover, ... they can actually be seen and communicated with by those who have medicinally reinforced eyes and appropriate resources of communication. And there is no lack of such 'specialists' in many African societies. (Wiredu 2010:38)

The world of spirits or what Wiredu prefers to call the world of 'extra-human beings' is conceived to be continuous and analogous to that of the living and the interactions between the two worlds are regular and on a day-to-day basis. The 'ancestors' keep watch over the affairs and wellbeing of their living. The ancestors are always rewarding good and punishing gross transgressions, while the living through ritual and acts of remembrance keep the 'living dead' alive by making sure they do not recede into a state of oblivion. The final sting of death is therefore kept at bay through these rituals and periodic ceremonial acts of remembrance. The idea of a separate world of spirits existing outside this commonsense world is therefore a misnomer in most African traditions.

Contributing on the same question of 'African metaphysics' and its nature, Ramose (2011:6) argues that, if by metaphysics we are concerned with what is beyond experience then 'the expression "African metaphysics" becomes problematical or at worst a misnomer'. Ramose makes the following submission:

> Whenever there is reference to African metaphysics this is often followed by the qualification that African metaphysics is 'this worldly', meaning by this that even the invisible beings are deemed to belong together with the living in the same world of be-ing; the world of substantiality manifesting itself in various forms. The critical point about the qualification is the

> underlying presupposition that be-ing manifests itself through beings that are always appearing as something. On this understanding, it seems reasonable then to surmise that African philosophy entertains only ontology but not metaphysics. (Ramose 2011:7)

Ramose indeed confirms the point being argued by Wiredu and reiterates that it is impossible to conceive of 'beings' existing outside space. To exist is to be somewhere in this world and this is why the spirits in Africa are indeed regarded as 'this worldly', although, due to their nature, they are not subject to the laws that constrain the movement and efficiency of ordinary objects. The key term in the above submission is 'surmise', where one may jump to conclude without evidence or serious objective scrutiny. The inference that 'African philosophy entertains only ontology but not metaphysics' could have unintended implications if read literally in terms of denying Africans the ability to reflect in philosophical terms on the nature of their 'inventory'. In other words, my point is that this conclusion can potentially be misconstrued to mean that 'Africans are unfamiliar to thinking with concepts of the highest abstraction' or simply that 'the metaphysical bent is absent from their thinking' (Wiredu 1996:99). These are two possible conclusions that could be capitalised on by those who have always fought to exclude Africans from the higher planes of reflection involving abstract reasoning. I have no doubt, however, that this is not the intended conclusion. The point that Ramose is making can be described as meaning that Africans, in the words of Wiredu (1996:99), 'do not employ in their thinking certain kinds of abstract concepts, namely those that cannot be defined in terms of deriving from human experience'. Africans have a different conception of metaphysics and this conception accords ontological significance to beings, particularly the spirits and living dead, as part of this world and not as 'other worldly beings', but they do grapple with questions about the nature of these beings. The point being made is that there is a distinctively empirical bent in the discourse relating to spirits in Africa as these are often spoken about as beings that can be seen and recognised in their bodily appearance as so and so and even in dreams.

In general terms metaphysics is based on the assumption that there is a general framework which every culture uses to make sense of reality and that picture of the world has a strong bearing on how the people organise their lives. For example, our picture of the world affects how we understand ourselves, our concept of person, how we claim to know and what counts as knowledge, and the whole question about the meaning of existence. It is important to assert that metaphysics permeates every facet of human life hence the need to understand its central concerns. So much material of philosophical import remains hidden in African cosmologies in general and the need to retrieve it to help understand societies in Africa and inform ideas on progress and development cannot be underestimated. This chapter, which focuses on Shona metaphysics attempts to delve into the underlying ideas that inform thought and practice among the Shona. Since metaphysics is a branch of philosophy that deals with the ultimate nature of reality, this chapter is an attempt to articulate the Shona conception of reality; that is, their conceptual framework relating to the entire sphere of reality and its operations. Shona metaphysics is here understood as the way in which the Shona understand and interpret reality; it describes the way they perceive and make sense of the world around them. As a rational reflection on the nature of existence and reality, metaphysics occupies a very important position in terms of understanding all other facets of Shona philosophy. At all times it is important to remember, as Wiredu (1995) submits, that what is distinctively African in metaphysics in Africa today derives from African traditional thought.

The concept of Mwari[1]

> From time immemorial human beings appear to recognise a persistent feeling that our existence is tied to something which is both immanent and transcendent. (Ramose 1999:67)

This universal fact of existence is the point of departure in my exposition of the concept of Mwari among the Shona. Mwari is the name given by the Shona to their High God whose shrine was at Matopos. Ranger (1974) acknowledges that a number of scholars have tried to trace the origins of the name Mwari and its meaning without much success, but what seems to be beyond any doubt is the point that the Shona shared a belief in Mwari before Christianity was introduced to Zimbabwe. As Daneel points out:

> For centuries they [the Shona] have believed in Mwari as the final authority behind their ancestors, a High God who was perhaps less directly involved in the affairs of individual lives than the ancestors, but one who could be consulted on matters of communal import. Far from being a remote deity, Mwari was believed to control the fertility of Shona occupied country, to give rain in times of national crisis. Thus the pre-

Christian belief in a Supreme Being contributed considerably towards shaping the destiny of the Shona people. (Daneel 1970:15)

Following below is one example on how scholars have tried to provide an account on the possible meaning and origin of the name Mwari. Of course I should hasten to say there are many conjectures that have been put forward to trace the etymology and historical roots of this name, but none of those accounts seem to have resulted in any consensus (see Daneel 1970; Fortune 1973; Ranger 1974). According to Des Fontaine, the Shona belief in Mwari holds that:

> In the beginning he was here, that is, somewhere above the world of which he is the unseen owner. He provides the feast of Nature, giving men the fruits of the earth, and yet is not of it, nor bound to it. Yet, Mwari is not a fetish God, bound to some stick or stone. The worship of Mwari may have come from the worship of the SUN; the word Mwari is thought to be a derivation of 'KUMWARIKA' ('to have watery eyes' as one would get from staring into the sun). There are, however, no indications of sun worship in the Mwari cult of today. Mwari is petitioned for the fertility of crops and barren women. (Des Fontaine 1974: 15; Caps original)

Going through the quotation above there are a number of things that have to be pointed out. The immediate issue concerns the use of the pronoun 'he' and the term 'Mwari cult'. I have dealt with the latter in my endnote. Concerning his reference to Mwari as 'he' this appears to be something borrowed from Christianity for it goes against the seemingly agreed position that for the Shona, Mwari was neither male nor female. In fact Daneel (1970:16) submits that Mwari was both male and female. The depiction of Mwari incorporates aspects that were associated with both genders in traditional Shona society. Mwari was referred to as the God of fertility which is an aspect associated generally with women as mothers and Mwari was also referred to as the head, father, and owner of the skies which are aspects that were associated with men among the Shona. Mwari was also known by a range of names such as *Dzivaguru* (the great pool); *Nyadenga* (Possessor of the skies); *Wokumusoro* (the One above); *Musikavanhu* (Creator of mankind) (Daneel 1970:16–17). Of philosophical significance is to examine how through these names the nature of Mwari was projected and what important insights could be drawn from these names. It is interesting to note that some of these names of Mwari have found their way into the new Christian religion as they were appropriated by the missionaries when they translated their scriptures into Shona. The convenience of such appropriations lies in the missionary attempt to render their new religion and its scriptures acceptable to the Shona. Looking at the names of Mwari it is clear that the Shona shared a belief in God who was both transcendent and immanent. This was a God who could be spoken to and who spoke and pronounced on matters affecting the people at all times, yet it was also a God that unlike human beings and ancestral spirits was shrouded in mystery; a God that was neither male nor female because it was not fully knowable.

The names used by the Shona carry certain metaphysical presuppositions about Mwari in terms of the kind of being Mwari was thought to be. *Dzivaguru* brought out the Shona belief that Mwari was the giver of rains – Mwari was the life-giving force, while *Nyadenga* and *Wokumusoro* expressed their belief in a God who is of the above and who provided the wonders that no mortal can lay claim to such as the skies. *Musikavanhu* portrayed the special God to whom humanity owes its origins. The name *Musikavanhu* has often been misconstrued since some scholars have translated it literally to mean 'creator' as Daneel has done. This is a common occurrence due to the influence of Christianity, a religion to which some of these writers were probably exposed to for historical reasons. However, as Bullock (1927) rightfully points out the name *Musikavanhu* most likely means a moulder of matter into men, rather than a creator. According to Bullock (1927:121) 'the Chishona name Mwari means the begetter or bearer; or, if embellished in our (Christian and Western) terminology, the creator. Mwari conveys the idea of generation, not creation from nothingness'. Interestingly a similar point is made by Wiredu (2002a) regarding the Akan of Ghana and their conception of God. According to Wiredu (2002a:21) 'Creation is often thought of, at least in run-of-the-mill Christianity as the bringing into existence of things out on nothing'. But the Akan God is not thought of as such a creator. In fact, for Wiredu, the notion of creation out of nothing does not even make sense in the Akan language. The Akan Supreme Being is thought of as a cosmic architect rather than a creator out of nothing. There is thus an affinity between the Shona and the Akan concept of God, although throughout Africa the average understanding of God today is one that has been influenced through and through by religions such as Christianity and Islam. For this reason there seems to be, as Wiredu notes, a superabundance of characterisation of African thought in terms of inappropriate or at best, only half appropriate concepts particularly in areas such as religion. The point is that some indigenous linguistic expressions are not readily translatable into foreign languages without loss of meaning or without the risk of distorting them completely. This is also true of so many other concepts in African philosophy.

There is no doubt the different names given to Mwari are in themselves renditions of the range of all imaginable qualities about the nature of Mwari and things that Mwari had and could accomplish. For the Shona, Mwari was credited not only with 'creating' the person but also with providing the feast of nature or fruits of the earth (Bullock 1927:121). It was believed that Mwari would continue to provide for the people unless someone within the community upset Mwari by committing acts that were deemed unnatural, such as incest which angered Mwari, which then provoked punishment in the form of pestilence or the withholding of the life-giving rains. The Shona had an established system of communicating with Mwari which involved specialist priests and priestesses who resided at the famous Mwari shrine at Matopo Hills. Within the hierarchy of beings, Mwari was at the top and as such dealt only with issues of grand importance affecting the entire community, leaving the rest to other minor spirits. This was because 'Mwari was not interested in individuals. Such affairs are within the province of other spiritual powers, but Mwari is too far above mortals to be interested in particular men and even tribes' (Bullock 1927:123). It was therefore the responsibility of family spirits or ancestors to deal with every detail of their living descendants but done, of course, in liaison with Mwari. This is because the Shona believe that the living dead are part of their life and have a direct responsibility to protect and guide the living at all times. As Mbiti points out, the living dead

> are the closest links that men have with the spirit world... [they] are bilingual: they speak the language of men, with whom they lived until 'recently'; and they speak the language of the spirits and God, to whom they are drawing nearer ontologically... these are the spirits with which most Africans are concerned: it is through the living dead that the spirit world becomes personal to men. (Mbiti 1969:83)

For the Shona, like most Africans, the spirits are a reality that must be reckoned with whether they make sense or not from the positivist outlook. Like most Africans, the Shona view their society as a trilogy of beings comprising the living, the living dead and the yet to be born. Ramose (1999:62) refers to this structure as the onto-triadic conception of being. However, since the other two levels of being in the trilogy pertain to beings that are either unknown or unseen, this structure can also be referred to as the 'ontology of invisible beings'. The living, the living dead and the yet to be born and their relationship operated within an overarching system anchored in the belief in Mwari who, according to the Shona, was the sustainer and provider of life. Having examined the idea of Mwari, it is important to look at how the belief in Mwari, was related to spirits and kings as ritual elders of their communities.

Spirits and traditional leadership

Studies on Shona traditional religion have pointed to the existence of a coherent system of beliefs and ideas about Mwari including the existence of spiritual beings. Since Mwari was concerned with rain, the wellbeing of crops and local politics, there was in existence a close synergy between the priests of Mwari, the tribal spirits, and the king as a representative of the people. The king of the Shona was also a spiritual leader and he symbolised the unity of the Shona people through the royal court and Mwari. As 'the dominant ritual elder of the tribe' (Crawford 1967:26), the king had the responsibility to coordinate spiritual functions at tribal level. The king was a descendant of the royal ancestors of the tribe who constituted the foundation and source of his power. Land or territory was hugely significant for the Shona as it was not only the source of livelihood but also the abode of the ancestral spirits and an integral part of the people's identity. People were not only identified by totems and laudatory names (*zvidawo*) but by the great names of the geographical places where they came from. Without land, chieftaincy had no legitimacy as became the case in most places after colonisation. Bucher (1980:34) recounts a very interesting story of a man who was reprimanded by the chief for not saluting him and the man angrily retorted: 'Where is the land?'. In other words, the man was simply reminding the chief that he no longer had any legitimacy in the eyes of his people because the land which gave meaning to his power had been lost to the colonial settlers. The lump of soil that he held at his installation to symbolise the title to territory had gone and with it his legitimacy.

It was partly because of the question of legitimacy in the absence of title to territory that chiefs led the first Ndebele-Shona uprisings of 1896–7 against the settlers. The people could not see any reason to respect the chiefs when they could not defend the territory bequeathed to their stewardship by the founding ancestors. The chief's 'ownership' of the land and its people derived from his supposed connection with the mythological founder-ancestors of his chiefdom (Bucher 1980:32). They are called mythological because the narrative concerning the history of these chiefdoms is often couched in myths and mysteries of heroism beyond ordinary and normal human capabilities. Kingship therefore rested in the ancestors, and rightful heirs to the throne were supposed to be connected by blood and totem to the founding ancestors. No kingship was conceivable without ancestors who constituted the rightful owners of the territory and invariably bestowed political legitimacy. This is why the *mhondoro* or tribal spirits had such an important place in Shona religio-political processes as a spiritual consultant. The people turned to the ruler because he had the closest access to the medium of the *mudzimu* spirits of his ancestors who could contact the High God and in that way gained respect from his people, but the ruler was not regarded as divine in terms of Shona traditional religion (Beach 1980:104). Kingship belonged to people on the basis of lineage in that one who could become king belonged to the line of the founders of the kingdom or the royal ancestors of the clan. In theory, the ruler was hedged by rituals that stressed his supreme power, but in practice rival houses were often waiting to stage a successful coup (Beach 1984:28). Kingship among the Shona was immersed in metaphysical beliefs involving not only ancestral spirits but magic and witchcraft. By working with renowned magicians, kings were able to fortify themselves through the acquisition of powerful magic and witchcraft popularly referred to in Shona as *kuromba*. A traditional leader had to have extraordinary supernatural powers often superior to those of his rival and other witches otherwise he would not survive. What Vansina observed about the Bantu of central Africa was also true of the traditional Shona. According to Vansina:

> A leader was always a focus of envy. A battery of charms helped him to repel the attack of witches, and his own witchcraft killed competitors or subjects. His success was attributed to the favor of supernatural agencies, a favor won by furtive human sacrifices through witchcraft 'at night'. Such beliefs explain why competing leaders often used accusations of witchraft against each other. (Vansina 1990:97)

What Vansina describes fits very well with the Shona tradition of *kuromba* (to fortify oneself with a battery of charms, furtive practices and magic often harmful to opponents). This practice of harnessing occult forces to buttress one's power and maintain a hold on leadership positions has not died down even in modern politics. The spirit world has and is still believed to carry a significant influence in the life of the living and machinations to harness the powers of that world have survived through time from the pre-colonial state to the present. Metaphysics therefore provides a framework within which to understand the ideas of power and the practice of politics in much of postcolonial Africa including Zimbabwe. The history of Zimbabwe is a story of how politics has been closely connected to the metaphysical particularly the belief in the power of magic and spiritual forces. Eminent scholars such as Ranger (1985b; 1999), Lan (1985), and Chung and Kaarsholm (2006) among others have written extensively about the liberation struggle in Zimbabwe detailing the close cooperation between ancestors, their descendants, that is, the living dead and the living in the pursuit of freedom. Many liberation war songs speak to this kind of synergy. Commenting on the place of spirits in Shona lives, Lan (1985) argues that the Shona have always seen the relation between their past and their present as mediated by ancestor spirits as the custodians of the land. Ranger (1985b) reminds us that even during the war of liberation spirit mediums offered guerrillas a certain historical legitimacy in their struggle while offering the peasants some sense of control over these armed youths. The spirit mediums therefore effectively established what he calls the 'moral economy' of the war in the country. The fighters had to enter into dialogue with the ancestors to justify and explain their actions and to seek ancestral help. Such beliefs have their roots in the pre-colonial Shona society finding their origins in the belief in the power of ancestral spirits. Like many other African groups, the Shona strongly believed that the 'real' world went beyond the apparent world (Vansina 1990) and it was in the 'real' world that the power to influence events in the physical world could be derived.

The strength of the belief in the power of the 'real' world manifested itself among the Shona through the existence of multiple sites of religious ritual and reverence. Every kingdom had shrines and places of power such as caves, hills, pools and even trees associated with various ancestral and nature spirits. At the apex of them all was the Shrine of Mwari. It was the duty of the king with the help of the elders and spirit mediums to coordinate activities relating to these places. Van Binsbergen (1981:101) defines a shrine as an observable object or part of the natural world, clearly localised and usually immobile, which is a material focus of religious activities perceived and respected as such by the participants. As Colson argues:

> places of power are permanent features of the landscape regarded as inherently sacred or as the loci of spiritual power. If they are associated

with particular named spirits rather than generic spirits or unpersonified force, these spirits are usually mythologised as ancient heroes who existed before present political units or communities came into existence or they are conceived of as spiritual forces of non-human origin. (Colson 1997:48)

Sacred sites or places were thus treated with respect and only a selected few with spiritual connections to the great spirits (*mhondoro*) believed to inhabit those places were allowed to lead rituals and to take people to such places if they needed the intervention of the spirits. Natural sites, as shrines, were therefore approached cautiously, usually by delegations sent for the purpose, who were guided in their pilgrimage by mediums or priests chosen by the spirits as their intermediaries (Colson 1997:48). Spiritualism among the Shona also manifested in the range of items and artefacts considered to be of religious or ritual significance. Nelson (1983:5) reminds us that the famous soapstone birds, eight of which were found at Great Zimbabwe, served as representations of the royal messengers to Mwari in rituals of spiritual communication. According to Huffman (1981:131) even the spatial organisation at Great Zimbabwe depicts the articulation of two main dimensions: attitudes about status and attitudes about life forces. Archaeological evidence confirms that the Acropolis was organised according to beliefs about life forces. To understand Shona metaphysics one therefore has to make sense of the whole religious and mystical nuances of the artefacts, beliefs, and symbolisms of the various items considered sacred in Shona culture, as well as narratives connected to artefacts found at the ancient ruins dotted around the country including Great Zimbabwe. Like any community of people, the Shona have their own ontology and metaphysics and having talked about the ancestors and ancestral spirits it is important that I conclude this section with a note on terminology. I have in mind the terms 'ancestor' and 'living dead' which have already appeared in this discussion and will be encountered throughout the work.

Questions have been raised concerning the use of the term 'ancestor' and its appropriateness particularly when referring to the living dead in Africa. Scholars have highlighted that the term 'ancestor' is a misrepresentation of the ontological status of the invisible beings and that it implies too strongly a Western notion of death that fails to accord sufficient presence to the invisible beings, who though dead, remain among the living in a different form (see Ashforth 2002 and Kopytoff 1971). African lineages are communities of both the living and the dead but 'the term "ancestor" sets up a dichotomy where there is no continuum' (Kopytoff 1971). Kopytoff (1971) submits that to insist on the conceptual primacy regarding the distinction between the living and the dead amounts to a distortion of the African worldview, a distortion that prevents a proper understanding of the ontology of invisible beings in Africa. For Kopytoff (1971), not only is the term ancestor – meaning an ascendant who is dead – denotatively inappropriate but also misleading. This conceptual problem can be traced to the Western ethnocentric conviction that ancestors must be separated from the living elders, which has in turn influenced the way Africans approach beliefs about life after death and how they theorise about it. For Kopytoff (1971) 'once we recognise that African "ancestors" are above all elders and to be understood in terms of the same categories as living elders, we shall stop pursuing a multitude of problems of our own creation'. In other words, because of the attempt by scholars to make sense of African beliefs using borrowed terminology from the Western worldview, the entire conceptual framework which deals with the 'ontology of invisible beings' has been distorted and rendered problematic. It is against this backdrop that I shall continue to use the term 'ancestor' for the simple reason that it is a compromise term and has become accepted in modern circles to refer to the dead in Africa. Hence, everywhere the term occurs in this work it should be read as if it contains special markers; that is, as if it is written in inverted commas to signify the fact that it is a problematic concept, particularly for Africa.

The concept of *chivanhu*

In contemporary Shona society the concept which seems integral to the process of understanding Shona tradition including metaphysics and its paraphernalia is the concept of *chivanhu*. There is little doubt in my mind that the term *chivanhu* and its rendition is a direct offshoot of the colonial experience connected with the installation of a tradition–modernity ideology in colonial Africa. *Chivanhu* is a term that consists of the prefix '*chi-*' meaning 'it', referring to the traditional beliefs, customs and practices, and '*vanhu*' which means people. As such the term *chivanhu* refers to the traditional beliefs, customs and practices of the Shona people. To analyse the cultural landscape in Africa today one has to take seriously the submission by Bell (2002) that the encounter of the African world with European modernity is in and of itself a philosophical text to be read, critically appraised and understood. Not many would disagree that through this encounter, a new world has been forcibly created as a consequence of the West's imperial adventure, and the categories (political, economic, cultural) in terms of which that world has increasingly come to live have been put in place by characteristic modalities of modern power. (Asad 1992:340).

This is a point that has been dealt with in the previous chapter. What is of significance at this point is to acknowledge the historical effects of modernity in the socio-cultural sphere of African lives, and the various processes of cultural metamorphosis it has triggered and continues to influence across Africa.[2] Although I prefer to talk of modernity in the singular form I am also aware that modernities are multiple and varied as the encounter of the different worlds with European modernity was never the same. I therefore believe Chatterjee's submission that:

> There cannot be just one modernity irrespective of geography, time, environment or social conditions. The forms of modernity will have to vary between different countries depending upon specific circumstances and social practices. (Chatterjee 1997:8)

So much has been written about modernity from the socio-historical and philosophical perspectives and for that reason I shall not embark on a detailed exposition of modernity. Africa has experienced and continues to undergo continual constitution and reconstitution as it reacts to developments and cultural processes that define this modern world. Borrowing from the work of Rengger (2000) and notwithstanding the contested nature of the concept, modernity is hereby understood in two basic forms: modernity as mood and modernity as a socio-cultural form. 'Modernity as mood' focuses on the way we understand and react to what is held to be the implications of the modern; it is, in other words, largely a philosophical, theological, ethical and, perhaps, ontological question. The second, by contrast, focuses on particular changes in the material, technological and, or socio-economic realm said to be constitutive of the modern (Rengger 2000:4). As socio-cultural form, modernity refers to modes of social life and organisation that emerged in Europe from about the seventeenth century onwards and which subsequently became more or less worldwide in their application. As mood, modernity is basically a way of doing things – a kind of spirit that people assume; and a way of looking at the world true to the ideals of the Enlightenment and its driving philosophies. In the words of Lawrence:

Chapter 4

> Modernity as mood – better captured by the German word Stimmung – celebrates a political-theoretic vision of progress encapsulated in ideas of liberty, rights and emancipation. It is a clearly optimistic view, especially in relation to the past. (Lawrence 1999:4)

It is this 'mood' that is of significance to this work in the way it manifests itself in Africans' reactions to and conceptions of their past. There is little doubt that postcolonial Africa is a complex metaphysical and social landscape characterised by the interplay of forces generated from the cultural ripples of the encounter of the African world with Western modernity. I agree with Rengger that 'any account of modernity is in fact a compendium of both modernity as mood and modernity as socio-cultural form' (Rengger 2000:4). From the foregoing, African modernity can then be defined to be modernity as experienced from the point of view of the Africans. It is, as Masolo states, 'a reworking of the familiar into new and changing times and conditions' (Masolo 2000:165). In other words, African modernity can be conceptualised as the African reaction to its own 'new situation' (as a result of the colonial encounter), as well as a conscious appropriation of modes of thinking, ideas and socio-cultural forms of existence typical of modernity. African modernity describes the process of Africans attempting to reconstitute themselves and define their own social reality in dialogue with the modern. Whilst modernity is often misconceived as antithetical to tradition, the position adopted in this work is that the two are not mutually exclusive because in every modernity there is tradition. As Gross (1992:4) rightfully points out, many traditions continue on in the nooks and crannies of modern life. They exist privately even where they have eroded publicly. Some traditions survive by going underground, others by reconstituting themselves in such a way as to live on in new forms and guises.

Concerning modernity Mudimbe, (1997:xii) notes that 'every modernity is, from an existential point of view, a form of cultural hybridation witnessing to contemporary dynamics of dialogues between peoples and histories'. With this brief analysis of modernity it is important to return my focus on the term *chivanhu*. There is no doubt that *chivanhu* as a concept arose in direct response to and as a consequence of the colonial experience. This process could have been driven by the colonials in their penchant for projecting the so-called exotic and the primitive in African lives. But it is also possible that in their attempt to resist cultural annihilation and hold on to their identity, the Shona may have seen it appropriate to demarcate what they felt was their own authentic traditions so as to preserve and transmit them to new generations. In both cases, whether the initiative was driven from outside by colonial ethnocentrism or by the instinctive quest to preserve one's identity in the light of impending and threatening change, the point remains that it was within the context of the politics of tradition versus modernity instituted during the colonial encounter that *chivanhu* was installed and carved its identity as the opposite of Western modernity.

As a classificatory term *chivanhu* is a name that refers to some existing entity and, since the aim behind any practice of naming is to identify, distinguish and classify the objects of experience, it is crucial not to ignore the politics behind its popularisation as a name. Processes of naming are important in the construction of social reality since the object named is thus situated in the order of the world and the structures of meaning invested in by a particular community. Although I can only surmise the context of its origin, I am convinced that the term was initiated to mark off the West from the non-West and probably served different ends for both the colonials and the African cultural enthusiast. Considering the ideological prejudices of the colonial era, the term *chivanhu* can be pejorative from its association with a long tradition of thinking of Africa as a continent to be understood in terms different from the rest. An analysis of the mentality that popularised its usage is crucial in understanding the concept. The term *chivanhu* as applied in colonial Zimbabwe (and to this day) is not a term innocent of politics but a description of the supposedly primitive Shona culture in contradistinction to modern Western culture and science. It is a term located squarely in the ideological politics of the colonial script and is therefore not free of stereotypes about African culture and mentality. In spite of this the concept remains useful in terms of making sense of the discourse of culture among the Shona. There is no doubt that there still remains a great challenge of how postcolonial Africa can engage with its past, and talk about it in language and terms that do not perpetuate colonial derogation, stereotypes, assumptions, attitudes and misrepresentations of indigenous thought and culture.

The popularisation of *chivanhu* as read in such phrases as *chivanhu chedu* (our cultural practices, customs and beliefs) can also be understood within the context of the cultural and philosophical discourse of negritude and African personality which were themselves reactions to the threat posed by colonial culture and values. However, what is of significance in this work is to examine aspects of what that *chivanhu* comprises of. I have decided to spend some time examining this concept in order to highlight the fact that indeed a gulf in conceptual thinking that has its roots in the colonial encounter, while problematic, can still provide an important window of analysis in making sense of those aspects of African culture prevalent today classified under the banner of *chivanhu*. Furthermore, since the term has been and continues to be applied to mark off traditional Shona practices from those of Western origin, philosophers can use this distinction to gain a better understanding of those aspects of Shona culture often emphasised as defining it and thus used to distinguish it from the so-called modern Western culture.

What I wish to emphasise is that although the term *chivanhu* is sometimes used pejoratively to ascribe the negative connotation of backwardness, it can also be read neutrally (even though it owes its existence to the colonial dictionary) to emphasise Shona cultural identity and those belief systems and customs that distinguish them as a people. It is in this second sense that *chivanhu* can be used as a galvanising concept for revitalising culture in contemporary society and shaping its discourse in terms of negritude or the popular African renaissance. This is where *chivanhu* can be used to feed into the discourse of politics and identity. The subject matter of *chivanhu* includes basically the sum total of most of those ideas which go into explaining the Shona worldview, including religion, belief in Mwari, ancestors and the living dead, spirits and forces, magic and the practice of medicine, witchcraft, sorcery, and divination among others. At the centre of this worldview are important institutions that mediate communication between the living and the spiritual realm. These are the spirit mediums, healers, magicians, oracles, rain spirits, and soothsayers among others. It is impossible to conceive of the metaphysical aspects of *chivanhu* without the intervention of these spiritual beings. They are the central pillars in the practice of *chivanhu* as well as its symbolic expression. Any activities in which these beings are invoked can rightfully be described as *chivanhu*.

In traditional Shona society even the social rules that regulated conduct found themselves buttressed and reinforced by the metaphysical dimension that in part defined *chivanhu*. Traditional Shona spirituality provided the foundation and justification for a number of practices. Such things as respect for elders, communal solidarity or belonging, the feeling of brotherhood and respect for persons had their basis in traditional spirituality. It was this metaphysics that explained why certain practices and forms of behaviour remained intact and unquestioned. In this sense *chivanhu* formed the seedbed or the 'fertilising soil' out of which *hunhu* would grow but as it appears today that 'fertile soil' has been eroded. *Hunhu* was strongly reinforced by and oriented towards a collective social morality. The close connection that existed between

Shona metaphysics, epistemology, morality and social theory made this possible. It is precisely for this reason that it may prove difficult to revive *hunhu* without making similar efforts to restore *chivanhu* particularly its positive elements. Attempting to do so can be analogised to the effort to reformulate Christianity without Jesus Christ as its central figure. In other words, without the biblical Christ there is no Christianity to talk about. Throw him away and you throw away Christianity. Throw away *chivanhu* and you throw away *hunhu* and instead something else remains, in this case *chirungu* (Western values). This is what is happening across many African communities that have emerged from colonialism. As a result of the negative perception of *chivanhu* proceeding from over a century of onslaught from Christianity and Westernisation which has been taking place since colonisation, the majority of people are no longer enthusiastic about *chivanhu* and care less about its survival let alone its revitalisation (see Mungwini 2011b:781).[3] Given this trend it is not inconceivable that generations to come will not be able to understand central aspects and ideas that defined this particular Shona outlook or worldview. It is for this reason that projects to preserve such ideas through writing become imperative. Since *chivanhu* continues to face the same fate confronting African indigenous ideas and traditions across the continent, the risk remains high that this foundation upon which Shona ontology was defined and conceived could be lost forever. To understand the history of thought in the traditional Shona society it is important to be able to preserve in writing those conceptual schemes through which they, as a people, sought to interpret, evaluate and manage their life and surroundings. The Shona worldview including the 'ontology of invisible beings' presents us with what Bucher (1980:14) calls 'a complete system of religious assumptions, a veritable *weltanschauung*, which is intended to answer men's most existential questions'. It is within this complex system of assumptions about existence and the nature of beings and how they interact that one may, for instance, make sense of notions such as causality, fortune, marriage, health and procreation, disease, death, and social relations in general.

Causality among the Shona

Chiripo chariuraya zizi harifi nemhepo (something must have killed the owl; it cannot be wind) is a Shona proverb that captures in a significant way the Shona conception of causality. In other words, nothing happens without a cause. Why has a particular event happened to a particular person at that particular place and at that specific time? This question lies at the heart of the Shona understanding of causality. For the Shona there are reasons that must be sought for things that happen apart from the ordinary. The search for a cause rises to another level when what has happened is considered as beyond the immediate and ordinary. There is a general unwillingness to attribute things to chance because of a belief that for everything that happens there is a cause. This belief is not unique to the Shona or even Africans alone, but is also found in the Western tradition as expressed in the famous Aristotelian axiom *quidquid movetur ab alio movetur* (whatever is in motion is necessarily moved by something other than itself), a principle of motion and causality that was examined in more detail by Thomas Aquinas. Where the Shona find themselves limited in accounting for phenomena, they immediately appeal to the extrasensory world to provide the explanation. Because of their picture of reality which views the world of spirits as intertwined with the world of physical existence, the Shona find it rationally appropriate to attribute causal events in the physical world to spiritual beings. Most of their explanations fit into what Sogolo (2002) describes in his scheme of causality as primary and secondary causes. Secondary causes are the straightforward physical causes of events like poison from a snake bite causing death to a person while primary causes are invoked to account for the reason why the victim fell victim to that venomous snake and why no remedy could work. For primary causes supernatural forces including spirits are appealed to as causes and among the Shona the popular term used to capture such forces is *mhepo*, which literally means 'winds'. The idea follows from the realisation that by their very nature, spiritual forces operate like wind which is intangible and can blow from any direction. When something bad happens unexpectedly to an individual the person can retort in Shona: '*idzi imhepo chaidzo*', meaning 'truly these are winds'. In reality what the person would be saying is that whatever happened to him/her is the work of evil spirits since no physical being is capable of doing such things. Unexpected events or mysterious happenings, bad luck or misfortune are things that are attributed to the workings of the spirit world. The contiguity between the two worlds, that is, the physical and the spiritual world within the realm of Shona metaphysical thought, provides individuals with a mental framework where things that happen are either directly or remotely connected to the spirit world. On the other hand when an unexpected feat of success or good luck also happens to an individual the Shona attribute it to good spirits, particularly the ancestors and God. The ancestors are said to have provided or intervened, *kupuwa nemidzimu,* meaning the ancestors have provided.

Since ancestors are the good family spirits, whatever credit they are given for bringing about fortune or good luck is automatically attributed to God, because the ancestors are understood as the intermediaries between God and the people and so whatever God wants to give to people is channelled to them through the hands of the ancestors of one's lineage. Each family relies on the good work of their ancestors and their level of alertness and ability to listen to their descendants, relaying that to God and then passing the feedback to the living. As such those who always remember to appease the ancestors and to keep the lines of communication with the ancestors open are the families that are often expected to experience good fortune in whatever they do. Like living beings, ancestors are understood to experience changes in mood, they can either be happy or angry and their emotions express themselves to the living through events of fortune, good luck or misfortune and suffering.

Causality in Shona life: An example

To highlight the notion of causality and its centrality in Shona life the following example is selected for analysis:

> A village fisherman drowns in the river while fishing possibly entangled by his own fishing net. Questions are raised about why despite years and years of fishing experience the man died on that particular fateful day. Why him and not any other person? What really blinded him to the point of drowning in a portion of the river he knew so well? With his knowledge of water and his ability to swim how could that happen? What is it that prevented other people from coming to his rescue? What blinded them?

All these questions would lead to the final and more crucial question of *'who could be responsible for this and why?'* Of course this is a question involving both secondary and primary causality as identified in Sogolo (2002:192). It points to the existence of a complex system of accounting for events that invariably constructs the world of the Shona as subjected to agentive forces, both physical and invisible, that determine basic outcomes and realities in their existence. There is common acceptance that power is wielded by both tangible beings or entities and invisible entities and there are indeed forces operative behind the visible nature of things over and above what we can see. The search for reasons behind the misfortune invokes the underlying belief in witchcraft which in turn renders the entire institution of magic not only appropriate, but highly effectual for the purposes of providing an 'adequate' explanation. Finding adequate reasons to explain why, for example, some individuals are drawn towards danger while others are made to walk away from it effortlessly immediately strays into the domain of metaphysical explanations. It is therefore true to say it is in part due to what the people consider as appropriate and therefore legitimate questions to raise which determine the adequacy or inadequacy of a causal explanation. For those communities preoccupied with the positivist outlook epitomised in modern science, some of the questions raised by the Shona would count as non-questions. But to the traditional Shona, addressing physical causes without the spiritual component that binds the living to the forces roaming in spaces around them is considered inadequate as it ignores a vital and probably more powerful component of existence.

The belief that invisible forces can be directly responsible for happenings in the physical world has not spared even the so-called modern gadgets like cars which are the symbols of science. For example serious vehicle accidents in which many lives are lost seem to attract both technical and spiritistic explanations. The most popular position taken by many regarding such things as bus accidents where many innocent people are left dead is that of *kuchekeresa* which boils down to an accusation of ritualised murder directed at the owner of the bus company. This illustrates that even in modern business and politics, the work of spirits and occult forms cannot be discounted (see Matereke and Mungwini 2012). Causal explanations are never limited to what can be perceived but always seem to beg a metaphysical or spiritual explanation.

Within the Shona worldview spirits occupy a central place and play a significant role in accounting for both fortune and misfortune. A healthy relationship must therefore be maintained between every family and their lineage spirits. Misfortune is usually taken as a sign of strained relations between the individual and his/her ancestral spirits. When relations are strained the spirits abdicate on their responsibility for around the clock protection and surveillance leaving the individual vulnerable and exposed to things that may bring about grief, bad luck, and witchcraft attacks or sorcery. It is in this light that the Shona notion of causality becomes intelligible.

Death and immortality

> Death awareness is a natural sequel to the development of self-awareness – an intrinsic attribute of humankind. The consciousness of man's transience in its known earthly form is thus a universal phenomenon and one which poses intellectually tantalizing questions for [philosophers] (Palgi and Abramovitch 1984:385).

In order to make sense of the ideas of death and immortality among the Shona it is important to understand their view of a person. In other words, finding an answer to the old metaphysical question of what a person is becomes imperative. It is probably true that one of the most enduring problems in metaphysics is the problem of the self or person. Although the question over which elements come together to constitute a person seems fairly easy to answer among the Shona, a major problem immediately arises when one moves to the next level to try and describe the nature of each of those elements and to provide a rational account of how those different components interact as they fulfil the different roles they are ascribed.

The concept of person

Wiredu observed that:

> African inventories of the constituents of personhood generally feature, at the minimum, a body, a life force, and a personality principle. Generally, one of the non-bodily components is regarded as coming directly from the supreme being and is frequently characterised as the speck of the divine substance in a human being. (Wiredu 2009:13)

The position articulated by Wiredu seems true of the Shona. The human being is made up of the physical body (*muviri*), soul/spirit (*mweya*), and blood (*ropa*) which gives one their *rudzi* (lineage or identity). It seems parallels can be drawn between the Shona conception and similar ideas about the person from other parts of Africa. What is of significance is not the disparate names they give to the various components or constituent parts but the overall picture which emerges where the person comprises of a combination of the material and the immaterial substances. For example, in his examination of the concept of a person among the Akan of Ghana, Wiredu (1996:157) submits that a person is the result of a union of three elements which, although different, are not necessarily disparate from each other. The three elements are the life principle (*okra*) which comes directly from God, the blood principle (*mogya*) which comes from the mother, and the personality principle (*sunsum*) which is linked with the father. On the other hand, Gbadegesin (2002:172–182) examines the concept of person among the Yoruba of Nigeria and concludes that the person is a unity of four elements, which are the physical body (*ara*), the heart (*okan*), the life-giving element (*emi*) and the head (*ori*). Of course I shall not enter into the details and controversies in terms of how these elements are understood, but what is of interest to me is the fact that in both cultures the person seems to be a composite of elements that are physical and spiritual with some of the elements capable of assuming what seems to be both spiritual and physical roles. However, it is important to highlight at this point that other than the physical and spiritual components that are emphasised there is more to a person than simply being a biological entity hence the normative dimension should never be discounted in the understanding of a person. I will return to this issue later in the chapter on indigenous Shona morality.

Among the Shona, although the blood at conception comes from both parents, it is from the blood that comes from the father that one gets the totem and clan identity. As such those who share the same totem are regarded as sharing the same blood (*ndeve ropa rimwe*). Other components of the body that are often emphasised are the head which is the city of reason and the heart which not only drives blood circulation but is also regarded as an intelligent source of emotions including right and wrong. The Shona often proclaim in their conversations statements to the effect that '*mwoyo wangu waramba*', literally translated 'my heart says no', presupposing therefore that there is inherent within the heart the capacity for rational moral decision making. What it would mean then is that with these advances in modern medicine today, like heart transplants, if a ruthless dictator were to receive the heart taken from, say, a well-known wholly compassionate and altruistic individual he would be expected to inevitably undergo profound change in character and emerge a good, compassionate, caring person, but this seems far from the truth. To that effect it seems what is attributed to the heart in common parlance therefore makes no rational sense. Furthermore, in Shona speech a conflict in thinking is often projected between the mind and the heart, for example in the statement *pfungwa dzangu dzati ita but hana yangu yaramba*, which is translated as my mind said go ahead but my 'inner conscience' in the heart said do not. This conflict, which is often expressed

Indigenous Shona metaphysical thought

in serious moral decision making, is again confirmation that the Shona accord certain rational capacities to their heart (*hana*) as the home of 'conscience' or inner intelligence. It seems the roles played by the heart and the mind are often conflated thus adding to the confusion over the nature and role assigned to the organs.

Let me now turn to examine the body and the spirit. To provide a better analysis of these two I shall again draw from popular Shona expressions that seem to capture their notions of the body and the spirit. I shall consider the following three statements:

1. *Chinonzi munhu mweya.* (The real person is the spirit.)
2. *Chinofa muviri mweya haurovi.* (It is the body that suffers death not the spirit.)
3. *Pachuru apo ndipo pavete sekuru.* (It is in that grave that grandfather is sleeping.)

While it can be claimed that the third statement expresses a specific form of figurative language considered appropriate for talking about the dead, the implied literal meaning cannot be discounted given claims about the dead appearing in person and talking to the living and the strong resistance to cremation of the dead among the Shona. It is believed that the living dead, that is, as embodied spirits, can actually be seen and communicated with by medicine men and those with special powers, and when those beings are described, the account is given in material terms or physical images. They are described as having a body; they occupy space and even converse. This is particularly problematical given that the Shona also seem to suggest that at death the body decomposes and only the spirit lives on as implied in statements 1 and 2. Even if the spirit were to live on without the body, the major problem is how that spirit can be identified by the living without the physical body which gave the person his or her physical appearance or identity before death. The fact that the Shona continue to speak of the dead as individuals and refer to them by name indicates the extent to which death is at one point seen as simply a process of transition into another world and therefore does not mark the end of both bodily and spiritual existence. After a period of about a year following a person's death, a ceremony is held to help the spirit get admitted to the ranks of the living dead of the person's lineage and at the same time the spirit is also welcomed back into the family as a guardian spirit to look after the family. This form of existence is aptly captured by Mbiti in his account of the living dead. Even though it remains difficult to fathom how the 'dead' can be regarded as still living and active in day-to-day activities of their

Chapter 4

families such difficulties only arise for the scholar. To the ordinary person (including some scholars), the belief in the real existence of the 'dead' is regarded as unproblematic in the same way some famous physicists are ardent believers in God and miracles. As Mbiti correctly pointed out:

> Whatever science may do to prove the existence or non-existence of the spirits, one thing is undeniable, namely that for the African peoples the spirits are a reality and a reality which must be reckoned with, whether it is a clear, blurred or confused reality. (Mbiti 1969:91)

This belief, whether scientific or not, deserves serious attention as it continues to influence questions of human dignity and rights. Several development projects in Africa have had to contend with the consequences of this reality when construction work has had to be halted for periods in order to appease the spirits of the dead buried there or to allow for their relocation before construction could resume. This in part explains why comprehending the true nature of a person's beliefs, though problematic, remains important.

According to Ramose, almost all accounts on the nature of person have to contend with what he calls:

> [the] empirico-philosophical question, namely, does the human being consist of a destructible component, the body, and an indestructible component which might be called the soul? If so, how is the soul knowable? Does it make any sense to talk about the soul if the grounds for its knowledge are dubious? (Ramose 1995:233–4)

The important thing to note is that even though talk of the soul may not make much sense to those of an empirical persuasion, it does seem to make sense to most people outside that bent and for that reason it is worthy of our attention. There is no doubt that the physical and metaphysical aspects of reality and their inseparability are given expression in the notion of self or person. The African idea of self, and by extension that of the Shona, is an affirmation of the point that metaphysical concerns will remain an integral part of what preoccupies us as humans for a long time to come partly because we are ourselves an unresolved metaphysical puzzle or paradox. No doubt humans have been able to agree on the nature of certain aspects of reality in the universe but it seems there has not been much consensus on what matters most – the question of who we are, that is, what is a person? To this end Kant is perhaps correct to warn that we should not expect the human mind to give up metaphysical questions or researches at any time.

Death and cremation

Among the Shona, the 'ontology of invisible beings' has a very strong influence on how death is conceived. The presence of the 'dead' among the living is taken for granted and on the basis of the accepted ontological hierarchy the 'dead' are not completely dead for they remain alive in the chain of being. In other words, death is not considered as an end but simply a transition into another plane of being within the cycle of life that connects the yet to be born, the living and the living dead. To cremate the dead is not only immoral but it destroys the cycle of life for burial is simply a process to facilitate transition to another form of existence that is much more powerful and of a higher rank than that of the living. Contributing to the debate on cremation in Zimbabwe, one renowned sociologist and founding president of the Zimbabwe Traditional Healers Association, the late Professor Gordon Chavunduka, argued:[4]

> Cremation is totally against cultural traditions. The philosophy of death in Shona society says it takes about a year for a spirit to leave the body and join the spirits of the ancestors. If the body is cremated, that spirit would be blocked. Although it would remain alive, it would be angered that traditional burial rites had not been followed properly and could return to punish the family and community.

It is interesting to note that as one continues with the news extract from which this quotation was taken, the two Harare officials who were advocating the need for society to accept cremation do admit to their unwillingness to be cremated in the event of their deaths. From the above submission, it seems logically appropriate to infer therefore that at burial the Shona are not putting a 'dead' person down because the soul/spirit has not left the body until after about a year when rituals are then performed to release it into the spiritual realm and to welcome it back into the family. But the other question which arises is what happens if the ritual for releasing the spirit is never performed? Does the spirit remain with the body meaning that the person literally remains alive forever? This again adds to the confusion raising more questions for which no answers are readily available. If cremation is conceived literally as the act of destroying the dead person then it is believed to upset the whole logic of existence. The Shona also conceive of burial as the act of reuniting the dead with the land and the earth where they came from. It is by the act of investing the dead back into the soil that the inseparable bond between the yet to be born, the living, and the living dead is reinforced. This is the reason why colonial land policies with their subsequent relocation of communities were such a devastating stage in the life and existence of the Shona. The land, the spirits of the living dead, the yet to be born, and the living constitute the community. When the living maintain balance and harmony in these elements, nature provides in abundance for all. When nature provided in its various ways through abundant rains, bumper harvests, plenty of fruit and animals for meat, the Shona believed that it was the ancestors and God showing their gratitude to the people for upholding the law of the land.

Belief in witchcraft and occult forces

> Yet it should not surprise us that education and science, the two most potent symbols and purveyors of progress and modernity, should not eradicate belief in the unseen, in the magical, in powers that transcend ordinary human control and comprehension ... Africans have no monopoly on witchcraft, occult forces and discourses. Moreover, contemporary witchcraft, occult practices, magics and enchantments are neither a return to 'traditional' practices nor a sign of backwardness or lack of progress; they are instead thoroughly modern manifestations of uncertainties, moral disquiet and unequal rewards and aspirations in the contemporary moment. (Moore and Sanders, 2001:2–3)

This passage which introduces the topic of witchcraft and the occult among the Shona has been carefully selected to highlight the enduring nature of this subject and to dispel the myth that the subject of witchcraft and the occult is a marker of primitive African societies as envisioned by colonial anthropologists. Western discourses on Africa have to a larger extent conditioned the African perception and reaction to African metaphysical beliefs and forms of knowing. However, despite this problem it is important to realise that witchcraft and occult beliefs are complex, on-the-ground realities that African philosophers cannot afford to ignore. They constitute an important facet of how the Shona defined and continue to define reality and experience. Omoregbe highlights an important dimension of African metaphysics as it relates to the explanation of the ultimate nature of things. For him and within the African context there are mystical or supernatural forces which defy any scientific analysis or explanation. These forces surpass and sometimes counteract physical forces. They can be manipulated by man and employed for both good and evil purposes, such as protection, prevention of calamities, cure of diseases, procreation and bringing about sickness, death, and other kinds of misfortune to people. (Omoregbe, 1990:26–27)

Beliefs about the existence of spirits, witchcraft, magic, sorcery, that is, occult practices in general, are practices that are intimately linked to the Shona people's cosmology and their way of dealing with the complexities of daily existence. These are key to understanding metaphysical aspects of *chivanhu*. Beliefs of this nature largely complement physical causal explanations by providing answers to the famous 'why' question asked of any mysterious or any out of the ordinary happenings that befall individual members of society.

In their book entitled *Witchcraft Dialogues: Anthropological and Philosophical Exchanges,* Bond and Ciekawy (2001:1) make the following salient comment: 'In this post-European colonial era, "witchcraft" and "sorcery" have become emotive and provocative terms, shunned by many Africanist scholars'. Not only does the study of witchcraft carry with it a heavy burden rooted in past prejudices and invidious comparisons but:

> for many scholars it evokes the period of colonial domination, their subjugation, and that of their beliefs and practices. It is often viewed as fitting into the repertory of negative images of Africans representing a perverse concern with the exotic that belittles the capacities of the human intellect to approach problems through reason. (Bond and Ciekawy. (2001:2)

Despite the fact that witchcraft is acknowledged as a universal phenomenon, colonial literature has attempted to portray it as a practice unique to indigenous colonised societies and as a mark of their primitivity. This is despite well-documented evidence on the prevalence of witchcraft beliefs and the famous witch hunts of the middle to early modern periods in Europe from the 15th to the 18th centuries. According to Bailey (2003:xxi), the 15th to the 18th century is known as the era of 'the great witch hunts' in Europe – a period which saw the execution of tens of thousands of people for the supposed crime of witchcraft. This period is remembered in history for the famous *Malleus Maleficarum* (Hammer of Witches), a manual or treatise on witchcraft and witch hunting written by the Dominican inquisitor Heinrich Kramer in 1487 to provide guidance on the identification, conviction and persecution of witches across Europe. It is therefore correct to assert that throughout history most cultures have held ideas about witchcraft and have grappled with the belief that there are certain individuals capable of accessing or harnessing supernatural powers to cause harm to others. In Europe such people were believed to be in league with the devil and bent on destroying the Christian society on earth (Bailey 2003:xxi). One can therefore submit that the concept of witchcraft and the idea of who counted as a witch in Europe were to a large extent influenced by the ideas, beliefs and practices of early Christianity.

Due to the varied cultural contexts, perspectives and perceptions on witchcraft are numerous and varied although it can be demonstrated that because of the spread of Christianity several other cultures and their ideas about witchcraft have now been influenced by the Christian notion of witchcraft. This is particularly important to remember when dealing with many of the concepts that are in use today in Africa across the academy. Although this is indeed a difficult task, what I seek to do is to articulate an understanding of witchcraft that is rooted in African traditions and practices. To this end the philosophical task is to try and distil the meaning of witchcraft from the standpoint of the indigenous Shona peoples and how that belief constitutes the key to an overall understanding of Shona cosmology. I agree with Ranger's (2006:351) observation that while it is hugely significant and philosophically correct to be absolutely clear on the concepts one is dealing with, it is somehow extraordinarily difficult to make distinctions between 'magic', 'witchcraft', 'sorcery' and 'religion'. Part of this problem arises due to the nature of the subject that I am examining which in itself is shrouded in mystery. Another insurmountable hurdle when dealing with these concepts is one that relates to the effect of what Naseem (2002) calls the contemporary confluence of cultures also noted much earlier by Mazrui (1986) as Africa's triple heritage. In other words, it is crucial that in any analysis one should historically acknowledge and take seriously the effect of the West and Islamic traditions on contemporary African ideas and concepts.

With regard to the Shona conception of witchcraft it is therefore important not to lose sight of the colonial and missionary imprint. As Ranger (2006:351) points out, colonial administrators and missionaries lumped together every supernatural manifestation–and many natural ones– as 'witchcraft', combining activities and ideas which originally had been not only separate, but opposed. The early missionaries and colonialists made no attempt to distinguish the different aspects of magico-medicinal practice among the indigenous peoples. Chavunduka confirms that 'the witch, the patient seeking relief, and the practitioner attempting a cure, were all treated alike. They were all regarded by missionaries as worshippers of devils' (Chavunduka 1978:77-8). The overall effect was that, following from this Christian logic, all indigenous practices whether nefarious or beneficial ranging from religion, magic, sorcery, witchcraft and medicine were grouped together as diabolical. The catastrophic effect of conceptual blunders such as these, obviously committed through either willful ignorance or sheer arrogance, is part of the problem that African philosophers have to contend with in their quest for conceptual clarity.

While there is no universal definition of witchcraft there is a sense in which it can be distinguished from sorcery and magic. However, I should be quick to acknowledge that the meanings of these terms are not only culturally dependent but they are also often vague and tend to overlap. Bailey (2003) provides such a distinction between sorcery and witchcraft; a distinction that I find very useful. Although witchcraft is a form of harmful sorcery which involves the manipulation of spiritual forces and the casting of spells in order to kill or cause suffering or misfortune, there are practices of sorcery that do not aim to harm others. The tendency to conflate sorcery with witchcraft is in part to do with the etymology and origin of the terms. Bailey (2003:121) argues that 'the English term sorcery derives from the French term *sorcellerie,* which means both sorcery and witchcraft'. However, from the fact that a distinction can be made between harmful and harmless sorcery I shall maintain in this work that the only harmful sorcery is witchcraft.

Magic on the other hand is a term that is derived from the Greek term *megus* meaning 'great' science (Guiley 2009:159). Guiley (2009:159) defines magic as 'a superior power created by the combining of inner power with supernatural forces and beings such as angels and demons'. Of course from her definition I can discern the cultural influence of Christianity. However, Guiley (2009:159) makes a very fundamental point that there are many systems of magic in existence each with its own procedures, rules, and proscriptions. Generally, the origin of magic lies in human beings' attempt to control and manipulate natural forces for their own survival. Guiley (2009) cites the anthropologist Bronislaw Malinowski who defined magic as having three functions and three elements. The functions are to produce, protect, and to destroy while the three elements are spells or incantations, rites or procedures and altered states of consciousness attained by various means such as chanting, fasting and visualising symbols among others (see Guiley 2009:159). From the above-mentioned functions of magic it is clear that magic is not inherently good or evil but it reflects the intention of its practitioner. This is the ambiguity of magic. In Shona culture indigenous magicians are known to openly declare to anybody who consults them that '*Ini ndiri muroyi ndapikwa*', which literally means 'I am not a witch but I can be hired to bewitch and you carry the blame'. This is what makes people ambivalent about the indigenous practitioners of magic since they can be available for hire by individuals with evil intentions. From the way magic is practised, and depending on the intention of the user, there is evil magic which can be associated with harmful sorcery and therefore witchcraft. But so long as magic remains harmless and is used with good intentions to benefit society then it is different from witchcraft. The practitioners of magic are neither wholly good nor wholly evil beings but due to their expertise they are both feared and revered. Unlike ordinary beings they have the ability both to avert and to cause danger. They can do strange and extraordinary things with their powers. Guiley's (2009:160) depiction is spot on: 'individuals such as magicians thus are dangerous because they work in this uncertain world. As adepts, they are themselves the agents of change and even chaos'. It is probably because of this indeterminacy and unpredictability connected with their practice that practitioners of magic are more often than not identified as witches too. However, although I have attempted to make these distinctions between witchcraft, sorcery, and magic for the purposes of analysis, the only point that scholars in this field can agree to is that witchcraft, magic, and sorcery are universal phenomena but there is no universal definition for any of them.

In Shona the term for witchcraft is *uroyi* and it captures a variety of activities involving nefarious practices aimed at destroying life and to causing harm through the manipulation of evil spirits and the use of magic. There are varieties of witches but they are all brought together by their desire to destroy life. I shall therefore adopt Bailey's (2003) definition of witchcraft for it comes closest to the way the Shona understand it. According to Bailey (2003:xxiii) witchcraft is 'a set of actions, practices, and behaviours that certain individuals actually perform to supposedly terrible effect' through the use of harmful sorcery, evil magic and the manipulation of spiritual and evil forces. *Uroyi* is the Shona word for both the anti-social act of harming other individuals and for the anti-social animus in the person carrying out the anti-social act (see Ranger 2006:354). For the Shona the witch stereotype is the antithesis of what a person should be. The witch is one who works in the dark and consorts with certain unclean animals such as hyenas and owls, one who is motivated by envy and always seeking to destroy the community rather than build it. The witch is the best possible example of the enemy from within as witches most often target family or blood relatives including those around them.

From the above exposition of witchcraft and its related concepts I can conclude that the subject of witchcraft and the occult in Shona societies like anywhere else, is particularly difficult because it deals with a phenomenon that is shrouded in mystery and one that literally keeps slipping out of sight. Although so much has been written on the Shona belief in witchcraft and occult forces (Bourdillon 1976; Chavunduka 1978, 1980, 1994, Gelfand 1973; Ranger 2006), the truth is that much of what one has to deal with and unravel remains shrouded in secrecy and mystery. However, one may not be far from the truth to assert that witchcraft beliefs are common in Shona communities and most people go about their day-to-day business conscious of the threat that witchcraft poses to their own lives and the wellbeing of the community at large. Witchcraft distinguishes itself as one complex set of beliefs that attempts to account for all the inimical happenings and misfortunes in everyday life whose comprehension is beyond the ordinary. The belief in witchcraft is closely connected to the invisible ontology and it constitutes an integral part of the Shona explanatory and interpretive framework that is so important in making sense of their world and social relations. This belief also provides, in the words of Bond and Ciekway (2001:323), an entrée into the people's (and in this case the Shona's) ethical and moral systems. By paying close attention to the Shona belief in witchcraft, philosophers will be able get a better picture of how the Shona, within the limits of their cultural horizon, bring together the visible and invisible ontology to inform their concrete existential circumstances. As a phenomenon, witchcraft provides the avenue through which complex ideas of spirituality, misfortune, suffering, and death can be interpreted and reinterpreted in the quest to restore equilibrium to the forces that regulate life within the family unit and community in general. Evil forces and the constant struggle against them are seen as an integral part of what defines life among the Shona. It is for this reason that while witchcraft is feared it is all the same an acknowledged phenomenon of life that like day and night is a constant reminder of the struggle of existence. Witchcraft is a subversive force that unfortunately has to be constantly struggled against and like any belief it affects people's choices and decisions. As an integral part of what defines their cosmology, the major issue for most of the Shona is not the existence of witchcraft but how to cope and survive in a world characterised by these unpredictable forces. In other words,

Chapter 4

the real question is how to regulate it, hence the intervention people seek from various churches especially African independent and Pentecostal churches and at times the institution of witch hunts by hiring the so-called exorcists or people who claim to have powers to flush out witches and to kill, banish, or shame them.

Stories involving malevolent acts that manipulate spirits coupled with the use of magic to harm other people are issues that one can expect to read about in daily newspapers that circulate in Zimbabwe and by extension most African countries. Even across the religious landscape the subject of witchcraft dominates. The so-called modern institutions like Christian churches devote a significant amount of time in their sermons to addressing issues of witchcraft. In fact, it can be partly argued that what makes modern charismatic churches and other Pentecostal churches popular today are their claims to be able to deliver people from the bondage cast by occult forces and witchcraft that prevent people from prospering by holding them back in perpetual poverty and misery. Meyer (2004:465) claims that one of the reasons for the extraordinary popularity of the Pentecostal church is its claim to be able to reveal the occult forces behind money, power and goods. It is therefore clear that Christianity has not displaced traditional metaphysical beliefs including beliefs about the occult, but has instead created a platform on which they make perfect sense. Witchcraft and mystical experiences are a set of experiences that elude scientific and commonsense explanations because of their sophistication, but they continue to occupy a central position in the existential realities confronting the Shona. It is this lack of 'openness' that makes the subject problematic when it sits next to other experiences that modernity considers as open, objective, universal and translatable such as science.[5]

On 14 October 2011, a daily paper, *New Zimbabwe*, carried the following story: 'Female 'rapists' charged with 17 counts'. The paper reported that for two years, investigators had been on the trail of female 'rapists' who offered lifts to male hitchhikers on the country's highways before taking them to secluded places where they are given some *muti* (Viagra) to drink and then forced to be intimate with them, usually at gunpoint. These ladies would then collect the semen in the used condoms. Police found 31 used condoms, four of them half full with semen. Police believed this 'semen harvesting' was for ritual purposes. A professor of sociology at the University of Zimbabwe speculated on the purpose of the sperm harvesting spree by the three arrested prostitutes and said that sperm was associated with the regeneration of life, which would translate into business growth. 'People believe that sperms can make someone's luck improve', he said, adding that unscrupulous businessmen were behind the sex attacks. A local journalist said: 'It's believed that because sperm sources do not dry, anyone who uses sperms in ritual practices can earn money continuously while those who use it for power can have a grip on the people they control forever. It is suspected that among those buying the sperms are politicians and business people'.[6]

This story, which is just one among many such stories, brings to light what one may call the prevalence of and recalcitrance of occult beliefs and witchcraft practices in contemporary and modern Shona society. The belief in witchcraft continues despite the enactment of laws such as the Witchcraft Suppression Act which was introduced by the colonial government and subsequently retained by the postcolonial government. According to Ter Haar:

> colonial governments did not take any position on the reality of witchcraft, trying only to suppress witchcraft accusations in an attempt to make African societies conform to European ideas of right and wrong. As a result, African communities felt abandoned to the capricious powers of witches, against whom they had no legal defence. (Ter Haar 2007:17)

This situation unfortunately did not change after independence and resulted in many people attempting to take the law into their own hands with the help of some traditional leaders who felt strongly that they were better placed to deal with accusations of witchcraft in their traditional courts even though the constitution does not allow it. Due to the widespread belief in witchcraft among the Shona, the Witchcraft Suppression Act remains in the words of Ter Haar (2007:20), 'a law without public consent'. It is true that across Africa the invisible ontology remains strong and belief in witchcraft provides Africans and Africanists alike with fertile conceptual terrain for constructing, considering and contesting the multiple manifestations of modernity that positively flourish at the crossroads of local and global worlds (Sanders (2003: 339). Far from being an archaic practice suited for primitive societies, the belief in witchcraft is as contemporary as the belief in science, although many claim the belief to be irrational and retrogressive. Having looked at these central metaphysical ideas it may be important to consider in brief other key ideas in Shona metaphysics.

Chapter 4

Other metaphysical concepts

There are other metaphysical issues such as the idea of change, freedom and determinism, time, appearance and reality that one may be able to reconstruct by considering a number of proverbs and sayings that capture these notions. For example, the Shona conceive reality as something that is ever changing and which never stays the same. A proverb such as *chinobhuruka chinomhara* (whatever flies comes down to perch) expresses the idea of things being in a state of constant flux. The inevitability of change is often expressed as a warning and veiled admonition to individuals who think of themselves as invincible. In other words, change is taken as a reality in life since nothing ever stays the same.

Another proverb is '*zuva igore rinovira rava nemarevo mavi nemauya*' which can be translated literally as, 'a day is like a year that one cannot predict how it will end; it can either end well or end in tragedy'. It highlights people's powerlessness in knowing and controlling natural events or happenings around them. It is closely connected to the Shona belief in the reality of invisible beings and forces as unpredictable and behind-the-scene determiners of the future. In other words, due to the complexity of the world and its operations which are not dependent on human wishes but are influenced by powerful forces and spiritual beings, it is impossible for anybody to be in control of how things may unfold with any certitude. You cannot predict what befalls you in a day although effort is often made to mitigate the severity of the consequences. The day is so long a period that you can experience both fortune and misfortune without expecting it and therefore individuals should never think that they have everything under control because there is always the unforeseen.

Appearance and reality is another important metaphysical notion that the Shona are very familiar with. Things are never taken as they appear and for granted. What appears to be may not be, as the proverbs *dhimba kushaya besu usati inyana* (that bird might be small in size but never mistake it for a chick), and *usaona imbwa kuchenama ukati inokusekerera* (a dog that bares its teeth need not be smiling). These proverbs indicate the extent to which the Shona can go in trying to distinguish between appearance and reality an important philosophical question in metaphysics. Even the world is considered to be hiding many of its own secrets, hence the need to penetrate to its heart and centre through divination, magic and spirit mediums. The Shona belief in the 'ontology of invisible beings' can in part be explained on the basis of their desire to comprehend or influence this complex universe and it is also at the same time an admission of their finite nature as beings in the face of the universe. It is important to conclude this discussion on Shona metaphysics by highlighting what has been observed about African metaphysics; in general, and which, for me, applies with equal validity to the Shona as a people. Asouzu observes that:

> Its shortcomings notwithstanding mythological African metaphysics ... is a metaphysics that is instrumental to the African in tackling fundamental issues of ethics and society and as such has been instrumental to questions of cohesion, social control, law and order within African societies. The fact of the African living in harmony with his/[her] environment and the world is rooted in a metaphysics that sees this as a necessary off shoot of man's relationship with the forces that control these spheres of reality. (Asouzu 1998)

Metaphysical beliefs contribute some of the fundamental ideas to what makes the Shona society what it is. These metaphysical assumptions are the foundation upon which other philosophical ideas about morality, knowledge, and aesthetics are buttressed. Despite the cultural metamorphosis triggered by colonial conquest and the contemporary confluence of cultures in Africa, there are aspects of traditional Shona metaphysics that continue to define the life of most Shona peoples. These enduring ideas and thoughts of the Shona about existence and the nature of reality are ideas integral to understanding their philosophy and they continue to inform their behaviour as a people.

Notes

1. I have decided to use the capital letter for the name Mwari, the Shona High God, to emphasise parity in religious depiction of Gods across the mainstream religions and those referred to as other religions. This is an idea I borrow from Soyinka (1999:32) who argues 'the convention that capitalises this [Christian] and other so-called world religions is justified only when the same principle is applied to other religions, among them, the Orisa'. The other important issue I need to highlight is that while most of the colonial scholars I make reference to write about the 'Mwari cult' I have deliberately taken a decision not to make use of the term 'cult' because of the ideological baggage it carries. Inherent in its usage is the apparent refusal by colonial scholars and anthropologists to see the Shona belief in Mwari for what it is – a form of religion. And since there is no universal definition of religion, the refusal to describe the Shona belief in Mwari as a religion and opting

to call it a 'cult' is reminiscent of the hierarchical reasoning affecting many aspects of African culture. The same can be said about similar concepts such as 'occult'. Commenting on its usage Ter Haar and Ellis (2009) correctly argue that the continued use of the term 'occult' is flawed owing to its association with a long tradition of thinking of Africa as a continent to be understood only in terms different from those applied to the rest of humanity today.

2. For an in-depth exposition of the argument on modernity and African culture I refer you to my two articles 'Surveillance and cultural panopticism': Situating Foucault in African modernities' *South African Journal of Philosophy*, 31(2), 2012, 340–353 as well as 'Orality and ordinary language philosophy: Revisiting the intellectual heritage of Africa's indigenous cultures', *Southern African Journal for Folklore Studies*, 21(2), 2011, 1–11.

3. In this article I examine the question of whether *hunhu* can be revitalised without first trying to strengthen *chivanhu*, something that will remain a stumbling block to any attempts to strengthen indigenous African values particularly in modern society where what is indigenous to Africa is often regarded with contempt because of the myth created by colonial history.

4. Chavunduka was commenting on the debate on cremation that had started in Zimbabwe in the face of the rising deaths mostly AIDS related and the shortage of burial sites in the city of Harare. It is critical to note that his position not only represents the feeling of many but it sheds light on how the Shona conceive of death not as the end, but as a necessary process of transition that allows one to continue to exist and to be connected and to commune with one's living lineage. Of course it also captures not only the respect accorded to the dead but also the inherent fear of interfering with or disrespecting and desecrating the bodies of the dead. However, nowadays a number of Shona individuals especially the prominent ones and those exposed to the influence of other cultures that practise cremation are accepting the practice. For a full discussion see Lawrence Bartlett, 'Zimbabwe–AIDS: Cremation a burning issue in Zimbabwe as AIDS toll rises', Agence France-Presse, August 29, 1999 http://www.freerepublic.com/focus/news/819957/replies?c=1

5. See also Matereke, K and Mungwini, P. 2012. 'The occult, politics and African modernities: The case of Zimbabwe's Diesel N'anga', *African Identities*, 10(4), 423–438.

6. This case illustrates the modernity of witchcraft and the recalcitrant nature of the belief in the causative effect of invisible forces and magic. It indicates how traditional rituals and cultural beliefs and symbolisms about bodily fluids are brought to bear on the modern market to enhance power and prosperity. It is for this reason that I argue that traditional metaphysical beliefs have proven resilient in the face of modernity among the Shona and even across much of Africa – a factor that has now made Pentecostal and African independent or spirit churches very much relevant across Africa, as they claim to be able to deal with beliefs in magic and spiritual machinations still rife among the peoples. For the full story you can read more at: http://www.newzimbabwe.com/news-6272-Female rapists charged with 17counts/news.aspx (Accessed 14 October 2011).

5

Knowledge among the indigenous Shona

The question of knowledge

> 'All men by nature desire to know'. So said Aristotle (1924: Book 1) and he was right. Information seeking is a pervasive activity of human life ... Our interest in information has two sources: curiosity and practical concerns ... We commonly seek the truth, or a close approximation of the truth ... Question asking is a universal feature of human communication and the prototype of a truth-seeking practice. (Goldman 1999:3)

This submission by Goldman underlines the historico-philosophical reasons of my argument for the universality of knowledge which informs this work. In the quote above, Aristotle (384–322 BC) indeed confirms what is arguably one of the most important aspects of humanity – the quest for knowledge. Had the verdict been pronounced with the universality it presupposes today, the epistemic marginalisation of other peoples and their forms of knowing would not have happened. However, as Ramose (1999:2) makes clear, the definition of man by Aristotle 'was deeply inscribed in the social ethos of those communities and societies which undertook the so-called voyages of discovery apparently driven by innocent curiosity', but which, for one reason or the other, metamorphosed into violent colonial incursions. Equally significant is the fact that the belief that all men are rational animals 'was not spoken of the African, the Amerindian, the Australasians: all the indigenous peoples of their respective countries [including women] from time immemorial' (Ramose 1999:1). Sadly, this belief became the basis of yet another monumental superstition that the indigenous peoples of the world, including Africans, were incapable of producing knowledge. The resultant effect of all this is the epistemically skewed world we inhabit today in which indigenous peoples continue to struggle to legitimate their accounts of knowledge. It is against this backdrop that the quest for indigenous forms of knowledge and philosophy should generally be understood. What motivates my discussion in this chapter is the position that all human beings from time immemorial have sought knowledge both for practical purposes and in order to satisfy their curiosity. It is on this basis that I shall attempt to outline aspects of indigenous Shona knowledge.

Epistemology is a branch of philosophy whose main focus is to analyse and evaluate claims of knowledge. An entry into the Britannica Online Encyclopaedia of philosophy traces the term epistemology to the Greek words *epistēmē* ('knowledge') and logos ('reason'), and accordingly the field is sometimes referred to as the theory of knowledge. Epistemology being the study of the nature, origin, and limits of human knowledge has a long history; it is as old as humanity itself. The emergence of the social construction of knowledge movement and the so-called ethno-knowledges has called into question all the claims of universalism in knowledge. Equally significant is the growing realisation that claims to universality about knowledge and particularly the universality of science have now come to be understood within the context of the politics of the North versus the South which saw the ideological deployment of universality in almost every significant aspect of life by the North as part of the process of dominating other cultures. What I mean by knowledge is universal is that it is found everywhere, but not in exactly the same mode or fashion. However, this does not discount the possibility that knowledge which originates in one corner of the world can also spread to influence the thinking of other peoples of the world and they can come to share in that belief. At that level this form of knowledge will have claimed universality in terms of its application and or adoption. However, such adoption leading to this universality can take place at two levels. First, it can happen by way of forced coercion where cultures are forced to abandon their own forms of knowing and adopt another position from a certain culture that happens to be more powerful or influential. The second way in which such universality can be attained is through the gradual and deliberate adoption of certain forms of knowledge as people discard and settle for those forms of knowledge which best answer their problems; through a process of mutual selection and/or natural diffusion of ideas across cultures that are inherently respectful of each other. The resultant positions if adopted by all can be called universal. This universality is achieved against the backdrop of the existence and availability of alternative and interacting epistemologies from different communities. It is this universality that is enriching to the world and it is something attainable in principle. I say in principle because humans will always have differences in what they hold and what they deem to be knowledge on account of the differences in the assumptions that underlie their epistemological quests, such as their metaphysical beliefs and worldviews. As long as such metaphysical differences remain, and these will forever be there, then our perceptions of the world including the sources of what counts as valid knowledge will be different. On that account there will always be various knowledges in existence.

An examination of African traditions and their epistemological status therefore constitutes an important project. It is the duty of the philosopher and African epistemologist to take part in the production, validation, refinement, and distribution of knowledge embedded in his/her traditions. The observation that ways of acquiring knowledge vary according to the socio-cultural contexts within which knowledge claims are formulated and articulated is crucial to this discussion. It opens room not only for the recognition of different sources of knowledge but it also provides good grounds to begin to take seriously the symbolic significance of the term ethnoepistemology and the possibility of a world free from epistemic hegemony. This is a world home to and amenable to different knowledges.[1] In other words, to speak of ethnoepistemologies is not only to legitimise the existence of varieties of knowledge but more importantly to recognise the role that history and place play in the formulation of knowledge. Okere argues, and correctly so, that:

> all philosophy is local and even individual before it can be universal; and nothing can be genuinely universally valid unless it was first authentically personal and inserted within a given culture. If this is the case for philosophy, it is likely to be the case for human knowledge, since every form of human knowledge must be situated or generated from within a culture or bounded by presuppositions, prejudgments, interests etc. (Okere 2005:21)

It is with this in mind that I feel adopting the term ethnoepistemology to describe the different forms of knowledge emanating from different cultures around the world is appropriate. I borrow the term ethnoepistemology and its usage from the work of Maffie. Given the global politics of knowledge, the term ethnoepistemology is understood here not in the pejorative sense in which it has been used by Western anthropologists where epistemological activities of non-Western cultures were designated as mere ethnoepistemologies while the epistemological activities of Western thinkers were taken as epistemology proper. Rather I employ this term with the same sense it carries in its other variants like ethnoscience, ethnobotany, and ethnomusicology among others. I therefore employ the term not only to draw attention to the cultural rootedness of knowledge but also to emphasise the locally contingent character of the knowledge making process. As Maffie argues:

> The world contains a variety of dynamic knowledge practices, sites, or perspectives and these are all equally inescapably local. All knowledges and epistemologies are local in the sense that they proceed from specific vantage points and have their social basis in a particular culture, class and gender. (Maffie 2009:61)

All knowledges are constructed by people in places with specific practices, and situated in power relationships, value assumptions, and historical frameworks. As such every culture develops and boasts of its own ethnoepistemology. Hence we can speak of various ethnoepistemologies across the world. In this regard Western epistemology becomes simply 'one among many alternative, contingent epistemological projects advanced by and hence available to human beings' (Maffie 2005). By taking this line of argument my aim is to avoid the problem of thinking in predominantly Western terms when approaching the question of knowledge. In other words, by adopting the term ethnoepistemology the ground is already laid for addressing the epistemic concerns of different communities while avoiding the tendency to use the West as the standard against which all other cultures have to be judged for their logic and adequacy. It is to avoid falling victim to what Gordon (2011) calls the imperial significance of standards where one form of knowing (in this case the African) seeks justification while the other (that is the West) is self-justified.

The term 'ethnoepistemology' is also implicated in the emancipatory discourses consistent with the anti-imperialist philosophies of liberation that characterise fields of study such as postcolonial African philosophy. As an attempt to contest the universalist pretentions inherent in Western epistemology and to expose this particularity, the term ethnoepistemology resonates with the emancipatory quest of 'shifting the geography of reason'.[2] 'Shifting the geography of reason' is neither a call to do away with Western knowledge nor is it an attempt to downgrade the role of reason in legislating on our various epistemic practices. Rather, it is an attempt to pursue the decolonisation of knowledge by 'liberating reason from its career in the service of domination' (Banchetti-Robino and Headley 2006:9). From the point of view of the African, decolonisation (whether of the mind or knowledge) 'takes place not only in facing the experience of colonialism, but also in recognising the pre-colonial, which establishes the destructive importance of so-called ethnophilosophy and sage philosophy, as well as nationalist-ideological philosophy' (Bernasconi 1997:191). This is why a history of the African past remains a crucial component of the process of liberation. To liberate reason is therefore to bring an end to the monopoly that continues to define the domain of knowledge by literally widening the scope and nature of philosophical ideas. This is where revisiting the African archive as a source of ideas that can potentially change the way human beings perceive and relate to the world, particularly in the face of monumental challenges such as climate change, becomes important. In order to realise a truly global knowledge landscape it is important that the ethnoepistemologies of previously marginalised communities be revisited. This, as Van Hensbroek (2013:33) correctly argues, is 'an endeavour to correct historical injustices' and to 'democratise intellectual production' in our world.

African epistemology

At this point I shall proceed not in the way most would naturally anticipate where a definition of African epistemology is given first and one is thereafter provided with more insights by way of fleshing out its nature. I have rather decided to begin by drawing from humanity in general and specifically on what philosophy can learn from humanity. This is important given the contestations that have characterised philosophy and the role that it should play for our common future. Here, as Okere (2003) urges, I distinguish the reality of philosophy from the promise of philosophy, that is, the history of philosophy as we know it, and the promise it holds, the great hope it imbues, and the as yet unachieved potential of philosophy. Often times we read of 'what philosophy can teach humanity' but I think it is time that 'humanity teaches philosophy' something. Philosophy needs to be equipped to face the new historical realities of a world in which there is no longer a place for that one hegemonic culture. At this point allow me as a point of emphasis to reiterate the point I made in the introduction that:

> Even when many 'others' become convinced that a certain mode of doing Philosophy is interesting and useful, that does not make this way of practicing Philosophy a universal standard. Philosophy is always there in the plural. (Van Hensbroek 2013:32; caps original)

Therefore as we contemplate this otherwise most important aspect of philosophy called epistemology it is critical to remind ourselves that Europe is not, as it has been portraying itself for centuries, the home of reason. Humanity is the only correct and true home of reason (Tabensky 2008). For that reason the true value of philosophy lies in its potential to bring humanity together in understanding and reflection. This is why claims to the monopoly of knowledge should naturally fall by the wayside to allow for the multifarious views on knowing. As Wimmer correctly argues,

> there are good reasons to hold that philosophy today and in the future will have serious shortcomings if it continues to discuss global questions only within the framework of concepts and methods derived from occidental lore. (Wimmer 2010:21–2)

In my view this submission by Wimmer summarises in precise terms 'what humanity can teach philosophy'.[3] Reason is not a prisoner of geography and neither does it become something different because it is exercised in the tropics (Ki-zerbo 1981). Whether a person inheres from the tropics, the polar or temperate regions, it matters not as we are all endowed with the ability to think and therefore the capacity to produce knowledge. I agree with Ramose (1999) that human reproductive power seems to have provided the all incisive blow to the myth that only a particular segment of humanity was exclusively and truly human while the rest were sub-human, if human at all.

> The discipline of philosophy has to reconstruct its own ideology, in order to establish an egalitarian basis of communication between philosophies from different parts of the world, a basis for polylogue communication. (Wimmer 2010:24)

At the centre of Wimmer's call is the attempt to warn against the tendency to perpetuate the belief that there is one true philosophy and one science which can provide humanity with fundamental truths about the world. I should reiterate the point that philosophy must renovate itself in response to the new historical realities of our world. 'Pointedly speaking, European philosophy and science presupposes necessarily European culture' (Wallner 2010:14) because philosophy is an expression of a specific cultural need and cultural conviction.

In epistemic terms, the validity of Wimmer's submission finds its expression in so-called alternative epistemologies such as feminist epistemologies and epistemologies of the South. The main point of entry for these epistemologies is not to offer 'alternative analyses of such traditional epistemological topics as memory, perception, truth, belief, and so on, or coming up with startling new solutions to the Gettier problem' (Mills 1988:237) but to transcend the framework within which these questions have been framed by arguing that such a conceptualisation is provincial in that it only reflects what one predominant group in a culture (Western males) has seen and defined as the central concerns of epistemology. Effectively then, the concerns will not be the problem of other minds, but the problem of

> why women were not thought to have minds; not the investigation of the conditions under which individual memory is reliable, but an investigation of the social conditions under which systematic historical amnesia about the achievements of African civilisations became possible. (Mills 1988:238)

In this chapter my focus is on the latter. Instead of tracing the roots of the historical amnesia concerning African civilisations I wish to challenge and thereby attempt to reverse this amnesia by drawing attention to the alternative modes of knowledge existent in indigenous cultures of Africa. My interest therefore is not to resolve the traditional problems of epistemology as defined in the Western canon but to map out some of those traditional forms of knowing which have been denied epistemic authority despite being in existence for centuries. Of course my view is that conceptions of knowledge, of what it means to know, of what counts as knowledge, and how that knowledge is produced are as diverse as the cosmologies and normative frameworks which inform human thinking (Santos, Nunes and Meneses 2007:xxi). It is true that in the process of establishing its epistemic authority, Western knowledge, through its practitioners, engaged in what Gieryn (1999) describes as boundary work, meaning 'a ceaseless policing of borders and a persistent epistemological vigilance in order to contain and repel the always allegedly imminent assaults of irrationality' (see Santos et al. 2007:xxx). In epistemic terms this boundary policing which took root in Africa from the colonial encounter has witnessed efforts by representatives of science and its canon to distinguish and mark off their domain of knowledge from that of so-called quacks and charlatans involved in what they demarcated as pseudo-science. This included almost all traditional forms of knowing whether traditional medicine, magic, and even religion and spirituality. It was under such ceaseless efforts that the fate of most traditional forms of knowing including even that of the African knowing subject was almost sealed.

Now let me get back to the question which I should have probably started with. This is the question what is African epistemology? In my opinion Kaphagawani and Malherbe (2002) have provided one of the clearest responses to this question by stating:

> Although epistemology as the study of knowledge is universal, the ways of acquiring knowledge vary according to the socio-cultural contexts within which knowledge claims are formulated and articulated. It is from such considerations that one can sensibly talk of an *African articulation and formulation of knowledge*, and hence of an African epistemology. (Kaphagawani and Malherbe 2002:220; italics original)

It is therefore correct to declare that 'given the specificity of their location in the world and their experience in human history, Africans as a people have a specific way of understanding and explaining the world and the complexity of the human condition' (Nkulu-N'sengha 2002:40). Since by definition any form of thinking is an epistemic quest, I take the existence of knowledge in any culture as a historical truth. In this work I am concerned with the Shona conception of the nature of knowledge and the means used to gain knowledge, including the purpose of knowledge and the role it plays in human existence. Every group of people possess the desire to know, to explain the world around them, and to make life bearable within the environmental confines they find themselves, giving rise to the emergence of culture-specific knowledge. Every culture has a worldview around which their life activities can be understood and that is why metaphysics is integral to epistemology. As pointed out by Horton (1998), worldviews whether primal or modern function as theoretical constructs that explain, predict and control the world as experienced and understood by its inhabitants. It is crucial to keep in mind that revisiting the African philosophical past is an integral part of providing that missing history in African thought. Ki-zerbo confirms that

> history is a source in which we should not only see and recognise our own reflection, but from which we should also drink and renew our strength, so as to forge ahead in the caravan of human progress. (Ki-zerbo 1981:23)

Progress on the African continent is contingent on a number of factors including reconstructing African knowledge traditions in order not only to correct the story of human civilisation but to help Africans reaffirm their being as 'a people of equal ontological density to the rest and second to none'.[4]

Shona epistemology

Let me begin with a brief analysis of the key Shona terms relating to knowledge. This I do in order not only to map out the meanings of these concepts and their implications for the conception of knowledge but to show that such key terms were an integral part of the vocabulary of the indigenous Shona demonstrating their human capacity for knowledge. The Shona term equivalent to the term knowledge is *ruzivo* where the verb *ziva* means 'to know'. In the way it is used by the Shona, the term *ruzivo* is a comprehensive term that captures broad ideas pertaining to knowledge including, but not limited to, comprehension of facts, having critical insight, clearly thought out and refined ideas, depth of understanding, knowing how, knowing that, and wisdom. Wisdom has often been used as a respectful evocation of the cultural achievements of the ancestors. So to have wisdom was testimony not only to one's ability but also to the time and dedication taken to learn from the elders. Among the Shona both theoretical and practical knowledge was prized. Wisdom and knowledge of human affairs particularly those pertaining to important trades including how certain traditional and religious rituals and ceremonies are conducted was particularly important given the Shona cosmovision. Knowledge of clan history and descent was also crucial as it determined the politics of kingship or chieftaincy and entitlement to territory. By virtue of a cosmology in which everything hangs together to constitute one whole, the metaphysical dimension in particular influenced the articulation of knowledge giving rise to a knowledge-belief-practice complex in which the unseen and the physical worked as one. Even practical knowledge such as that of medicine, hunting, and even agriculture was tangled up in the web of metaphysical beliefs. Knowledge and expertise in all fields important for human existence was therefore buttressed by the belief in the 'ontology of invisible beings'. The term *ruzivo* is also related to another concept *zano* (singular form) and *mazano* (plural) whose English equivalent is 'idea' and 'ideas' respectively. A person who has knowledge possesses *ruzivo* which is constituted by *mazano* that is, important ideas whether practical or theoretical needed in life. Knowledge among the indigenous Shona had a strong social character. It was to be used in the pursuit of desirable social ends although of course selfishness, egoism, and malice could never be ruled out given contestations over power which invariably made access to esoteric knowledge including magic and witchcraft often times advantageous in terms of warding off one's competitors or adversaries.

Another key epistemological concept that I shall consider is truth. The Shona term for truth is *chokwadi*. There are other terms of course such as *zvomene*, *zvirokwazvo* and *ndizvo chaizvo* which emphasise the quality of being so. However, a closer look at these notions reveals that *chokwadi* can have a variety of meanings although it is often used to refer to that which corresponds to what is there or that which is the fact. Furthermore, it can also be used to mean that which is accepted by the majority of the group as when there exists consensus regarding a particular issue. In that sense *chokwadi* and its equivalent *ndizvo* (it is so) express a sense of agreement. Another phrase equivalent to truth is *kureva nemazvo* which means to report or state as it is. This latter position presupposes the existence of a 'path' which if one's account manages to follow without deviating makes the account true. Today this third sense is often captured by the phrase *kutaura nomumutsetse* meaning 'to report as if one is following a straight line'. This is most probably a more recent adaptation of the use of a ruler and the drawing of a straight line where to tell the truth is to follow the line of the facts as they are without deviating. It could also derive from the much more recent practice of stating that which is written down as when witnesses give statements in court and when they are called upon to testify are able to give the very same statements they gave at the initial investigation. However, what emerges is that in the various instances in which the term truth is applied, it tends to fluctuate in meaning from the correspondence theory of truth to an understanding of truth as consensus, shared opinion or viewpoint as when somebody says in Shona, *ndiri kutaura chokwadi changu* (I am proclaiming my truth). Here one is equating truth with a viewpoint, that is, with one's own honest judgement concerning reality. The following example captures one of the senses of truth used in common parlance. 'What Mary told us is the truth because she was not yet aware of the new facts which now appear to make her initial position false.' The question that we may need to ask at this point is how does this rendition of truth compare with the traditional Aristotelian view of truth stated thus: *To say of what is that it is not, or what it is not that it is, is false, while to say of what is that it is, or what is not that it is not, is true* (Metaphysics, 1011b). It does not need much analysis to realise that what is stated in the example above does not pass this traditional test for truth. And yet it would not be correct for sure to say Mary was lying. In the example above truth and being truthful are taken as synonymous. One other traditional view of truth is often captured by the claim that the statement 'Snow is white' is true, if and only if, 'snow is white'. Again examined against this view our example above does not measure up and yet it expresses something fundamental in terms of how the Shona conceptualise truth. In other words, to give an account based on the facts that were available which someone believed to be genuinely adequate (although they are wrong) amounts to being truthful and therefore to telling the truth. An honest account which eventually turns out to be false because it does not correspond to the facts is regarded as true. At this point it is important to note that among the Shona there is a connection between truth and morality, where honesty as a highly prized virtue is a measure of truth. There is therefore more to truth that just correspondence to reality or facts. Truth is not some abstract intellectual formulation unrelated to the questions of morality and intention. Interestingly, Wiredu (1996:105) also points out, among the Akan of Ghana, that there seems to be in existence a close association between truth and morality because 'the main preoccupation with truth in traditional Akan society was moral'. Truth is not just a consideration of facts but the act of giving a truthful account which is in essence a moral thing to do even if the facts could be mistaken. Without going any deeper regarding the various conceptions of truth in philosophy, variations such as these are important in that they draw our attention to the fact that key epistemic concepts can differ and thus invest crucial implications about knowledge on both the Western and African philosophical outlook.

Having examined these terms it is time to say something about empirical and rational knowledge. Among the Shona the idea that the power of reason and the senses provide people with knowledge was taken for granted. Knowledge by the senses was presupposed and the connection between the five senses and reason as routes to knowledge was never an issue for disputation. To confirm the central role of the senses in knowledge acquisition I have selected the following five statements for illustrative purposes each relating to a specific sense organ.

1. *Ndinotaura zvandawona.* (This is testimony of what I saw with my eyes.)
2. *Ndinotaura zvandanzwa.* (My claims are based on what I heard with my ears.)
3. *Ndakatochibata nemaokoko angu awa.* (I felt it with my own hands.)
4. *Ndakachiravira ndini.* (I tasted it myself so I know what it is like.)
5. *Ndinochiziva nomunhuhwi wacho.* (I could tell from its smell.)

Although these sound to be bold claims to knowledge they all remain susceptible to the traditional refutations put forward by sceptics against any knowledge claim based on the senses. Many of these problems characterise philosophical inquiry perennially. However, in as much as senses can be prone to error for various reasons and in so far as any perception is mediated by many other factors including the environment of the perceiver and his or her own mental state at the point of perceiving, it is crucial to realise that no community of human beings has ever discounted the role of the senses in the acquisition of knowledge completely for that would be folly. In fact, the irony is that any skeptical consideration hinges on the very senses it doubts. Like any testimony about knowledge the corroboration of what is perceived using the senses was from time immemorial an important process of affirming whether something was to be relied on as knowledge or not. However, over and above these seemingly straightforward sources of knowledge about the world there were other avenues to knowledge which the Shona regarded as equally important if not more important since they 'revealed' what the senses could not ordinarily master. It is at this point that the complex worldview including belief in the 'ontology of invisible beings' and all its metaphysical paraphernalia entered the epistemological platform. This rather mysterious and contentious source of knowledge will constitute much of my focus for the simple reason that it remains shrouded in controversy. Furthermore, it is the sort of knowledge that seems to have suffered the most from the encounter with modern science and its 'boundary marking' exercise. Despite the negativity it has suffered since the advent of modernity and Christianity in Africa, this form of knowledge has refused to be completely subdued or forgotten. It remains therefore an important tradition of knowledge and hence a form of memory and intellectual heritage that requires preservation.

Revealed and esoteric knowledge

> Interest in so-called paranormal matters such as out-of-body experiences, reincarnation, spirit mediumship, extra-sensory perception, possession and the like is generally shunted into the dark corner of the profession by mainstream philosophers, and considered part of a misguided, pre-scientific past. (Hales 2001:335)

Perspectives such as these have become part of what defines the attitude towards not only these paranormal matters but most indigenous traditions and practices in general. There is a general disinterest and animosity towards many things labelled traditional and the degree of disinterest goes a notch higher if those traditions are conceived as being superstitious in nature. This is what threatens to seal the fate of indigenous knowledge and forms of knowing in Africa. Abimbola and Hallen correctly observed that

> the use of the scientific method as a paradigm of thinking has led to misleading comparisons, obscuring rather than illuminating the methodologies of non-Western systems of knowledge. The method of such systems may be not only different to their Western analogues, but coherent and objective in their own terms. (Abimbola and Hallen 1993:214)

Equally worrisome is the fact that this attitude of disdain captured in the opening quotation is adopted irrespective of the fact that many people, and not only in Africa, are still believers in religion and paranormal experiences. Rather than being dismissive of such widespread beliefs on the charge of being unscientific, philosophy can do well to analyse them by shedding more light on the logic behind their persistence. It is within the province of philosophy to reveal the epistemic and ontological assumption driving such forms of thinking. It is for this reason that I believe that this often derided form of knowledge deserves particular attention. In fact 'inherent in the scientific tradition is a resistance to knowledge that is exclusive, esoteric, or secret in nature, even if it "works" – even if its applications are effective' (Abimbola and Hallen 1993:215). This negative attitude towards other forms of knowing has partly to do with the rise of science as a model of explaining reality. It is probably true that since its inception science needed to be ruthless with other forms of knowledge for its own good. This self-aggrandising attitude is aptly captured by Lauer as follows:

> Due to the historical circumstances in Europe that gave rise to the 'New Science' of the early 1600s, fifty years after the Reformation. In the early 17th century the intellectual establishment of Europe adopted a posture of disdainful mistrust and extreme scepticism toward any new system of justifying and authorizing knowledge about nature. This was a reaction to the traumatic effects of the Reformation in the 1500s ...The first modern scientists needed to adopt an exclusionary posture of self-validation in order to build confidence in their innovative methods and results. In the effort to establish their legitimacy, they rejected all competing techniques of knowledge-gathering as wholesale quackery and nonsense. (Lauer 2006:3)

It is important to remember that the effect of this negative attitude towards other forms of knowledge was transferred with added ferocity to other cultures outside Europe, such as to those cultures in Africa. To make sense of the knowledge condition in Africa one would always need to understand the politics of knowledge and be prepared to go against the grain to confront the prejudices of science and its methods. However, such a feat will require commitment and dedication given the seemingly widespread acceptance of science and its canon as the only reasonable and reliable path to proper knowledge.

The place of secrecy

Etymologically the term 'secrecy' is derived from the Latin term *secretus* which means 'set apart,' 'withdrawn', 'hidden', 'concealed', 'private'. In examining any form of specialised knowledge in indigenous communities such as the Shona, particular regard must be paid to the role played by secrecy in the control and dissemination of specialised knowledge. This is because the notion of secrecy is key to understanding those forms of knowledge classified as esoteric knowledge. Helms (1988:13) cited in Hingley (2009) defines esoteric knowledge as 'knowledge of the unusual, the exceptional, the extraordinary; knowledge of things that in some way lie beyond the familiar everyday world'. Crucial to this kind of knowledge is the way in which the knowledge is controlled by a priviledged group of elders in terms of access and this is where the idea of secrecy arises. Nooter (1993:55) argues that 'in African epistemology ... secrecy operates in complex, subtle ways, being a key strategy in much secular and ritual experience, including traditional forms of education and the arts'. Secrecy was associated with what was of absolute value to the survival of the community. According to Nooter (1993:55–56; see also Bellman 1984:4), although in the eyes of the West, 'the word 'secrecy' tends to summon up sinister, negative connotations of espionage, of subversive or self-serving illegal political groups', in Africa secrecy is viewed less as sinister than as a necessary part of social reality and a defining element of certain systems of knowledge. There was therefore a close connection between highly valued knowledge and the degree of public disclosure allowed about it in traditional Shona society. Like in many cultures around the world expertise was qualified by possession of specialised forms of knowledge, skilled performance, the recognition of status, and the politics of exclusion. Access to various forms of knowledge considered invaluable and esoteric was regulated through ritual and initiation practices. There was knowledge including access to special geographical sites which only those with privileged positions conferred by tribal seniority and ritual enjoyed. Specialist and exclusive knowledge such as that of medicine, magic and ritual was the preserve of a selected few in society. It was believed those priviledged individuals were called into such practice directly by the spirits or initiated into the practice through ritual training under the guidance of mediums and tribal elders publicly recognised as custodians of sacred spaces. The Shona as a people were also aware of the fact that knowledge could be dangerous if it fell into wrong hands since it could be used for personal gain and to the detriment of others. Therefore, the liberal disclosure of knowledge was considered irresponsible and punishable by the spirits hence the strict control of knowledge in terms of who got access to what knowledge was very important. As Nooter (1993:49) citing Jose Nevadomsky reminds us, 'where knowledge is of absolutely crucial importance to the survival of the kingdom and the wellbeing of its caretakers, secrecy is paramount and precautions against reckless revelation are uppermost'. Secrecy was not unique to the indigenous Shona, it pervaded most societies and does so even to this day. The central importance of secrecy is aptly captured by Roberts when he argues:

> Secrecy is the essence of politics, for it implies a hierarchy of privilege and dependency: some people know something, others do not. Secrecy

is power, for those who know secrets may withhold or reveal their knowledge. The knowledge at issue is not the common sense by which people set their expectations for leading ordinary lives; to be kept secret, knowledge must be worthy of control. (Roberts 1993:65)

In this sense a knowledge system, through the process of deliberate exclusion, remained powerful, protected and highly sort after making its holders highly invaluable. Secrecy in indigenous Shona communities, if considered in today's terms, was also a form of patenting valuable knowledge from unscrupulous abuse or exploitation. It was at the same time a traditional method for the rationalisation of hierarchy and difference through the division of labour. Particular individuals whether by blood line or descent were renowned for specific trades such as magic or traditional healing while others were selected through some of form of 'calling' to serve the community by providing moral and spiritual guidance. Reference to such individuals was made in the chapter on indigenous Shona metaphysics.

Divination and knowledge

Divination as a practice and source of knowledge has a long history in many societies. In ancient Greek mythology on wisdom and foresight this practice can be traced to the Greek deity Prometheus who is credited with introducing mortals to the art of divination. Peek (1991) and Graw (2009) agree that divination is perhaps one of the most intriguing forms of human knowledge practice and is a primary means of understanding certain dimensions of epistemology in society. Nkulu-N'sengha (2002:40) argues that divination is not mere faith but 'a learned discipline based on an extensive body of knowledge, which involves at once natural and supernatural phenomena, the material and immaterial, and visible and invisible dimensions of reality'. As a means of obtaining knowledge, divination draws from the repository of cultural insight and meaning production which exists in a particular society. Peek (1991:3) describes it as 'a system of knowledge in action'. This is because every divinatory tradition constitutes a specific hermeneutic horizon in which questions of existential concern are addressed. In other words, divination and the knowledge that follows from it were integral to the life and function of the communities in which it was practised. The practice of divination and the search for meaning which ensued was anchored in the general metaphysical outlook which defined that particular society. An understanding pervaded most African societies including the Shona that the true reasons for all events can be known, but sufficient knowledge is seldom available through mundane means of inquiry; therefore, divination is employed to ensure that all relevant information is brought forward before action is undertaken (Peek 1991). Divination as a procedure yielded a form of knowledge called revealed knowledge. By revealed knowledge I refer to a sub-category of esoteric knowledge and other forms of specialised knowledge gained by means of techniques including divination, clairvoyance, magic, and spiritual possession that tap into the power of the invisible world to reveal knowledge to human beings as visions and in dreams.

Metaphysical thinking among the Shona and particularly the belief in the ontology of invisible beings to a large extent shaped the context of knowledge production and the means by which it was articulated. As such it seems logical that the criteria by which that knowledge is to be judged should out of necessity take into consideration cosmological beliefs including the paranormal generation and transmission of knowledge. It was because of the intertwined nature of the physical and the metaphysical that the Shona system of knowledge was essentially a knowledge-belief-practice complex, that is, a system in which particular ontological beliefs determined the nature of knowledge. The logical-analytical and the intuitive-synthetic, apriori and aposteriori forms of knowledge were not distinct and unrelated modes of knowing, but constituted one complex continuum needed for adequate mastery of the universe.

Among the Shona, divination was a means by which people sought to transcend the limitations of human sensory knowledge by reaching out for intervention or direction from the realm of the invisible beings. Divination may take many forms but the most popular image of a diviner is that of an individual who throws divining dices or bones called *hakata* in Shona. These bones or dices are regarded as a means of communicating and instruments through which messages from the invisible world can be decoded. For the Shona, *hakata* constituted a means of communicating with the spirits in that they literally wrote down the answers being sought for the diviner to see. As primary investigative tools, *hakata* were therefore special instruments; however, they remained completely blind and could not be expected to 'see' until they had been prepared for contact with the spirit world through special rituals (Gelfand 1959:109). Divination operated through the repeated throwing of the *hakata* to produce certain patterns believed to be visual commentary from the spirits which the diviner was then able to interpret in terms of its relevance to the problem being dealt with (La Gama 2000). To check the validity of the message received the diviners had to cast their divining bones a number of times to confirm the outcome. On the other hand those seeking advice from the diviner were also encouraged to visit more than one diviner to ascertain the facts and to satisfy themselves on the findings. This, in the positivist sense, was the procedure available to ascertain truth and a part of the verification process.

According to Peek (1991:2) 'divination systems [were] not simply closed ideologies founded on religious beliefs but dynamic systems of knowledge upon which the proper ordering of social action [was] based'. The search for deep understanding and the attempt to get to hidden knowledge was itself philosophic since it called for reflective and interpretive endeavours about life and action.[5] Divination processes were therefore marked by established procedures for arriving at truth, and if truth is to be taken in its pragmatic sense then divination could be a contending source of knowledge since solutions to practical problems were preferred. Saying this does not in any way ignore the fact that its credentials to knowledge will always remain contested because of the problems related to how to ascertain truth and the reasoning process behind interpreting oracles. And if the means of arriving at truth and the reasoning behind the procedure are questioned then that form of knowledge is also put in doubt. But the question to be addressed first is whether there is any universally agreed and completely adequate foolproof notion truth. Without addressing this question it would be pretty prejudicial to dismiss the assumptions and findings of this 'sacred science'. Not only does Peek (1991:14) believe that African divination systems are a genuine form of knowing but he also makes a passionate plea to African scholars to 'reject the biases which have misrepresented African epistemologies' and instead 'return to our elders to ensure that African systems of knowledge are part of the total record of the human enterprise'.

The question of efficacy

There is no doubt that the most crucial question concerning revealed knowledge has to do with the question of its validity and usefulness. To address this issue my analysis will be based on two issues: the question of truth and the question of intelligibility. I use these two ideas because they are fundamental in determining what effectively counts as knowledge. My point of departure is that different peoples develop their 'theories of knowledge and rationality as well as dispense their epistemic evaluations and judgments of reasonableness within a context of background assumptions about the nature of things' (Maffie 2000:250). Now let me start with the notion of truth by drawing from anthropology as the study of being. We read of Western anthropologists who were reportedly disappointed by certain cultures' total 'disregard for truth', cultures that they unfortunately described as being averse to truth because those anthropologists were looking for a conception of truth that suited their own culture. I have here in mind the work of Smith (1980) on comparative perspectives on truth. Smith draws our attention to nineteenth century missionary reports expressing the following outright condemnation:

> More unerradicable than the sins of the flesh is the falsity of the Chinese; ... their disregard of truth has perhaps done more to lower their character than any other fault. [And secondly] the ordinary speech of the Chinese is so full of insincerity ... that it is very difficult to learn the truth in almost every case. In China it is literally true that a fact is the hardest thing in the world to get at. (Smith 1980:428)

The point that Smith is making is that what the West has primarily settled for as the meaning of truth (in the sense of correspondence with reality) is something that the Asian cultures did not share. They had a different understanding of truth which these early missionaries and anthropologists could not fathom. Examples such as these are numerous elsewhere including in Africa where certain attributions were made or withheld simply because of a cultural misreading of reality.

Smith goes further to trace the historical shifts in the meaning and application of the term 'truth' over the years within the West itself and concludes that:

> There was a time when truth had a wider referent than it has in Western philosophy today ... At some point truth had a triple reference: to things, to statements, and to persons ...It was modern science that caused the west to contract its notion of truth until in philosophy it is now thought to refer strictly and properly only to judgments (statements or propositions). (Smith 1980:426–434)

If indeed Smith is correct in his analysis then even the notion of truth within the West itself, in the sense it is popularised and applied in the academy today, is not just a recent development but it is more significantly unrepresentative of the entire history of Western thinking. Smith argues that those conversant with the history of thought and indeed with what I can call the 'folk thought of their own people' will be aware of the various meanings of truth that today have been trivialised and are often relegated as metaphorical. If truth has come to be more and more restricted in its meaning to refer to propositions, with all other senses of truth being taken as metaphorical, then the mistake other cultures can make is to accede to this narrow and monolistic perspective of truth. I am particularly concerned about this new scientifically grounded concept of truth because it has been applied indiscriminately and continues to be used to judge the knowledge systems of other cultures and their claims to knowledge. There is no denying that propositional truth in the sense of correspondence is the most popular version of truth today, but this should not be allowed to suppress other definitions of truth be they ontological or moral. Smith refers to a point in time in the history of Western thought when truth was also a property of persons and not just of propositions as when Christ is said to have proclaimed 'I am the way, the truth, and the life' (John 14:6). He goes further to remind us of the etymology of the word, that 'the Latin term *verus* means true; it also means real, genuine, and authentic – properties that obviously are not restricted to statements' (Smith 1980:426). This observation on its own is ample evidence to many of us that truth can carry varied meanings across cultures although it is possible that there can be certain converges in some of the meanings.

With this analysis the point I wish to make is that before we dismiss other forms of knowledge as pseudo-knowledge on the account that they do not measure up to the correspondence theory of truth we need to take time to understand the folk uses of truth and the various meanings it carries not only across different cultures but also within one culture through time. That the West and through the influence of science and positivism has settled primarily on the correspondence theory of truth should not in any way distract us from affirming other ways of conceptualising truth and therefore other forms of knowledge. I think, for philosophers in Africa, Wiredu (1984) has taken the lead on this issue with his highly illuminating analysis of the Akan conception of truth. In assessing the validity of indigenous knowledge systems it is therefore important not to lose sight of the fact that the West is

> a culture whose conception of [truth including] rationality is deeply affected by the achievements and methods of the sciences, and one which treats such things as a belief in magic or the practice of consulting oracles as almost a paradigm of the irrational. (Winch 1964:307)

While it is critical that beliefs and ideas should be checked against reality it is a mistake to assume, as most today are predisposed to do, that science provides that objective truth about reality against which all beliefs and ideas can be checked. Adopting the paradigm of science to measure what Winch (1964:308) calls 'the intellectual respectability of other modes of discourse' is itself problematic as it hinges on the belief itself unfounded, that scientific claims correspond to reality.

Now let me turn to the second point of intelligibility since for anything to be knowledge it must be rational and therefore intelligible. The question of intelligibility arises at two levels: is the practice of divination and by extension the revealed knowledge it yields intelligible in the logic of modern science? Secondly were divination and the knowledges it produced intelligible to the indigenous peoples who practised it? Framing the questions in this way allows for a clear distinction between those who lived the practice and those looking at the practice from outside. If intelligibility is taken as a measure of the acceptability of a set of ideas to explain reality within a cultural context then it is not hard to see clearly where the problem may lie. In other words, if intelligibility is the extent to which the explanations provided fit within the worldview accepted by a people without contradiction then the problem with divination and revealed knowledge could not be with the indigenous peoples since they held it in high regard. The problem therefore lies with those assessing this practice from the vantage point of a different logic. Take for example, the idea of miracles and the theistic God and how they make sense within the Judeo-Christian belief tradition across the world and then raise the question of how they would fare if a different logic were appealed to. To argue that ideas and belief systems have to be assessed without discarding their cultural relevance is not to advocate for some form of extreme relativism but it is basically an attempt to remind ourselves of the need to guard against a summary dismissal of all other beliefs and ideas that do not correspond to what science 'reveals' to be the case. The point I wish to underscore is not only that different cultures have different ways of understanding reality but that there is benefit to humanity in particular if philosophical effort could be taken to understand why significant importance continues to be attached to certain practices and forms of knowing despite the protestations from science. In other words, it remains crucial for philosophers to articulate the foundations of such beliefs and practices in order to understand them on their own terms without subordinating them to the 'universal' paradigms of knowledge. At a more fundamental level I think there is a need to be circumspect about many issues including the logic of science itself lest we fall victim to what Feyerabend (2011) calls the 'tyranny of science'. Crucial to the growth of knowledge today is the need for openness, that is, the willingness to accept whatever is positive from the experiences offered by the world's varied cultures. I think that as we assess the validity of traditional forms of knowledge it is important to remember that there is more than one philosophical and epistemological trajectory open to humankind. Different types of knowledge and forms of knowing enrich rather than impoverish humankind. Advocates of intercultural philosophy would attest to that.

As a final remark on this issue, it may be worth pointing out that today's burgeoning Christian faiths in Zimbabwe, and across Africa, which in part owe their origin to the resilience and strength of African metaphysics (particularly the occult) have become in themselves champions of revealed knowledge. Owing to their claim to know and to be able to reveal the nature and source of occult forces in people's lives, the Christian churches, particularly the Pentecostal ones, have become an important force not only in the renewed quest for revealed knowledge but in its widespread acceptance. Meyer (2004) claims that one of the reasons for the extraordinary popularity of the Pentecostal church in Africa is its claim to be able to reveal the occult forces behind money, power and goods. In light of this it is clear that Christianity has not displaced traditional metaphysical thinking, including beliefs about the occult, but has instead created a platform on which they make perfect sense. In this way it has become one of the strongest contenders for revealed knowledge in modern society with its ever-growing set of diviners and charismatic prophets. The question that one may ask therefore is whether this phenomenon should be ignored or acknowledged as a competing source of what people regard as valuable knowledge. Although its logic remains shrouded in controversy there is little doubt that this divinatory practice and the revealed knowledge it yields is solving real and practical problems of life and testimonies to that effect are abound.

Proverbs and knowledge

Relevant inferences concerning the nature and conception of knowledge among the indigenous Shona can also be derived from their proverbs. In fact, proverbs themselves can be distilled to provide indications of various aspects of Shona thought from their epistemology, ethics, and aesthetics. I will draw from a selection of three proverbs to provide an indication of what the Shona held concerning the nature of knowledge, its acquisition and even the role of the individual in the knowledge making process. The question here is what was knowledge like in the eyes of the indigenous Shona, and what do the proverbs as artefacts of language and repositories of experience reveal.

The first proverb I will consider is: *Mazano moto anogokwa kune vamwe*. Literally translated it says 'knowledge is like a fire, you borrow glowing charcoal from a neighbour to light your own'. Knowledge, like fire, is a precious gift to be shared for the benefit of the entire community. It is also the light that fights the darkness of ignorance and therefore an essential component of human existence. Once you light your fire others can also rely on you to light their own and in the process keep the entire community safe and warm. Seen in this light knowledge among the Shona was therefore something to be shared, with those who have it being ready to give it to those who are still looking for it. No individual was expected to have solutions to everything on his/her own hence the need to collaborate with others. To negotiate and overcome the challenges and trepidations that life threw at them, individuals needed both practical and theoretical knowledge and this knowledge was shared in the community. However, just like making a fire, each individual had the responsibility to initiate the search for knowledge.

The second proverb is *Kusaziva kwakafanana nekufa*. Literally translated it says 'staying ignorant is the same as being dead'. What distinguishes a living human being from a dead one is the constant search for knowledge. Knowledge is the source of be-ing and vitality. Those who do not seek to know are literally dead. Active engagement, exploration, discovery and generation of knowledge are the true essence of humanity. It is only through proving astuteness of mind and providing informed contributions to problem solving that one demonstrates what it means to be alive. This proverb also underscores the value of knowledge since to know is to defeat ignorance and therefore death of the mind. The search for knowledge was considered an unending quest, a worthwhile enterprise, and the hallmark of life.

One of the often highlighted aspects of knowledge is its fallibility and the need to avoid dogmatic tranquility on whatever we hold. This is the point which the sceptic makes – that the chance of error is always there in any knowledge claim. It seems from the available proverbial lore that the Shona were not oblivious to this invaluable aspect of knowledge. The proverb *Mungwaru haati chandareva ndicho asi benzi ndichandagwinyira* which is translated as 'the wise person never counts what he/she says as the final word; only a fool thinks that what he/she knows is final'. The possibility of error is inherent in knowledge. To be a wise person is to be a person who is capable of imagining one's views being mistaken. The spirit of scepticism and not dogmatism distinguishes the wise from the foolish. The discovery of error was not to be stigmatised but something that society should readily accept. The Shona were aware that knowledge is something which grows and therefore keeps on changing. For knowledge acquired through the senses, this was probably an admission of the possibility of error associated with the senses. The proverb warns against steadfastly holding to a position or viewpoint.

Having considered insights from these three proverbs, I conclude my discussion with this fundamental observation concerning African epistemologies for which the Shona are but a subset.

> Far from subscribing to the rigid dichotomies of the dominant epistemological import from the west, the popular epistemologies of Africa build bridges between the so-called natural and supernatural, physical and metaphysical, rational and irrational, objective and subjective, scientific and superstitious, visible and invisible, real and unreal, explainable and inexplicable; making it impossible for anything to be one without also being the other ...Understanding the visible is hardly complete without investigating the invisible. (Nyamnjoh, 2004:166)

This indeed is a different way of knowing and with a logic of its own. My concern with indigenous knowledge and forms of knowing was to draw attention not only to the fact that these different epistemologies exist but that they should provide us today with a platform to learn other possibilities for making sense of the world and the meaning of life in particular. In other words, we need these indigenous epistemologies for the challenges they pose to our thinking and the light they throw on our conceptions of the world. To ignore them is to impoverish ourselves. It has also emerged in this chapter that knowledge among the indigenous Shona was a domain through which the spiritual realm participated in the lives of the living by directly informing them through dreams, signs, divination and other mystical means. Traditional Shona society, just like other African societies, was founded on a community of shared beliefs, in the wisdom of age, the binding force of tradition and the 'ontology of invisible beings'. This cosmology had a strong influence on their conception of knowledge.

Notes

1. I use the term knowledges and by extension speak of epistemologies because I take seriously the observation by Lewis Gordon that 'the formulation of knowledge in the singular already situates the question of knowledge in a framework that is alien to precolonial times, for the disparate modes of producing knowledge and notions of knowledge were so many that knowledges would be a more appropriate designation' (Gordon 2011:95).

2. I have here in mind the argument by decolonial theorists particularly the Caribbean Philosophical Association. The phrase 'Shifting the geography of reason' is the motto of the Caribbean Philosophical Association (see Gordon 2005) and what it seeks to achieve on the epistemic front resonates with the efforts of many philosophers from the African continent and other thinkers from the global South.

3. I have taken the phrase 'what humanity can teach philosophy' from Barbara J. Thayer-Bacon's paper entitled 'Humanity educating philosophy' in which she argues that 'because we are embedded and embodied social beings who do not have transcendental, objective, "God's eye views" of the world in which we live, we need each other to help us be potential knowers able to make knowledge claims. Others help us become aware of our own situatedness and help us develop enlarged views'. As members of humanity we have much to teach each other including philosophers. See https://www.bu.edu/wcp/Papers/Educ/EducThay.htm (Accessed 03 September 2015).

4. This is one of Magobe Ramose's favourite expressions which I have borrowed from him. For me it captures a fundamental truth that Africans should take seriously all the time given the historical experiences of slavery, unjust wars of conquest and subordination.

5. See also Emmanuel C. Eze, 1998, 'The problem of knowledge in "divination": The example of Ifa', in Eze, E.C. *African philosophy: An anthology*, Oxford: Blackwell (173–175). In this article Eze argues for the possibility of taking Ifa divination seriously as a source of knowledge because of the profound training and interpretive skills exhibited by its practitioners. Although divination practices

differ across Africa his position concerning the philosophical and epistemological status of divination as a means of getting to the truth is very important.

6

Indigenous Shona morality

The nature of African morality

The question of an African morality is one that arises against the background of the denial that a system of morality existed in indigenous communities, like the Shona, in Africa. No society can exist without a set of rules to guide their conduct or the behaviour of their members no matter how rudimentary. Wiredu (2002b:287) declares without any degree of equivocation that 'morality in the strictest sense is universal to human culture'.[1] From their indigenous wisdom, the Africans articulated an 'art of living' including morality, on whose basis social relationships were defined. To argue for the legitimacy of an African morality is to draw attention to the existence of 'a set of principles, values, and norms that guide or are intended to guide the conduct of people in a society' – a set of principles on whose basis beliefs about right or wrong conduct that results in rules being issued and norms established, is grounded. By African morality 'we are also talking about good or bad character, which is ultimately crucial in the observance of rules and in conforming to the norms' (Gyekye 2000:73). The existence of such rules is testimony to the prevalence of abstract thinking among the indigenous peoples from time immemorial. In this chapter the terms ethics and morality will be used interchangeably. I find Gyekye's submission on how these terms are often used to be very informative. According to Gyekye:[2]

the term 'ethics' is technically used by philosophers to mean a philosophical study of morality – morality understood as a set of social rules, principles, norms that guide or are intended to guide the conduct of people in a society, and as beliefs about right and wrong conduct as well as good or bad character ... Even though morality is the subject matter of ethics, it is most often used interchangeably with 'ethics' it can be said that the two terms, morality and ethics, refer essentially to the same moral phenomenon – human conduct – and, thus, can be used interchangeably. (Gyekye 2010)

Even the etymology of the two terms ethics and morality brings out this affinity between them. Etymologically, the term 'moral' comes from the Latin *mos*, which means custom or habit, and it is a translation of the Greek term *ethos*, which means roughly the same thing, and is the origin of the term 'ethics'.[3] In this work, I shall employ the two terms ethics and morality interchangeably as I attempt to articulate the Shona conception of morality. I have no doubt in my mind that a system of morality existed among the Shona of pre-colonial Africa. The fact of being in existence and occupying a particular space as beings living in community with each other created the conditions that made a system of morality a prerequisite for any such life to be possible. It is this system of ethics that a number of African philosophers have sought to articulate. Murove (2009a) draws our attention to the fact that in the history of ethics much emphasis has been given to presenting Western and Eastern moral traditions in form of anthologies for the world to read while little was being said on African ethics and what it could contribute to humanity. This unfortunate tendency has perpetuated the impression that there is nothing that the world can learn from African institutions of morality. On the same issue Gyekye argues that

> like African philosophy itself, the ideas and beliefs of the African society that bear on ethical conduct have not been given elaborate investigation and clarification and, thus, stand in real need of profound and extensive analysis and interpretation. (Gyekye 2010)

Adding to the corpus of literature on the subject of African ethics may take various efforts including the articulation of the morality of any of the disparate indigenous communities of Africa in the same way attempted in this chapter. That kind of literature will provide insight into the thinking of Africa's indigenous peoples and inevitably shed light on their ethical systems. My exposition of the Shona and their moral thinking follows similar efforts by other philosophers who have contributed to our understanding of African philosophy in general. Morality across Africa has been defined as a social morality that is characterised by an unrelenting preoccupation with human welfare, harmonious social relations, and human solidarity. The individual identifies and defines him/herself through communal social belonging since social relationships are regarded as necessary and not contingent. In moral terms, what defines the individual in the African context is characterised in the words of Wiredu as

> a set of concentric circles of obligations and responsibilities matched by rights and privileges revolving around levels of relationships irradiating from the consanguinity of household kith and kin, through the 'blood' ties of lineage and clan, to the wider circumference of human familyhood. (Wiredu 2002b:291)

A common social life forms the basis of the ethic of responsibility that characterises African communities. African morality also places high value on good character. For Gyekye (2010) good character is at the heart of the African moral system and is the lynchpin of the moral wheel. It is for this reason that as part of their socialisation of the young, the elders emphasised the cultivation of virtues of character from which they argued good actions would follow.

While a lot of literature exists on African morality this chapter limits its attention to works that have attempted to articulate an understanding of morality within Southern Africa to which the Shona belong. The most comprehensive philosophical work to date that focuses on morality in Southern Africa is Ramose's *African Philosophy through Ubuntu*. His work examines the philosophy of *ubuntu/hunhu* within the context of Southern Africa and concludes that African morality revolves around and is defined by the principle of *ubuntu/hunhu*. In the opening paragraph to his chapter entitled 'The philosophy of ubuntu and ubuntu as a philosophy' Ramose declares:

> *Ubuntu* is the root of African philosophy. The be-ing of an African in the universe is inseparably anchored upon *ubuntu* ... *Ubuntu* then is the wellspring flowing with African ontology and epistemology. (Ramose 1999:49)

By implication it follows that *ubuntu* is the root of African morality. Ramose (1999) draws our attention to the maxim '*umuntu ngumuntu ngabantu*' whose Shona equivalent is '*munhu munhu nevanhu*' to highlight that within these communities in Southern Africa, 'to be a human being is to affirm one's humanity by recognising the humanity of others and, on that basis, establish humane relations with them' (Ramose 1999:52). This rendition of *ubuntu* underscores the importance of the normative dimension in the understanding of being. A person is indeed a person through other persons. The recognition of others as moral entities and the establishment of harmonious relationships with them are integral to the constitution of a person as a person.

The other more recent effort to articulate an African moral theory with particular reference to Southern Africa is the work of the South African philosopher, Thaddeus Metz. Although he has written extensively on this subject, my specific interest relates to his article on the African moral theory. Inspired by the consequentialist and deontological theories, such as utilitarianism and Kantianism in the Western philosophical tradition, Metz (2007) attempts to construct an African moral theory of right action that is 'comprehensive' and that could be applied with equal significance in Africa to resolve moral problems. Having analysed various perspectives of what is considered right in African moral thought, Metz (2007:334) arrives at the conclusion that the fundamental principle that can better capture a theory of moral action in Africa, south of the Sahara, is the principle: 'An action is right just insofar as it produces harmony and reduces discord; an act is wrong to the extent that it fails to develop community' (Metz 2007:334). Metz comes to this principle by examining the values and forms of ethical thinking that one finds in indigenous African communities as he constructs what he called 'a normative ethical theory with an African source'. Concerns have been raised regarding some of his claims and his attempt to come up with a grand norm or a 'comprehensive' basic norm to underpin African ethics. Ramose has attempted one such rejoinder in his 2007 article by the title 'But Hans Kelsen was not born in Africa: A reply to Thaddeus Metz' published in the *South African Journal of Philosophy*.

Although it is not the aim of this work to enter into that kind of debate, significant points along the lines of those raised by Ramose in his response are worth considering. The main concern relates to the attempt to model African ethics alongside its Western counterpart, where prominent theories of ethics from the West with their scientism such as utilitarianism and Kantianism are taken as models against which an African theory of morality should be constructed. It seems to me that the major point of contention stems from the comparative approach somewhat discernible in the essay by Metz in which he seeks to develop an African moral theory in terms of some well-known Western theories of morality. By proceeding in this way, the approach taken presupposes a *philosophia universalis* in the form of a Western moral theory and philosophy in terms of which the rest of the world philosophies should be understood. This point is made acutely clear by Wallner (2010:13) when he argues that comparatively orientated philosophy is problematic in that 'intellectual outcomes of other cultures are interpreted as facets of the one and only truth that eventually will be grasped by Western philosophy'. But the reality is that there are outcomes of thinking or ideas from other cultures that cannot be properly interpreted in terms of the Western forms of thinking (Wallner 2010). It seems the end result of Metz's approach was to arrive at an African moral theory inspired by occidental thinking. Western philosophy is taken as the structure of understanding into which African thinking is then constructed to fit. While this effort can be explained as emanating from our natural urge for comparisons, the trouble comes at that level when what is different and distinct in the case of Africa is then recast to take the preferred Western format. This is where the significance of the historical context out of which African moral thought finds its origination may be compromised. The danger is that what we may end up having in the form of the 'comprehensive moral theory' or 'comprehensive basic norm' may be different from what it is supposed to represent and in that sense becomes a distortion. To most African philosophers the tendency to regard the West as the model against which Africa and its institutions have to be understood was the reason why most colonial anthropologists are accused of inventing much of what they attributed to Africa. However, as philosophers it would be folly not to take efforts made by different scholars to understand this complex African heritage seriously. The point is that, all attempts to reconstruct the past rely on the science of interpretation and interpretations of most things from the past remain at best approximations. There is little doubt that Metz's effort and approach is crucial in that it has contributed immensely to the subject of African morality by bringing in a different way of looking at the subject and in the process drawing attention to some important aspects of African morality and its logic. Having said this, it is now time to turn my attention and focus on what the Shona hold concerning morality. To do so I shall consider their conception of what it means to be a good person and what constitutes the good life in society. Philosophical inferences and deductions on Shona moral thought will derive mostly from their concept of personhood as well as from a selection of proverbs and sayings that formed instructional instruments for moral teaching in pre-colonial society.

Morality among the Shona

One of the earliest sources of literature that attempts to articulate an indigenous moral theory of the Shona is *Hunhuism or Ubuntuism: A Zimbabwean indigenous political philosophy* by Samkange and Samkange published in 1980. The two scholars attempted to come up with a moral theory that would inform politics and life in Zimbabwe at independence and for that reason they refer to *hunhuism* as an indigenous political philosophy. It is clear that the idea was to articulate an indigenous philosophy that would inform the process of social and political transition in Zimbabwe from colonial rule to self-rule and the normative framework that was to define the new society. In their book they raise and try to answer a number of questions such as the following: What political philosophy or ideology should inspire the new Zimbabwean in this new era? – that is, the era of independence. Is there a philosophy or ideology indigenous to Zimbabwe that can serve its people just as well as, if not better than, foreign ideologies? In an attempt to respond to these questions Samkange and Samkange (1980) proposed and propounded *hunhuism* as the philosophy upon which existence in the emerging nation of Zimbabwe was to be buttressed. This was the first time, to my knowledge, that *hunhuism* was coined and proposed as a driving philosophy or moral ideology for the peoples of Zimbabwe. Of philosophical significance to this work was the attempt by these two scholars to provide an ideology suited to building society anew on the basis of its own indigenous conception of what it means to be human. *Hunhuism,* as an ideology of political, economic and social existence informed by *hunhu* (humane-ness), aptly captures the essence of being and existence among the Shona. Samkange and Samkange's work can be conceived historically as belonging to the discourse of African personality including negritude – philosophies which were behind the drive for authenticity in Africa. As an ideology, *hunhuism* was aimed at articulating a particular vision of the Zimbabwean society and its moral and political trajectory at the beginning of the new era of independence. Given the worldwide influence of the great African political theorists and Afrocentrists of their time including Senghor, Nkrumah, and Nyerere among others, it is not difficult to understand why the Samkanges thought *hunhuism,* being the sum total of a form of life and system of values indigenous to Shona culture, would constitute the driving philosophy and ideology for the newly independent nation of Zimbabwe. In fact, what prompted them to articulate this ideology of *hunhuism* was the perceived need to build a new Zimbabwean society distinct from the colonial structure and its morally bankrupt ideology of discrimination and the inferiorisation of certain groups of people. The new society was to be distinguished by its own *hunhuism* as its authentic and indigenous value system. Its attractiveness as the hallmark of a good person and its ability to foster harmonious human relations were the reasons that the two Samkanges were convinced that *hunhuism* needed to be strengthened as the political and moral foundation for the new polity. To this day *hunhuism* remains central to the intellectual and cultural project of 'postcolonial' Zimbabwe as attested by several scholarly documents and recommendations in education and social policy. One such official document with recommendations about revisiting the philosophy of *hunhuism* and making it the driving philosophy of education and society is the most recent Commission of Inquiry into Education and Training of 1999 popularly referred to as the Nziramasanga Commission.

Kuva munhu muvanhu

Central to understanding Shona morality is the concept of *hunhu* also translated as *ubuntu* in other variants of the Nguni languages of Southern Africa. *Hunhu/ubuntu* is regarded as the foundation of African morality and by extension Shona morality. Samkange and Samkange argue that

> the attention one human being gives to another: the kindness, courtesy, consideration and friendliness in the relationship between people; a code of behaviour, an attitude to other people and to life, is embodied in *hunhu* or *ubuntu*. (Samkange and Samkange 1980:39)

Hunhu as the embodiment of morality within the Shona is expressed in a number of maxims: *iva munhu pavanhu* (be humane and always respect other human beings); *munhu vanhu* (a person is a person through other persons); *kuva munhu* (exhibit personhood); *chinonzi munhu hunhu* (what constitutes a person are good morals); *kuva munhu chaiye* (be a true person you must not be found lacking on the normative dimension); *'rarama somunhu kwete semhuka'* (exhibit personhood and recognise others as human beings, and never live like an animal). A person is usually called an animal to underline the fact that the individual in question has failed to exhibit elements considered appropriate for being a true human being.

The common element that runs through all these maxims is the principle which can be summed up as 'to live as a person is to live well with others' – *kuva munhu muvanhu*.

The Shona expression *kuva munhu muvanhu* (to live at all is to live well with others and for others) is here taken as the maxim capturing the essence and ultimate goal of Shona morality. This maxim sums up the overriding goal and essence of Shona morality where the phrase *kuva munhu muvanhu* is the normative measure of existence and personhood among the Shona. What it captures may not be different from the meaning expressed in that famous expression of African morality captured by Ramose (1999:52) as 'to be a human be-ing is to affirm one's humanity by recognising the humanity of others and, on that basis, establish humane relations with them'. '*Kuva munhu chaiye*' translated as 'to be a true human being' is, in moral matters, the ideal that all Shona individuals ought to thrive towards and a *telos* for which both parents and the community are expected to play a significant role in its realisation. This ideal is what individuals, despite their failings, ought to strive for. To become truly human is measured by the acquisition of virtues of character and qualities of personhood that are considered appropriate by the community. Since the Shona are communitarian in their social outlook, true humanity can only be achieved within the context of the community through particularly the individual's ability to enhance social wellbeing and not diminish it. It is good persons that add to the vitality of the community while bad persons work to diminish and destroy its vitality. A good person is one who is there for his/her community. Having *hunhu/ubuntu* means having commendable character and hence being virtuous. Among the Shona, the cultivation of character is the *telos* of moral education or a process of socialisation which is characterised basically by what Wiredu (2002b:288) describes as 'precept, example and correction'. It is expected that every elder should play their part in moulding the character of the young although primary responsibility lies with the parents and the immediate family members. The proverb *mbudzi kudya mufenje hufana nyina*, which can loosely be translated into English as 'a goat comes to learn about which species of plant leaves are edible by watching its parent' whenever used, draws attention to a comparison being made between the behaviour of a child and that of his/her parents. What that means is that moral upbringing, which ultimately manifests itself through individual character, is the responsibility of parents. Although not every parent is mirrored in the character of their children, the acknowledgement of the fact that moral education is through experience, habit and imitation is critical.

In the sphere of morality, character and moral education goes together with one central concept called *kutsiura* which means to 'correct' or more appropriately 'reproach'. The process of constant correction and reproach is regarded as central to a moral life and since individuals are prone to falter now and again moral education is regarded as a lifelong process. The moral significance of reproach (*kutsiura*) in society is reflected in the Shona saying '*ibwa inoroverwa pachinyiro*' which means 'to correct a dog behaving badly one must do it at the very point the dog misbehaves'. While this saying indeed demonstrates the Shona's knowledge of the behaviour of pets such as dogs that will not be able to understand the reasons for a punishment when it is meted several hours or days after the offence, it carries an unmistakable responsibility not to turn a blind eye or defer the correction of wrong behaviour. Of equal importance is that the term dog used in the proverb is also often used to refer to people whose behaviour is outrightly bad or antisocial. Among the Shona to talk of character is ultimately to talk of morality. This may not be unique to the Shona because as Gyekye interestingly points out:

> The Greek word *ethike*, from which the English word 'ethics' derives means 'character' (*ethos*). What we call 'ethics' Aristotle calls 'the study (or, science) of character', *he ethike*. For the Greek, as for the African and the Arab, the character of the individual matters most in our moral life and thought. (Gyekye 2010)

The cultivation of character entails the acquisition of desirable qualities or virtues. Virtues that form the basis of *hunhu/ubuntu* relate mostly to the way individuals respond to the needs arising from such things as their feelings, emotions, and desires. The way one reacts to the call of these self-directed feelings as an individual, to a large extent, determines their character. This is the virtue of self-control. Virtues of self-control, which are concerned with the mastery of the positive passions are often considered as the most fundamental virtues of moral character. A good person is one who is capable of enjoying relationships of mutual co-existence with others in the community. The Shona placed great significance on character in moral matters hence the saying *munhu asina nyadzi haasi munhu* (one who has no sense of shame is not a person) to which I now turn my attention.

Shame cultures and the panoptic effect

In *'Discipline and Punish: The Birth of the Prison'*, Foucault develops the concept of panopticism, which has become an influential idea in conceptualising issues and principles of social control and deviance. Foucault's panopticism is extrapolated from his interpretation of the historic ideal prison called the Panopticon developed by Bentham in the 18th century. Bentham's Panopticon is the architectural figure designed for a cost-effective and efficient method of monitoring prisoners around the clock under the pretext of an omnipresent observer. Although traditional Shona society was not the equivalent of a prison, the panoptic effect seems to be evident in its culture as a tool of moral surveillance among its members. The expression *'Munhu asina nyadzi haasi munhu'* which is translated to mean 'one who has no sense of shame cannot be a person' or 'it is shame that makes a person' is a Shona saying which is arguably at the core its shame culture. In order to influence social behaviour, cultures everywhere cultivate specific attitudes and regulate the expression of certain emotions. The significance attached to shame in defining personhood is so high that it may be appropriate to refer to Shona culture as a 'shame culture'. The idea of 'shame cultures' and 'guilt cultures' was first applied by Ruth Benedict (see Creighton 1990), as a conceptual framework within which the cultural embodiment of emotions could be understood. Western anthropologists have labelled Western cultures as 'guilt cultures' and other cultures such as the Asian and African ones as 'shame cultures'. Notwithstanding the controversy surrounding such distinctions and particularly the ethnocentric intimation in the claim that the emotion of guilt belongs to a higher level of moral development than shame, which then positions cultures integrated by guilt sanctions as superior to those integrated by shame sanctions (Creighton 1990: 280); there is no doubt that shame occupies a central place in moral education particularly in the cultivation of character among the Shona. Indigenous Shona culture could be described as a shame-conscious culture because of the importance attached to the emotion of shame in defining social relationships and the harmonious integration of people in community. The evolution of the self is always firmly attached to the community or social group and its practices, however numerous and various these may be. Everyone's existence is continually placed under the regard of others and the scrutiny of their eyes.

A host of indigenous regulatory mechanisms such as taboos, together with practices of designating social spaces, and conceptions of selfhood, created a social landscape that promoted a community of self-surveillance in which practices of self-discipline and self-monitoring were the direct product of the normalising gaze and power of society. Self-surveillance in indigenous societies whose social arrangement was communal was made possible by the cultivation of such emotions as shame which also fed off the overarching communitarian ethos. Vaz and Bruno's (2003:275) define self-surveillance as 'a form of self-monitoring or habituated anticipatory conformity'. It is the attention that individuals pay to their actions and thoughts when constituting themselves as subjects of their conduct. Self-surveillance is built on the cultural assumption that certain actions and thoughts are not appropriate for a desirable constitution of the individual. Through the ever-present gaze of their community, individuals perfect mechanisms for judging themselves according to what is prescribed as appropriate behaviour in their community always with an effort to constitute themselves as good members of the community. The 'I–we' relationship captured by the famous aphorism 'I am because we are and since we are therefore I am', which placed the individual within a network of relationships and obligations, had a desirable outcome on the formation of character. In other words, this 'I-we' relationship, which was not only restricted to mortals but stretched to encompass the living dead, was built on a particular metaphysics providing an important normative and interpretive framework within which relations were understood and defined not only between people but with the entire surrounding environment. Everyone was a child of the community; a community which played a significant role in the formation of persons.

As individuals went about their daily activities in pursuit of their needs, they were also conscious of the eyes and ears of the community. This was because of the existence of a strongly cultivated sense of responsibility based on shame. Shame can be described as a strong and painful feeling arising from negative self-evaluation and others' negative evaluations of the self. People feel ashamed if they look worse compared to others. Liszka submits that

> the sense of shame originates in awareness of the eyes of the outside world and is directed in toward the self. One feels shame when an improper action or failing is revealed publicly or to certain authorities or peers; it is a feeling especially connected with the group and is clearly associated with the fear of ridicule by others. (Liszka 1999:15)

The feeling of shame therefore draws attention to a deficiency in one's true character relative to the standards of the community or group in which one lives. This is what brings out the panoptic effect in Shona culture, a mechanism capable of promoting self-discipline and self-regulation in its members through the omnipresent eyes and ears of the community. In indigenous shame cultures such as the Shona, the panoptic gaze was exercised by venerable individuals in one's life in the form of both mortals and immortals. In the same way that Foucault's invisible guard in the panoptic tower deployed the gaze to control the inmates, cultivating the emotion of shame through character education worked well in making sure that individuals regulated their own behaviour as much as possible, although moral failure would always happen as part of human nature. So, even without any sophisticated psycho-social theory, indigenous Shona communities had long realised that the human being is basically an embodiment of emotions that could be harnessed to promote the wellbeing of the entire society.[4] Traditional Shona societies capitalised on the fact that social relations were lived and experienced through emotions. For example the indigenous Shona seem to have cultivated a very strong synergy between the emotion of shame and the entire subject of sex, an association which has to this day rendered the subject of sex difficult to address openly even as the communities face the devastating effects of the AIDS pandemic. Since issues of sexuality were an important measure of one's moral worth, sexual relationships and marriage were important aspects of moral education. Since sex was such a powerful and pervasive aspect of human nature, the Shona were aware that issues of sexuality could make or break society, hence they sought to regulate it through strong morals. Through the deliberate cultivation of the emotion of shame, the Shona were able to control and ensure sexual harmony in society without having to go out every day to hold sermons to remind members about sexual conduct and their obligations in the community.

The Shona word for shame is *nyadzi*, which has its variants *kunyadzisa* or *kusvodesa* and it means to be a disgrace to others especially one's family or community. People feel ashamed if they have done something that embarrasses themselves, their family or community. Menkiti (2004) reminds us that in African communal thought, personhood is something that the community can withdraw or refuse to confer on an individual on account of that person's behaviour. It is for this reason that individuals strive to demonstrate specific virtues of character and hold themselves back from entertaining certain forms of conduct especially those that are designated by the community as unacceptable. Among the Shona if you say to someone *haunyari!* (aren't you ashamed!), more often than not they will retort *kuti handina kupfeka here?* (Why should I? Am I naked?) While indeed clothes are a recent arrival, it is common knowledge that traditional societies went to a great deal of effort to try and cover their loins using animal skins. The important point is that the analogy drawn between shame and nudity highlights the sense in which shame and the emotion that comes from it equates to that of being naked in public. In other words, it is similar to the sense of embarrassment that one feels when doing a shameful act and being naked in public. Through the cultivation of the emotion of shame the Shona were therefore capable of harnessing the expression of certain desires and actions by relating individual actions to communal interests and expectations. The Shona saying '*nyadzi dzinokunda rufu*' ('the feeling of shame is worse than death') sums up the value that was attached to shame as a moral emotion. The point is that one would rather wish they were dead than do something that embarrasses one's family or the entire community. One feels so deeply embarrassed by what they have done that one wishes to be dead rather than face the community. To a certain degree this strong emphasis on shame which is even contained in traditional stories and folklore and which constituted important instruments of moral teaching can be blamed for most suicide cases in traditional Shona communities. It is true that most people who felt they had caused irreparable damage and brought shame to their families have contemplated suicide or actually committed suicide. Therefore, while the cultivation of such emotions helped individuals develop appropriate consciousness to police their own behaviour, playing on this important emotion made individuals more fragile and suicidal instead of preparing them to face up to their actions.

The morality of relations

> For a muShona of Zimbabwe what I am is also a matter of what relationships I am involved in, and my state of wellbeing, or otherwise, is much affected by the health of those relationships. (Silberbauer 1993:18)

The point is that the wellbeing of the individual is in part a product of the relations that prevail in the society he or she inheres. It is harmony which ought to characterise human relations. Disturbed social relations should not be allowed to persist even where there are disputes and suspicions of all kinds. This is why the village palaver, in Shona tradition, was such an important institution as a place for bringing belligerents to talk to each other with the assistance of elders in order to dissolve the tension. At the palaver, disputes were brought before the elders and debated. The reason for this was so that justice could be served and equilibrium, balance, and harmony could be restored. Morality among the Shona was therefore largely concerned with the state of affairs and the health of relationships that obtained among community members. The 'ethical community' comprised more than the living beings as it included also the living dead who were easily offended when people failed to follow moral principles or engaged in reprehensible behaviour. Bujo (1998) makes a similar point in his overall analysis of African ethics when he draws attention to the fact that the invisible beings play an important role in shaping morality by setting out moral directives for the welfare of the living. Among the Shona such moral directives were usually issued from time to time through the spirit mediums who served as the communication conduits linking the two worlds. Taboos of various kinds were promulgated in order to make sure that people did not offend the living dead by violating important moral precepts. An example of this would be to look at incest. If incest was committed effort was made by the elders of that community to atone for the wrong by appeasing the spirits so that they were dissuaded from retaliating by causing famine or crop failure in the entire community. The living dead were therefore an important part of the moral community and certain customs were followed and remained unquestioned because their authority rested in what was thought to be desired by the living dead. A good community was that which not only respected the living but one that respected the wishes of the forefathers as a way of honouring them for what they did as parents. Respect to the elders who are considered living representatives of the forefathers was critical and to this day most Shona find it objectionable to send their old parents and relatives to old age homes instead of staying with them. Sending them away is interpreted as turning one's back on the parents and the spirits that brought you into this world and it amounts to severing oneself from the family by disregarding the chain of being which begins at birth and ends with ancestorship. Morality demands that no person should be without a home and the living have an obligation to each other and to the living dead to show love.

Gelfand (1973) identified the concepts of brotherhood, the love of a good family life with close support for its members and good neighbourliness as pillars of Shona culture. The Shona extol the virtues of solidarity, fraternity and equality. A quick examination of the moral values that are cherished by the Shona reveals the link between such values and the quest to achieve harmonious social relations that is expressed in Shona as *kugarisana savanhu* (living like true human beings), *kuwadzana* (living well together), or *kunzwana* (peaceful co-existence), all which are variants of the same concept of 'living well with others'. This aspect is confirmed even for all Africans by Archbishop Desmond Tutu in his exposition of African morality when he argues:

> Social harmony is for us [Africans] the *summum bonum* – the greatest good. Anything that subverts or undermines this sought-after good is to be avoided like the plague. Anger, resentment, lust for revenge, even success through aggressive competitiveness, are corrosive of this good. (Tutu 1999:35)

To this day social harmony, solidarity, and good relations in Shona families and communities are regarded so seriously even to the extent of undermining the criminal justice system as defined by modern courts and institutions. For example, relatives oftentimes get away with crimes such as rape or stealing and are never reported to the police for fear of upsetting harmony and relations in the extended family. While these individuals are reprimanded in the family court, handing them over to the modern courts, which results in imprisonment, is often regarded as being too vindictive and therefore an evil that would militate against the attainment of the greatest good of all; social harmony. The lessons about *kusimudza hapwa* literally translated as 'to lift and expose one's armpit', which means failing to respect secrets, privacy or confidentiality within the family are crucial though at times they are detrimental to social wellbeing. My point is that while such teachings are important for moral integrity they also unfortunately constitute a shield that foments criminality and unethical behaviour.

Among the Shona *kuvimbika* (being one who can be trusted) is one other virtue that is highly regarded and the mark of a good person. *Kuvimbika* is an all-encompassing virtue covering such qualities as honesty, being trustworthy, being truthful, being faithful, and being forthright or straightforward such that other members of the community can count on the individual in almost every aspect of their relationship. This is the only virtue which when broken in a marriage is regarded by the Shona as the only reason good enough to justify divorce. But of course due to the patriarchal nature of Shona society this virtue, particularly in marital relationships, is placed heavily on the shoulders of women. After a divorce due to unfaithfulness in marriage it is not uncommon to hear the people say about the woman who did the cheating '*hapana nezvemunhu apa*' meaning 'the woman is not a person at all'. She lacks the most critical aspects of morality which define a person and distinguish a person from all other animals driven by instinct. *Kuvimbika* summarises the basic virtues that characterise a good person among the Shona. People who lack this quality are regarded with suspicion by the community. The quality of *kuvimbika* is such an important quality; it is indeed a summation of all the other virtues such that it counts as the basic qualification for one to be entrusted with any position of responsibility in society including even political office. Once one has lost this attribute one is regarded as unfit to hold any position of responsibility or public office for the person will have demonstrated that he/she is unstable and cannot be relied upon in almost every sphere of life. While those who commit crimes within the extended family can be protected from prosecution as discussed above, they would never regain this important virtue of *kuvimbika* and hence they remain social misfits who openly live with the weight of shame hanging over their heads for being evil persons. *Kuvimbika* takes effort to attain and to be conferred by the community but once lost it is difficult and almost impossible to reclaim, because it is a virtue of such high quality.

For the Shona 'living well with others' – translated as *kugarisana nevamwe* – is the essence of being. It is the embodiment of ethical living and all moral teachings and customs promoted by the Shona have this as the ultimate goal of morality. Even periodic and inevitable conflict must be used as the platform to establish harmonious relations. The level to which the Shona acknowledge conflict as a real factor of existence and then try to transcend it and establish harmony comes out in the following proverb: '*Mvura bvongodzeki ndiyo garani*' literally translated as 'when muddied waters settle they become clearer and cleaner'. In other words, even where conflict is inevitable, the ultimate prize must be to establish harmony; reconciliation is a fundamental aspect of Shona moral teachings. Moral reasoning among the Shona is therefore influenced by the search for harmony and the desire to maintain social relations. To this effect the Shona cherish a number of values and principles such as the principle of equal consideration of interests, non-discrimination, the importance of and the irreducibility of the human life, giving and sharing, harmony and friendship, hospitality, and respect for elders. At the heart of the quest to promote harmonious social relations is the principle aptly captured by the phrase '*dai wanga uriwe wainzwa sei*' (if it were you on the receiving end how would you feel?) This principle which is built around the logic of role reversal is key to understanding moral reasoning among the Shona.

The principle is very similar to the Golden Rule articulated in the Bible of 'Do unto others what you would want them do unto you'. While the similarity here can easily be construed as the effect of the spread of Christianity among the Shona, a more convincing explanation is that because we are all human we share certain interest and values on the basis of us being human. Chimuka (2008) goes to some length to analyse some crucial terms which also define Shona social life such as *kugara hunzwana* (mutual co-existence) and *kuyanana* (peaceful co-existence), *kunzwana* (civic friendship), *kudyidzana* (use of resources by all and for all), *kugamuchirana* (tolerance and acceptance). What emerges ultimately is the fact that moral reasoning among the Shona revolves around the establishment and quest to maintain social ties through mutual respect and co-existence. This is the reason why the community is conceived of as one big family comprising of *vabereki* (parents) and *vana* (their children) irrespective of whether or not there are any biological connections between the peoples.

Proverbs and Shona morality

Moral reasoning among the Shona can also be deduced from the proverbs in the form of the moral lessons they carry for society. In these indigenous societies the moral values and principles were crystallised as aphorisms, proverbs or even riddles (Silberbauer 1993). In fact, the majority of proverbs were to a large extent the repository of moral teachings for they emphasise certain values and decry vices as inappropriate for harmonious life in society. Sumner (1999:22) reminds us that 'every proverb is a carrier of the values of a society: that is no doubt the reason why it was selected by tradition in order to become a constituent part of the common memory of a particular human group'. I shall now consider a few proverbs in this regard to drive home Shona teachings concerning shared humanity, respect and sympathy, tranquility, vulnerability and interdependency, and the evil of selfishness. As indicated before, 'there is a special relationship between proverbs and philosophy to the extent that philosophy has its primary place in the medium of spoken language' (Kimmerle 1997b:64). Since proverbs are often formulated in a general way interpretation is required so that the relevance and strength of their advice can be revealed. I have selected five proverbs for analysis each extolling certain values in Shona morality.

The first one is *muroyi munhu kubaiwa anochemawo* translated to mean 'the witch is a person like anyone when hurt he or she groans in pain'. This proverb is directly connected to the Shona belief in witchcraft and individuals capable of manipulating forces to deliberately harm other people often resulting in death. Thus the witch represents the example of the worst possible person you can have in the community. This is an antisocial person, a person who cares neither about the welfare of others nor the good of the community. The proverb's moral lesson is that no matter how evil a person is, and despite any level of bitterness one may feel towards that person, it is crucial to remember that even the worst person deserves to be treated with dignity. What it teaches constitutes the basis for forgiveness and non-retribution. The social relevance of this proverb manifests itself when reconciliation and amnesty is granted to persons known to have killed other people. The point is that even the worst persons in the community deserve our sympathy. Every human being needs help.

The second proverb is *Chiri pamumwe chiri padanda* which means 'the pain on another person is like the pain on a lifeless log'. The reality is that the pain that others feel is the same as the pain you would feel because all humans are the same and nobody is a piece of wood. This is a proverb that is usually used to attack any signs of selfishness and unwillingness to assist that may be manifesting in the behaviour of certain individuals. A log has no feelings and so ideally it cannot experience pain and therefore the choice not to do something to a person who is suffering is to reduce that person to an inanimate object such as a log. It is to demonstrate a level of cruelty and selfishness that a proper human being is not expected to show. The proverb is also a reminder to any thinking person that to be insensitive to the plight of others stems from thinking that you are the only true person and that what other people feel or experience does not matter because it is their problem and not yours. Empathy, sympathy, willingness to assist and the promotion of wellbeing are crucial aspects of Shona morality. Being human prescribes that we behave in a certain way commensurate with the moral ideals of being human.

The third proverb is *chinokura chichirwa mwana wengwe wemunhu anodzidza murairo*. This is translated to mean 'what is taught to survive by fighting is the young of a leopard; a human child is nurtured in customs and morals'. *Murairo* or its variant *murawo* are Shona terms that refer to the law, that is, the rules of proscription and prescription operative in society. The proverb draws attention to the importance of education in children's upbringing. Society is not a jungle where individuals are to be guided by instinct and survival of the fittest. Human beings, unlike animals, have a different course of life even though they inhabit the same earth. People use reason and follow laid down rules of etiquette and not instinct in their engagement with each other. This proverb draws an important distinction between what is considered the essence of a human being and that of an animal among the Shona. Morals are what the Shona consider as key to the growth and formation of the person hence the need by the entire community to assist in the moral upbringing of the young. Knowledge of custom (*murawo*) was an integral part of becoming human among the Shona. To follow *murawo* (custom) is to have *tsika* (morals) and to have *tsika* is to be a good person. The term *tsika* is used by the Shona to describe 'knowing, possessing and being able to use rules, customs and traditions of society' (Pearce 1990:145). In general terms a good child is one who possesses *tsika*. It involves exhibiting desirable character traits significant in all aspects of life from politeness, civility, circumlocution, and the ability to keep all physical and emotional drives in check and knowing the right time and place to act, talk, ask and say things. To have *tsika* is to be a dependable person in almost all aspects of life particularly those relating to living and respecting harmonious social relations. For the Shona having *tsika* is the basis for living a life of tranquility and in peace with oneself and others as it is the highest form of being a good person.

The fourth proverb is *dindingwe rinonaka richakweva rimwe kana rokweviwa roti mavara angu azara ivhu* translated to mean 'there is a cheetah which enjoys wrestling another cheetah to the ground and rolling it in the dirt but when it is the one pushed and rolled in the dirt it complains that its beautiful coat is being soiled'. Of course all cheetahs are the same, they all boast a nicely spotted coat but only one of them complains as if it has a special coat. When the tables are turned and suddenly an individual gets a feel of what he/she has been putting others through, to try and complain would be the highest form of hypocrisy. This proverb touches on the value of equality and equal treatment. You must expect that that which you believe is appropriate to do to other people should also be appropriate when directed at you. Do unto others what you want them to do to you. The proverb teaches about a number of things including selfishness and the need to pursue justice or fairness. In modern day politics the proverb is usually used with reference to the hypocrisy of those nations and leaders who complain loudly when they experience the slightest infringement to their rights when they are known to be behind the suffering of so many through their policies. Living with others as a group demands mutual respect, modesty and equal consideration of interests.

The last proverb that I shall consider is '*kutsva kwendebvu varume tinodzimurana*' which may be translated to say 'when one man's beard catches fire others must help extinguish the fire'. What is being extolled here is a lesson on vulnerability and interdependency. This proverb brings out the morality of shared humanity and vulnerability. A man with a beard represents the image of a father and a person with responsibility. For his beard to be on fire means the man is in serious trouble. It is during that time when a fellow human being is in distress that our assistance matters most. The proverb extols the virtues of being able to share not only in the joy but also in the suffering of other people. The metaphor of a burning beard is the equivalent of a distress call. Life is mutual aid. Human beings thrive by relying on each other and knowing that others will be there for them when they need help. No person is an island unto himself or herself. Shona morality is a morality of shared humanity. It is built on the ability to share in the plight of fellow human beings. This proverb demands, in the words of Gyekye,

> mutual reciprocity as a moral mandate in a world in which human beings can easily be overcome or overwhelmed by the contingencies of their existence, a world in which human beings, weak and limited in many ways, are inured to vulnerable situations. (Gyekye 2000:109)

Shona ethics of nature

Harmony and communion with everything including nature is an important aspect of Shona morality, although sometimes the disruption of nature is necessary for the sake of attaining imagined harmony. This relational aspect in morality can be traced to what is called the Shona mind's orientation towards ecological concern and not ecological curiosity. A mind that fails to see itself as part of the natural environment is likely to engage in selfish exploitation of the environment premised on the spurious philosophy of *natura vexata* – to know nature is to expose and to conquer it. Mazrui cited in Murove argues that, ecological concern goes beyond mere fascination; it implies commitment to conserve and enrich. Ecological concern is an aspect of morality in its quest for empathy (see Murove, 2009b:325). This element of concern with the environment and being at one with nature characterised indigenous Shona societies before that harmony was uprooted or unsettled by new and alien policies on land and resource use that redefined the Shona's people's relationship to nature. Commenting on the cultural imprint of colonialism Mudimbe argued:

Chapter 6

> Although in African history the colonial experience represents but a brief moment from the perspective of today, this moment is still charged and controversial, since, to say the least, it signified a new historical form and the possibility of radically new types of discourses on African traditions and cultures. (Mudimbe 1988:1)

There are several ways in which the African world was transformed, some with positive consequences and others negative. One such change happened at the level of how the Shona related to nature and this change, judging from the climate change consequences we experience today, can be said to be negative.

A consideration of the Shona and particularly their ethics of the environment brings out the centrality of the 'ontology of invisible beings' in defining the overarching relations not only among humans, but also between people and nature. Not only does belief in the invisible beings invest all facets of life with meaning and significance, but it also ensures that specific non-human species and natural elements are bestowed with sacred mystique and as a result, protected through supernatural and other sanctions. As highlighted before, what every Shona elder would testify in the villages were amazing stories about how nature provided in abundance for all their needs in the pre-colonial times. All that can be explained with reference to the harmony that prevailed between the people, nature and the spirits in traditional Shona society. Writing on ecology through *ubuntu*, Ramose (1999) underlines the fact that the relationship of human beings to nature in traditional Africa was derived from the obligation humanity held to each other. As Ramose (1999:155) puts it: 'to care for one another … implies caring for physical nature as well'. Respect for nature followed by necessity from the respect that human beings owed each other for living in a community and sharing the same environment. Since the ultimate enemy of the human person is death, the obligation that human beings had to each other was to try and fight everything that brought about death while promoting everything that enhanced life. The entire cosmos including nature is a source of life and as such to protect nature is to preserve and perpetuate human life and defeat death. This point is made clear by Bujo when he argues that for the African person,

> one can only save oneself by saving the cosmos … it is the task of the human person to study the cosmos in order to identify plants, animals and minerals possessing that force which can liberate one from physical and psychological suffering. (Bujo 1998: 210–11)

Drawing from the example of a traditional healer in Africa, a practice that we have explored already, Bujo argues:

> The traditional healer in Africa does not only include the community of the living and the dead into his healing practice, but also uses natural elements like minerals, plants, pieces of wood, animal bones, teeth and hair, etc., in order to emphasise that effective healing is only possible where reconciliation with the entire cosmos has taken place. (Bujo 1998:211)

It is crucial therefore to realise that the African was aware that keeping the cosmos in its entirety healthy was a means of prolonging the life of human beings. Among the Shona a series of taboos in the form of proscriptions and prescriptions on how to relate to nature were common and violating them was punishable by the elders. For example, there were taboos about gathering wild fruit at certain stages of ripening, taboos on hunting during certain periods of the year and the size or age of animals that one could hunt, taboos about water sources and their use, taboos about access to certain forests based on age, gender, and purpose or profession. These mechanisms were an attempt to regulate the relationship between human beings and nature by maintaining ecological balance, which ensured that the constant battle against death was won and in the process life was prolonged. All beings, whether organic or inorganic, living or animate, personal or impersonal, visible or invisible, constituted one whole which the Shona were taught to respect and maintain since upsetting one component of this totality had the ultimate effect of undermining human existence and harmony in the community. Forests were naturally regarded as the abode of ancestors and so whatever was in the forest was under their stewardship. To respect the forests was therefore to respect the spirits and the forefathers whose spirits resided there. The entire cosmic community comprising all its beings is the foundation upon which an ecological ethics is built and for this reason I agree with Bujo's (1998) submission that ecological ethics is culturally conditioned rationality[5] and such is the Shona ethics of nature.

All in all the discussion in this chapter has highlighted the humanistic orientation in thinking that pervades indigenous Shona teachings on morality. The need to preserve society and the wellbeing of the entire community is the foundation upon which moral decisions were made. Not only do we get the Shona vision of the ideal society but equally important is their sense of personhood, the inherent dignity and worth of a person and the need to be able to count on fellow human beings as persons of equal nature. Our analysis has also acknowledged that personhood requires that human beings count equally irrespective of individual shortcomings. The ultimate moral graduate for the indigenous Shona was a person who possessed *tsika* and who exhibited that in the way expected by the community – a community that also included the invisible world of the living dead. Shona morality placed serious demands on the individual to respect other persons, laws, customs, and traditions of the society. This is where the charge of authoritarianism in traditional moral education has often emanated from. However, the position is understandable given the fact that in the absence of any written text the elders had to command a certain degree of authority so as to remain credible teachers in the face of ever inquisitive young minds. This is not to imply that there was no change, for change is the reality of life and nothing ever stays the same. In their collection of proverbs the Shona attest to the reality of change when they say '*chisingaperi chinoshura*' meaning 'what stays the same isn't normal'. This is the equivalent of Heraclitus' principle of reality – *panta rhei* – 'all things are in a state of flux'. Similarly, in the letter and spirit of this principle, I can confirm that with writing this book and reconstructing the indigenous philosophy of the Shona 'things will never be the same'.

From the past to the future

The point of articulating this indigenous intellectual heritage, particularly on this very important aspect of morality, is not merely to present a picture of indigenous Shona thought and to end there. There are important lessons which the Shona of today, Africans and the rest of the world could derive in terms of redefining our perception of each other as human beings and of the world. In *Leading Afrika* Rukuni (2009), a Zimbabwean scholar, joins the legion of scholars who have called for the revitalisation of some of the important values that defined indigenous African societies such as the values of *ubuntu*. There is general consensus that the world could be different if such values were embraced globally at both the level of leadership and by ordinary members of society. By embracing the values of *ubuntu* I have no doubt that there would be more dialogue than polemics on many of the issues confronting the world, including the problems of terrorism and climate change. These are the 'universal core problems' of today which philosophy must address (Dussel 2009). Most African countries today suffer greatly because those in leadership and positions of authority pay lip service to *ubuntu* as an important African humanistic heritage. These African values could redefine the relations between peoples and between human beings and nature in a fundamental way. Rukuni's call reiterates the position poignantly argued by Wiredu in the following submission:

> The sense of solidarity and fellowship which, as it were, spills over from the extended family to the larger community and the well-known spontaneity of our people ... combine to infuse our social life with a pervasive humanity and fullness of life which visitors to our land have always been quick to remark. This quality of our culture is obviously one which we must not only preserve but positively develop and deepen. It would profit us little to gain all the technology in the world and lose the humanist essence of our culture. (Wiredu 1980:21)

What we are witnessing today is the emergence of a new age of thinking where the conditions necessary to sustain human life on Earth demand a transformation in our ontological attitudes to nature, work, property, and other cultures (Dussel 2013:17). But the reality is that while our estrangement from nature is arguably on the rise, time has not yet run out for modern society to draw valuable lessons from indigenous traditions from around the world in order to arrest this estrangement. Cultures with different ontological and metaphysical orientations to those of Western modernity do have alternative modes of relating to nature. This is where dialogue across cultures becomes fundamental. In my essay 'Dialogue as the negation hegemony: An African perspective',[6] I argue that dialogue is central to what it means to be human. This is a value which was highly prized in indigenous African communities and to which modern society must turn. Dialogue, unlike argument, where individuals can speak at cross purposes, assumes prior recognition of our parity as human beings. It is in dialogue that humans are brought together to grow in understanding through the active process of reciprocal elucidation in search of knowledge, truth and justice. As I think of indigenous Shona morality or African morality in general and what contemporary society can benefit, it is in the values of ubuntu and what it means to be human that I see the future of humanity. This is what modern Africans and other cultures could salvage from Africa's indigenous cultures. The mentality of aggressive silencing of the other has proved to be detrimental to humanity and in times such as these it is important to return to the past and seriously consider our intellectual heritage in its entirety. What we seek, as Makang (1997) correctly states, is not to repeat the past but to make use of the wisdom from our foreparents to try and address the challenges we confront today.

Notes

1. The same point is made by his Ghanaian compatriot Kwame Gyekye (2000) in Lecture 3 of his book, *Beyond Cultures: Perceiving a Common Humanity*, where he argues that every human society has instituted some mechanisms to regulate the conduct of its members. This is another attempt to reinforce the point that morality should be regarded as universal in that no society can exist without such a system in place.

2. This quotation is taken from an entry by Gyekye (2010) entitled 'African ethics' in *The Stanford Encyclopedia of Philosophy*. Available at: http://www.science.uva.nl/~seop/archives/spr2011/entries/african-ethics/ (Accessed 14 May 2014).

3. See entry by John Hare (2010) entitled 'Religion and morality' in *The Stanford Encyclopedia of Philosophy* in which he looks at the etymology of the two terms. Available from: http://plato.stanford.edu/entries/religion-morality/ (Accessed 14 May 2014).

4. The argument presented in this section on Shona morality and shame cultures is developed more extensively in my two articles namely: 'Surveillance and cultural panopticism: Situating Foucault in African modernities', *South African Journal of Philosophy*, 2012, 31(2), 340–353; and in a book chapter entitled 'Aids and the challenge of rethinking sex education in postcolonial Africa: An Afro-philosophical perspective', which appears in a book by Ramose, M. B. (ed). *Hegel's Twilight: Studies in Intercultural Philosophy Series*, Vol 23. Amsterdam and New York NY: Rodopi, 2013, 193–211. In both of those works I have examined how traditional Shona society developed and deployed indigenous mechanisms of social control to foster harmony in the same way that modern surveillance systems such as CCTV and other monitoring mechanisms are meant to work.

5. The idea that ecological ethics is culturally conditioned rationality is taken from Bujo, (1998) in his book, *The Ethical Dimensions of Community: The African Model and Dialogue between North and South*, Nairobi: Pauline Publications Africa, 1998, 221.

6. See Mungwini, 2015. Dialogue as the negation of hegemony: An African perspective, *South African Journal of Philosophy*, 34(4), 395–407.

7

Indigenous Shona aesthetics

Aesthetics and African culture

Concerning art, Bell submits:

> What is expressed in the art of a culture, in its iconic tradition, is not accidental, nor is it simply the spontaneous expression of emotions and feelings; it is, rather, the conscious creation of considered and often wise reflections of a people on its age, and as such deserves to be taken seriously as part of the narrative portrait of the people's most important concern. This is as much the very stuff of philosophy as are the so-called 'critical' reflections which are made upon it. (Bell 1989:376)

This citation bears testimony to the fact that works of art express philosophical content for which an account must be given. Art, like philosophy, is a conscious creation that invariably reflects the cultural horizon out of which it comes. As they roam into the imaginative world of art, artists rely on the traditions, mythology, religious beliefs and customs of their community to inform the themes of what they depict in their works. Like the question of African philosophy in general, questions have been raised about the possibility of an African aesthetics. Such questions, which were rooted in the overall scepticism concerning the very be-ing of Africans and other indigenous peoples, have since been exposed for what they are and as such this work shall not seek to rehash any such debates even in the area of art in Africa, suffice to say that art represents the struggle by human beings to give meaning to experience wherever they find themselves. As Onyewuenyi emphatically states:

> We can and should talk of an African aesthetics because African culture has its own 'standards of value in judging art'; its own 'general principles' in explaining the value of any work of art. (Onyewuenyi 2000:396)

Art in and of itself presupposes the existence of consciousness and the inherent desire by human beings to communicate and make available through representations the otherwise private thoughts in their minds. I think we would do well to remind ourselves that 'art is part of life; art is living; that it is the critique of life; that art is the celebration of life; and that art is simply the experience or expression of life' (Bewaji 2003:142). In other words, art is life. African philosophers today are confronted by works of art, that is, by what Bewaji termed

> evidence of genius creativity and the legacy of a veritable African past which would have been totally obliterated in the work of racialist appropriation of knowledge, science, technology, rationality and creativity. (Bewaji 2003:124)

The challenge then is to get into the mind of these geniuses to try and read their minds as transcribed in their works of art which today constitute our only available text since the creators have long gone. It is within this framework that I examine the works of art from the Shona past to decipher the philosophy that lies hidden in those works of art bequeathed to us by the fore-parents. In this chapter, I therefore attempt to engage with the artistic creations of the Shona, as an example of an African cultural group, to reveal the philosophy that lies embedded in its traditions. If by aesthetics we refer to a science of perception about beauty then we should speak of Shona aesthetics. Aesthetics as a science of perception has always existed across all communities. According to the *Routledge Encyclopedia of Philosophy*:

> Aesthetics as understood today owes its name to Alexander Baumgarten (1714–1762) who derived it from the Greek *aisthanomai*, which means perception by means of the senses. As the subject is now understood, it consists of two parts: the philosophy of art and the philosophy of the aesthetic experience and character of objects or phenomena that are not art.

Chapter 7

An entry in *The Blackwell Dictionary of Modern Social Thought* by Bohdan Dziemidok describes aesthetics as follows:[1]

> In its modern meaning aesthetics is most frequently understood as a philosophical discipline which is either a philosophy of aesthetic phenomena (objects, qualities, experiences and values), or a philosophy of art (of creativity, of artwork, and its perception) or a philosophy of art criticism taken broadly (meta-criticism), or, finally, a discipline which is concerned philosophically with all three realms jointly.

In this chapter, aesthetics will be understood basically as that branch of philosophy that deals with the study of art and beauty. Kauffman (1969), who is among some of the early scholars to write on aesthetics among the Shona, cites Munro whose analysis of aesthetic processes can be useful to our understanding of Shona aesthetics. Munro provides a threefold framework which can be used in analysing the aesthetic expressions and experiences of different societies. According to Munro 'the aesthetic process involves morphology (classification of types and shapes of art objects), psychology (human reactions and patterns of behaviour in relation to art), and value theory (how art fits into various culture patterns)' (see Kauffman 1969:507). By evaluating each of these perspectives of art – the morphological, the psychological, and the axiological dimension – it is possible to gain a better understanding of a people's art and at the same time delve into the hidden ideas or thoughts embedded in those works of art. As Bewaji rightfully notes,

> studies in philosophy of art constitute efforts to unravel the relationship between the creative genius of specific human beings and groups of human beings and the fundamental presuppositions of such genius. (Bewaji 2003:1)

Art and philosophy

Although the history of philosophy of art is replete with controversies surrounding the definition of what constitutes art, one thing that is without dispute is the fact that 'art is a conscious human activity and works of art are products of that activity' (Tatarkiewicz 1971:138). This is where art is, to a certain degree, akin to philosophy. As Dutton (2006:376) reminds us, 'the arts in many ways rough and precise, were created and directly enjoyed long before they came to be an object of theoretical rumination', that is, by philosophers and art theorists alike. What has emerged over the centuries concerning art is that 'the manifold of what we call art ... takes on different forms in different epochs, countries, or cultures. It also fulfils different functions. It springs from different motives and satisfies different needs' (Tatarkiewicz 1971:147). This realisation is crucial for it creates room, not only for acknowledging diversity in works of art, but more importantly, it serves to expose the evil machinations of those who through definitional conspiracy have sought to exclude other peoples from the domain of art and making it a preserve of particular cultures. Through the application of creative skill and imagination humans across cultures are capable of producing works of art. Thus art is not a field governed and explained on the basis of one universal theory but it is 'a rich, scattered, and variegated realm of human experience' (Dutton 2006:376). Regarding artistic expression and the conditions that determine it, Bewaji makes the following crucial submission. For Bewaji, to suggest that there is artistic expression presupposes the existence of an artistic consciousness which issues from

> that inherently human desire to make something out of both something and 'nothing', to express the self both creatively and compulsively, to cognise the various aspects of reality as much as possible or as less as possible, given the limitations of our epistemic tools, but it must also have issued from a desire to leave something behind no matter how materially irrelevant or economically indifferent to the problems of the day. (Bewaji 2003:98)

From the foregoing, I can conclude that works of art from the African past which are the subject of my focus indicate to us the prevalence of conscious and creative individuals who took time to leave for posterity, a record of their thoughts and evidence of their contemplations about reality within the horizons of their culture. It is no accident that Ki-Zerbo declares:

> Man (read human being) is a born chronicler and the artists of prehistory are the first African historians [and philosophers], since they have left us a legible record of the successive stages of African man's relationship with his natural and social environment. (Ki-Zerbo 1981:671)

Chapter 7

What we should aim for, as philosophers of today, is to understand this corpus and use it to thread together the philosophical presuppositions inherent in these artistic expressions. Although my main interest will be on art with symbolic and religious significance, it is important to point out right from the outset that not all art in Africa belonged to this category. Traditionally, art has always been equated with skill manifesting itself through sculpture, visual arts, music and dance, poetry and theatre among others. Art in traditional Shona society took all these dimensions. Take the example of music. Although there were different forms of music the choice of music, dance, and even musical instruments varied according to social function and purpose. The role of music as a medium of connection between artistic expressions in ritual contexts is one of the things that have stood out in traditional Shona society and one which has continued into the present. This is where music is used as a catalyst in ceremonies or ritual and divination procedures. Since there are varied motives and needs that drive every form of art, making sense of the art of a people requires an understanding of their culture particularly their worldview. Art was employed in mediating life and existence within the context of a given worldview. The significance of the worldview in shaping expressive emotions in art is depicted in even the architecture produced by the people in terms of the dwellings or houses and monuments they constructed and through the choice of patterns or decorations they used on those structures. To this day archaeologists are not in agreement on how to interpret the conical towers at Great Zimbabwe, with some saying they are an expression of power and male fertility while others think they symbolise grain storage. But whatever interpretation is given it cannot ignore the culture and worldview of the people. Various forms of art traceable to the traditional past are still practised and continue to influence the nature of contemporary art. Art takes many forms and, as correctly pointed out by Des Fontaine, art in Africa was also

> expressed in objects which had no religious character, for example, architecture, the decoration of houses, mats, objects made from bark, cooking utensils, decorated pots, drums, axes, head-rests and so on. In a study of African art, it would be incorrect to omit these articles, as this might give the impression, erroneously held by many, that all African art has religious significance. (Des Fontaine 1974:1)

My reason for not focusing on all these other forms of art, including traditional music, is purely pragmatic in that space and time will not allow. Such explorations can be the focus of other projects in the future.

At this point, let me touch on the importance of traditional artistic forms such as carvings and drawings to an understanding of traditional life in Africa in general. As archaeologists would attest, much about the African past can be discerned from the relics of materials such as artistic creations, artifacts, rock paintings, and symbols left behind by the ancestors. These pieces of artistic creation which can be referred to as iconic forms of expression are varied and numerous in their form and depictions. They are found throughout African villages, and in the wild in caves that were once the abode of our forefathers. Today carved pieces of art continue to occupy a significant place in African lives but of course driven by a slightly different cause. Art has now been integrated into the mainstream economy and pieces of art are now found everywhere alongside highways, designated market points and in galleries as artists respond to modernity and its capitalist requirements in an attempt to earn a living from their genius.

Art represents one of the most important creations of a people; it is the genius of that particular society. Highlighting the significance of art to contemporary Africa, Wingo argues:

> Africa's ancient history is chiseled in stones, cast in brass and bronze, carved in wood, painted on stones and walls of caves, and frozen in songs and stories waiting for the brave to decipher. (Wingo 2004:430)

Confronted with this ancient heritage, the philosopher is challenged to enter into dialogue with this heritage in order to bring out ideas and hidden perspectives on the life and philosophies of the communities that created the art forms. Art is, therefore, a cultural resource pregnant with the people's history and philosophy. In an oral society where the technology of preserving ideas and maintaining records was not fully developed, the importance of the artist and his/her role may not be underestimated. Following Okpewho's (1977) argument, the traditional African artist can be regarded as an active mind who tried to 'give vitality and meaning to the community's life and myth with the aid of his creative vigor'. Operating within the dynamic context of his or her community, and being guided by the community's metaphysical beliefs and traditions, the traditional African artist could act as both a documenter of society's thoughts and an important agent in recreating and refashioning community myths and traditions. Hence, pieces of art are not only meant for aesthetic enjoyment or pleasure, they are in themselves documentaries to which contemporary historians and philosophers should turn their attention.

Okpewho (1977) went further to draw our attention to the synergy between art and the landscape out of which it grows. In other words, while the artist was indeed a product of his own community and the myths and traditions that it cherished, his or her artistic creations were also influenced by the nature of the surrounding landscape and wilderness in which the artist found him or herself. To quote Okpewho:

> There is a subtle but discernible relationship between art and the landscape out of which it grows. And it would appear that a good deal of the aesthetic nourishment of traditional African art derived from the nature of the surrounding landscape and the concomitant throb of animate company within it. (Okpewho 1977:307)

The influence of the natural environment, the beliefs of the community and its traditions on art and artistic expressions are thus significant. It is for this reason that Floistad (2007:3) submits that 'as a free play of imagination, aesthetic creations and experiences are dependent on metaphysics and ontology, epistemology, logic and moral philosophy'. Mystical ideas prevalent in a culture are represented in concrete works of art and those who are capable of subjecting these pieces of art to intense interpretation and scrutiny are able to reach at those ideas contained in those forms of artistic representation. Aside from being representations of life and thought in the life of the community, works of art also open doors to the dream world, a world of imagination and abstract thinking.

According to Bell,

> an iconic tradition is more than a collection of artifacts, stories, symbols and formalised ritual; it is a primary and reflective mode of articulation of human life and, as such, can be philosophical in nature. (Bell 1989:376)

The art in traditional African societies becomes a philosophical text from which the beliefs, mythology, patterns of life and forms of existence in a particular community can be discerned. If it is indeed accepted that philosophy begins in wonder, then the myths and various artistic creations are a crucial indicator to the prevalence of wonder among the traditional peoples, a genuine source of philosophy. Even the lover of myth is in a sense a lover of wisdom, for the myth is composed from imagination and is a product of creative human genius to account for reality and why things are as they are. The African works of art are not merely for entertainment or for pleasing the eye, but they are also an important means of transmitting cultural and spiritual values. They are, in themselves, an indigenous epistemology replete with cultural truths about humanity, the universe and the spiritual substratum. Concerning African art, it seems

> impossible to understand African artistic and aesthetic experience without an understanding of African mythology, religion, ontology, language, social and political doctrines as well as the African theory of knowledge. (Anyanwu 1981:282)

What this means is that, African art and whatever ideas it expresses, contain important leads on some of the most crucial aspects of life from religion to forms and practices of knowing such as divination, which were discussed in chapter five in detail. For Floistad (2007:10), African art purports 'to transfer the sacred to the social sphere guided by the vision of the collective'. It attempts to render the unfamiliar familiar, the abstract concrete, and to capture the spiritual to bring it closer to humans in a physical and sensory form. This is probably the reason why Senghor refers to 'African art as the language of ontology' (Diagne 2011:10). The African comprehension of reality can be reconstructed out of the works of art. Senghor is convinced that African art forms bear an important identity of Africanity and these art forms 'constitute the writing which allows us to read the metaphysics it transcribes' (Diagne 2011: 54). Senghor went further to claim that 'art is the evidence of African philosophy and, conversely, we do not attain full comprehension of African art without understanding the metaphysics from which it proceeds' (Diagne 2011:55). The knowledge of forces and the entire cosmology expressed in the 'ontology of invisible beings' is the key to unlocking the meaning of most artistic forms in Africa. This is the point made by Tempels in his seminal work *Bantu Philosophy* when he concluded that vital forces constitute the fabric of true reality. It could be argued that Tempels was convinced that

> to understand 'African life' in its multiple manifestations, whether in terms of religion, art, ethics, medicine, law or government, involves going beyond the ethnographic descriptions in order to reach knowledge of ontology that is the *ratio essendi* ('reason of being') and *ratio cognoscendi* ('reason for intelligibility') of things. (Diagne 2011:84)

There is an ontology of forces which literally affords meaning to almost all significant aspects of African life, an ontology that is expressly captured in art forms. In his work on the idea of African art, Anyanwu (1987:259) concludes by stating that 'art is rooted in life-force, and it is the art of living, of integration, of consecration and of association'. In other words, art like philosophy embodies the central tenets of the culture from which it comes.

Beauty among the Shona

The concept of beauty is at the centre of aesthetics and constitutes a comprehensive aesthetic idea for the Shona. It is not only seen in works of art but also in the qualities of persons and even the environment. Gyekye (1996:130) argues that 'beauty is traditionally and universally held as the central concept in aesthetic experience' and 'different cultures hold different conceptions about what beauty is and what features of the human experience can be called beautiful'. Just like most values, beauty is believed to be culturally embedded and socially defined. Among the Shona, the term for beauty and good is the same. In other words, what is beautiful can also be described as good. The Shona term for beauty is *kunaka* and several of its variants may be used depending on whether the beauty that one is describing is that of a person, an animal or an inanimate object. Since aesthetics is closely related to the notion of perception it may be important to examine in brief the Shona concept of perception.

Among the Shona the terms *kuona* (to see, to discern, to understand) and *kunzwa* (to hear, to taste, to smell, to feel, to understand) are used to capture what is described in philosophy as perception. The term *kunzwa* is a concept that can be taken as expressive of much that qualifies as designating aesthetic experiences. Since sense perception is central to aesthetic experience these two terms *kuona* and *kunzwa* are central to the understanding and expression of aesthetic experiences among the Shona. An object or a thing that is beautiful is one that is good and attractive and arouses a good feeling to the senses. Among the Shona, the beauty of an object is measured by the feelings it arouses as expressed in the range of superlatives used to describe it. Such superlatives are also applied to other living entities including human beings. Beauty in objects also relates to their instrumental value or function, whereas in human beings beauty is also used to capture the moral character of the individual in question. For example a drum is described as beautiful or good if it produces sound that is as good as is expected by the dancers. The Shona conception of beauty is often aptly captured in sayings and proverbs. An analysis of a few such proverbs can provide crucial information on how the Shona conceptualised beauty and how it fitted within their scheme of values.

The proverb *mukadzi munaku akasaba anoroya* (a beautiful looking woman is also most likely a thief or a witch). The belief is that facial beauty in and of itself is not the only measure of a beautiful woman. Extremely beautiful people usually have other serious shortcomings or blemishes in their character. Human beings cannot be perfect in all aspects. The tendency to pair beauty and witchcraft or bad morals was a way of encouraging individuals to go beyond physical appearance when judging the beauty of a woman. This proverb may also be taken as a ploy by the elders to protect so-called ugly women from being shunned for marriage by painting those physically attractive as having their own darker side. This proverb plays down physical attractiveness and subordinates it to moral uprightness when judging the beauty of a person. Thus beauty among the Shona ought to include the inner self or the character of the individual over and above the physical beauty.

The saying *Kunaka hakudyiwi* (beauty cannot feed or nourish anybody) is yet another Shona expression playing down the value of physical beauty in women. Literally, it draws attention to two values: beauty and industry. Within the traditional and subsistence context an industrious woman was valued and hence considered better than a lazy one. Instead of being preoccupied with one's looks as a woman, one should instead be doing that which can make the community survive. In other words, a hard worker is a better woman than one who is physically beautiful who spends most her time trying to preserve her good looks. This saying dismisses the tendency to make physical attractiveness a central issue in judging the worth of persons within society. A better woman is one who is able to provide for her family and the community through hard work and not one who wastes time trying to nurture and preserve her good looks.

Guyu kutsvukira kunze mukati muzere makonye (the fig appears attractive and appetising from outside but inside it is infested with disgusting moths). This proverb captures the basic philosophic problem of appearance and reality. In other words, all that glitters is not gold. In terms of beauty this proverb tries to capture the simple truth that individuals are not to be judged for their beauty on the basis of their looks or physical attractiveness. Instead, inner beauty or character was more crucial for beauty as it said something about the inner person. The Shona believed that being virtuous was more important than being physically attractive, hence they would always emphasise that '*mwoyo momunhu ndiye munhu kwete chiso*', meaning the true human is what lies hidden inside, that is, in one's heart not the facial appearance.

The fourth and final proverb I shall consider is *Matende mashava anovazva doro* (beautiful calabashes cause beer to go sour). Among the Shona the traditional brew was an important beverage as it served multiple functions including being a source of entertainment and a key beverage for all traditional ceremonies. Those who produced a good brew earned themselves a lot of respect and social approval as they brought joy to their community. As such, if a container used to ferment beer turned out to be the spoiler of the beer then it was to be discarded. There was no need to keep such a container for it brought misery rather than joy to the community. The same logic extended to the way people looked at physically attractive women particularly those with lighter skins. The implicit warning was that the chances of social disharmony are higher in those who invest in chasing after beautiful and physically attractive women for marriage. Because of her attractiveness, the beautiful wife is always faced with temptations and is exposed to the dangers of being the object of lust. Just like sour beer which does not bring any joy to the community, an attractive woman can mean trouble in the community. These proverbs put together capture an important aspect of beauty and its appreciation among the Shona. Beauty is a function of morality and purpose. These are the psychological and axiological dimensions that Kauffman referred to above. The extent to which the Shona went in subordinating beauty to function and morality is crucial to understanding Shona aesthetics.

Metaphysical dimensions of Shona art

Reflecting on the significance of art as a source of information about the African past Hampete Ba (1981:180) submits that 'in the traditional African society, often human activities had a sacred or occult character, particularly those activities that consist in acting on matter and transforming it, since everything is regarded as alive'.

As a result of their metaphysical wholeness Africans could capture and express myths about spirits and other legendary stories from the past through works of art. Traditional artisanal crafts are therefore one important source of ideas from which the traditional philosophy of a people can be reconstructed. Art among the Shona, like most other African cultures, reflects the influence of metaphysics, religious beliefs, and mythology. Highlighting the close relationship that exists between art and metaphysics Amaladass argues:

> Religion and art go together in almost all cultures. Religion uses music in rituals and liturgies and develops architecture to suit their liturgical needs. Visual art depicts their religious history. Art shapes religion, affection, beliefs, memories, and provides symbols. Religion without art could become ethereal spiritualism, and art without religion would turn into direction-less subjectivism, devoid of proper orientation. (Amaladass 2007:67)

The myths that manifest themselves through these works of art in traditional societies that had no writing, constitute a repository of the metaphysical and religious ideas of a people's past. Mythological and cosmological symbolism remains the key to understanding traditional African art. Art occupied a crucial place in the traditional belief matrix as it was the expression of religious fervour and the means to transcend reality, as such works of art are imbued with meaning. They can have a concealed meaning as well as a more obvious meaning. Art with a sense of humour can be used to capture the ironies of life but on the other hand the same art can be esoteric, vibrating with the mystical fervour that impelled the artist who produced it. Art represented an important way of making accessible or visible the mythological forces and powers that were at play in the universe and hence responsible for shaping life and its destiny. Myths were more or less theories about people and their relationship to the universe and its forces. Myths were therefore far from being meaningless fantasies as they captured important cosmic beliefs which contained an internal logic of their own. Although artists are considered creative individuals who use their power of imagination to create works of art, they are at the same time products of their own culture since what they produce are depictions of the ideas contained in the myths and fables of their culture. In this work I shall select for analysis the famous sculpture known as the Zimbabwe bird and its potential as a key to unlocking the cosmological thoughts of the indigenous Shona. Since the artists who invented or gave shape to those forms of artistic creation are long gone, it remains the task of the living to use their interpretive techniques to reconstruct the story and meaning behind those artistic representations.

Sculpture among the Shona is a form of art that has a long tradition or history. The Shona used and continue to use various materials including clay, wood, and stone to create their works of art. Through the use of these popular materials they were able to capture various aspects of the cherished traditions of their communities including, of course, the popular myths and beliefs of their community. The Shona artist, like his or her diviner counterpart, is closely connected to the spirit world in the sense that they both derive the inspiration for their practice from the spirits of the departed. The artist is a miniature creator breathing meaning and life into otherwise ordinary and simple raw materials of stone or wood and thus thought to follow in the footsteps of God himself. There is also a close connection between art among the Shona and rituals of ancestral veneration. Shona art has religious and symbolic aspects. Writing on Shona art and its metaphysical connection Dewey observes that 'spirit mediums and divine healers indirectly or directly are the main patrons of artists who make the ritual objects, since they use many themselves and also direct their clients to have them made' (Dewey 1986:64). In other words, the diviners and spirit mediums recommend certain objects of art to their clients as part of the ritual procedure to whatever problem they are dealing with. For example, most traditional Shona families had *tsvimbo yemudzimu* (a special walking stick for rituals) kept in the house and used in traditional ceremonies. These were designed by artists and people were then urged to purchase them. Most of the objects created by artists are therefore directly linked with spirit mediums and diviners as living manifestations of the religious myths that prevailed in that community. It is also believed that through dreams the spirits availed images and inspired artists to create objects of religious or spiritual significance, hence, artists were capable of creating objects that were so mysterious as to leave everyone around confounded. Mysterious creatures boasting bird, animal, and human like features all combined were not uncommon. It is believed that most ceremonial objects are not creations out of the ordinary human skill but physical depictions or emblems of the divine and its power.

The soapstone birds of Great Zimbabwe

> So what shall we call them, sacred or sinister, living or legend, historic or hideous? They keep us guessing, those birds! (Heather Jarvis in Hubbard 2009:109)

This quotation captures the mystery surrounding the Great Zimbabwe birds in a very telling way. The Zimbabwe bird is one outstanding symbol that is completely imbued with its own fair share of mythology and spirituality. Traced back to the famous iconic structure, the Great Zimbabwe monuments, the Zimbabwe bird is not simply an ordinary carving depicting a bird, but more importantly a symbolic representation of the soul, religion, mythology and origin of the Shona people. The true identity of the Zimbabwe bird has remained a mystery with others preferring to call it the Fish eagle (*Hungwe*) – which is a totem bird; while others contend that it is a Bateleur eagle (*Chapungu*) – a rare and often elusive eagle that is believed to be a divine messenger. Although most researchers agree that these famous soapstone birds (eight of them in number) represent birds of prey, it has not been possible to agree on the type of species. According to Huffman, an archaeologist who has done extensive work on the Great Zimbabwe monuments,

> it is not possible to identify any specific species because the carvings incorporate human as well as avian elements. One stone, for example, has lips rather than a beak; all have human limbs and four or five toes (or fingers) in front, rather than three talons forward like most raptors. (Huffman 1985:68)

The depiction of these birds as having both bird and human features adds to the mystery surrounding these soapstone birds. However, what is important to remember is that birds feature prominently in the spirituality of the Shona.

Speculation over the features of the birds still continues, but of particular significance are inferences that have been made between the significance of the bird in Shona mythology and the intercessory role they play between the living and the spiritual realm. Both the fish eagle (*hungwe*) and bateleur eagle (*chapungu*) are raptor birds that are believed to have a sacred connection with the spirit world. To further confirm the sacred nature of these carvings one has to put together and interpret the various depictions of the stones, which include the anthropomorphic features of the birds, and other features on the stones on which they are perched, together with their original location within the Great Zimbabwe complex. According to Huffman, most of the birds were found in the Eastern Enclosure of the hill complex– 'a place sacred both because of its position at the back of the king's residence and because in Shona religion the east is associated with life-giving forces' (Huffman 1985:71). The anthropomorphism in the soapstone birds themselves was 'an intentional blend of parallel concepts about the mediatory flight of eagles and of royal ancestors' (Huffman 1985:70). These birds were each perched on a pillar of about a metre or more in height. One of the birds has a crocodile creeping below the metre – long pillar on which it perches. That in itself also calls for an examination of the significance of the crocodile in Shona mythology. It is believed that the crocodile with its connection to the pools of the sacred *njuzu* (mermaid) spirits was an animal associated with power and royal ancestral spirits. Myth had it that the founding father of the Shona, the first man and rainmaker, came from the spirit world at the bottom of a sacred pool of water and the king as father of the nation is directly linked to that person (Huffman 1985).

> Crocodiles behaved like chiefs in that they are dangerous, ferocious, and fear no enemies, they live for many years, and, most importantly they can communicate with the ancestor spirit world at the bottom of deep pools. (Huffman 1996:29)

It is believed that at the installation of a king, the aspiring candidate had to catch a male crocodile himself and then a special dish to prepare him for leadership and royalty would be cooked with the stones retrieved from the crocodile's stomach. This procedure had the symbolic significance of transforming the chief into becoming a crocodile himself in terms of power and connection to the founding spirits (see Huffman 1985 and Matenga 2011). Ontologically, the king was far from being just a human being, the rituals of installation transformed him into a composite figure with spiritual and animal qualities, and to bolster this rare power, he was at all times surrounded by a team of renowned medicine men.

The Shona enter the world of spirits in part through the act of divination. The crocodile which features prominently on the carving on which one of those birds is perched is also an important item in the divination instruments called *hakata* in Shona. One of the four primary divination dices (*hakata*) used by diviners in their work has the image of a crocodile inscribed on it. The four *hakata* instruments for divination are made from wood, bone or ivory and each has a name representing key elements in life. The four are *chirume* (male and the crocodile); *kwami* (female); *nhokwara* (good luck); and *chitokwadzima* (bad luck) (see Matenga 2011). The crocodile and other symbols represent different and competing life forces whose meaning could be translated into relevant messages by those who had mastered the art of divination. Thus it is no coincidence that one of the birds was put together with the crocodile image.

Those who have attempted to interpret the Shona divination system and its matrix of symbolisms would be quick to highlight the importance of birds in social life. Some birds particularly the nocturnal species are associated with evil spirits, death, illness, misfortune and witchcraft. For example, the owl is a bird associated with witchcraft and bad omen such that to accuse a person of having an owl in his or her custody or being the lover of owls is in effect to accuse that person of witchcraft. On the other hand the *chapungu and hungwe* are good birds that are associated with the ancestral spirits and it is believed that ancestors can send them to protect and warn people of imminent danger. Matenga (2011:133) argues that 'the ominous appearances and postures of the bateleur eagle as a divine warning or premonition for danger or disasters is a conventional belief among the Shona as well as its role as royal messenger'. As an elusive bird species, its appearance or unique cry was often regarded as a sign that the ancestors wanted to convey something to the people. Stories of hunters who were helped to avert danger and freedom fighters who claim to have been saved by these birds from walking into enemy ambushes during the liberation war are not uncommon.

The Zimbabwe bird remains an important point of contact between the past and the present and a carrier of the Shona narrative both historical and mythical. If Huffman (1985:72) is correct, these birds could also be connected to number of 'individual mythical or important ancestors who lived before the establishment of Great Zimbabwe'. In that sense they would each stand for the great great ancestors who were the founding ancestors of the Shona people. As a national symbol appearing on the flag and on the Zimbabwean currency, the bird is now famously known just as the Zimbabwe bird. It is as if it is the only bird, 'the Bird' in Zimbabwe. The name captures its centrality to the history of the peoples of the country. The architect of colonialism in Zimbabwe, Cecil John Rhodes, was reportedly so obsessed with the bird that to this day one of the birds is still kept at his official residence in South Africa, which is also decorated by replicas of the bird (Matenga 2011). The colonial government went on to appropriate the symbol and used it as part of the official coat of arms of the Southern Rhodesia Government and the bird featured on many things such as coins, buildings, and corporate logos associated with the colonial government. According to Matenga following the establishment of the Rhodesia Responsible Government of 1923,

> the Zimbabwe bird entered state iconography for the first time, crowning the coat-of-arms with the Rhodesian (Latin) motto, *Sit Nomine Digna* (may it be worthy of the name) inscribed at the bottom. In 1932 it was struck on the reverse side of the coin – a silver one shilling denomination. The bird emblem now symbolised Rhodesia and came to be everywhere from buildings to corporate trademarks. (Matenga 2011:152)

Chapter 7

This adoption of the Zimbabwe bird by colonialists was ideological and an act of spiritual usurpation because the symbol that stood for Shona spirituality was now being appropriated in the construction of a perverted heritage and identity for the colonial regime. It was also another act of arrogance in the same mould as that of Cecil John Rhodes's choice to be buried at the site of the famous Mwari shrine. The Zimbabwe bird has therefore occupied a central place in the history of the country dating back to the ancient Great Zimbabwe state, through the colonial and into the independent state of Zimbabwe. In 2003, a national event was even held to commemorate the return of the other half of one of the birds that had been taken to Germany during the colonial era. Such is the significance attached to the Zimbabwe bird. Because of its connection to the Great Zimbabwe monument, and the founding fathers of that settlement, the Zimbabwe bird becomes not only a religious symbol, but also a symbolic locus of power connected to the divine rule of kings, a link between the physical and the metaphysical, and a historical symbol reconnecting the present to its past. Symbolism was an integral part of the indigenous peoples who were without writing as 'meanings and ideas were given expression through symbolic art' (Gyekye 1996:127). For example, prehistoric art in Africa is the equivalent of a modern documentary film where the story of the past is told through the various symbolic representations. Symbolism in African art therefore had a context and getting to understand that context is the crucial step in unfolding the mystery and meaning behind artistic expressions.

The visual creations such as the mythic birds of Great Zimbabwe share a similar significance to that attached to other symbols of representation like the cross in Christian mythology which to the Christians is, just as the Zimbabwe birds were to the Shona, imbued with power, force and energy. To Christians the cross is not just a wooden or bronze artifact, but a sacred object oozing with supernatural power and a compressed script of the entire story of human salvation. Although the power of and sentimental attachment commanded by the various symbols varies between cultures, there is little doubt that every religious art form enjoys more significance and is of uncontested value to those to whose culture it belongs. This in part explains why objects or animals venerated by other cultures around the world are of no significance and even make it to the dinner table each day in other cultures – for example, cows are sacred to Hindus, but are perceived as food in many other cultures. The point I am trying to make is that the metaphysical beliefs of any particular culture are to a large extent responsible for shaping the meaning and significance of symbols.

The raptor bird that I am discussing as the Zimbabwe bird is no ordinary bird for the Shona as it is part of the important story of their own survival as a people. Because there is metaphysical significance attached to them, the soapstone birds of Great Zimbabwe as they are famously known, continue to elicit attention. It seems what every scholar who has examined these birds has sought is to unravel the myth and provide a narrative that delves deeper into the mentality of those who created them. It is true that African sculpture which is often 'grandiose, noble, intimate, intricate and even disturbing' (Bewaji 2003:142) is of significant importance in the artistic terrain as it helps to record history and to serve as memories and monuments that commemorate achievements and beliefs from the past.

Much concerning the indigenous Shona worldview can be decoded from their artistic creations and the role those animals depicted in that artistic form played in Shona mythology. The Shona therefore created artefacts as symbolic tools to assist them communicate with gods and other spirits in their effort to obtain insight into problems encountered by the people and as a way of trying to solve them. The various creations are not ordinary art pieces but 'they embody abstract spiritual forces, serving as transitional cites that allow these ephemeral entities to communicate with the living' (La Gama 2000:55). Belief in Mwari, and the ancestors and the interconnections between the visible and invisible realms is a narrative that can be deciphered in the Shona people's artistic works. For example, by looking at the birds and their varied human features and in their original abode – the sacred enclosure– it is possible to make inferences about the spiritual significance of those birds as symbolic representations of both the departed ancestors and as avenues for communication with the invisible world. Whether the Zimbabwe bird is taken as a *Hungwe* or *Chapungu*, Shona mythology places particular birds at the centre of their religion. As a result of their ability to straddle the spaces between this physical earth and that beyond the clouds, a select few among all the bird species, were given spiritual significance as symbolic representations of the ancestral and royal spirits of the clan who could intercede with God on behalf of the living on various issues of significance such as protection from enemies, the provision of rains and a bumper harvest, as well as sustaining good life and wealth in general. Those birds are in themselves a language of Shona ontology and throw light on the Shona comprehension of reality. To enter into the world revealed by these forms of traditional art is in part the means to read the philosophy transcribed by these art forms.

The ontology of invisible beings and the belief in the universe as a constituency of contending life forces that can be harnessed for a positive outcome is at the heart of artistic creations such as the Zimbabwe bird with its pretty unusual features. Traditional sages spoken to during the compilation of this work to provide insight into Shona sculpture confirmed the spiritual dimension of most traditional art symbols as well as the spirituality surrounding those who produced them. Artists often attribute their skills to two types of spirits in Shona cosmology: the *shavi*, that is, the wandering or alien spirit, and the *vadzimu* or spirits of the ancestors. However, as Bewaji contends,

> this attribution of creative genius to the largesse from the ancestors, the gods, or other supernatural sources, serves to remove the artist from pettiness of accusations of sabotage, indecent criticism, oppositional inclinations, etc. (Bewaji 2003:214)

In other words, such attributions made it difficult for society to attack the artist once the artist's creations were attributed to the work of spirits. The inspiration to create works of art from simple raw materials such as soapstone and wood or clay was itself regarded as the preserve of a few who were capable of carrying their imaginations into the spiritual world. This in a sense falls within the common belief among the Shona that anyone who excelled in their chosen trade owed it to the spirits as it was the spirits that inspired and gave them strength and genius. I am told that even my grandfather, who was a famous blacksmith, was believed to have a spirit (*shavi*) behind his famous trade and occasionally he was required to brew traditional beer to honour the spirits that gave him strength to work the iron 'like none of his peers in the community could do'. Hence, the connection between any form of art and the spiritual world was commonplace in traditional Shona society.

Overall, the Zimbabwe bird in its artistic mould brings together speculations about birds and their intervention in human affairs as divine messengers; birds and their connection to the famous Mwari religion; and birds and the beliefs about rain ceremonies; while the anthropomorphic and other features link the birds to royal ancestry and myths of the sacred pools of the *njuzu* (mermaid) spirits and the crocodile origin of chieftaincy. However, like any important symbol in history, such as the cross in Christianity, what is of significant interest to philosophy here is not the veracity of these myths and narratives, but the central role the myths play in shaping the lives of the local people and their belief system which in turn informs how they relate to nature and give meaning to everything. It is in essence the continued power of mystery ever present in these artistic creations that give them cultural significance. This is where the philosophical meaning and significance of art becomes important. In this mythological form, art is able to transcend the ordinary art object and open the door into the spiritual world. It is true that we cannot perceive ideas, but what we perceive are certain phenomena that suggest to us certain ideas and that is what we get from art. Shona art, like all art in general, carries those who come into contact with it into the world of imagination expressive of the people's thoughts about nature and divinities. The imaginary realm into which the artist is able to transport its participants results in a variety of insights that when analysed, within the historical context of the origin of that art, can yield important philosophical inferences about a people and their life.

Notes

1. Dziemidok, Bohdan. 'Aesthetics' in Outhwaite, William (ed). *The Blackwell Dictionary of Modern Social Thought*. Blackwell Reference Online. Available at: http://www.blackwellreference.com/subscriber/tocnode? (Accessed 10 April 2012).

8

Conclusion

In the general introduction to the *UNESCO General History of Africa Volume 1*, Ki-zerbo (1981:3) draws our attention to the fact that 'unless one chooses to live in a state of unconsciousness and alienation, one cannot live without memory, or with a memory that belongs to someone else'. It is in view of this that African philosophers cannot afford to ignore their past or even to take it for granted. There is no doubt that some of the most provocative questions in African philosophy get their impetus and direction from historical memory. In Africa these issues pertain to, among other things, the range of political experiences and grievances which no progressive African can afford to ignore. There is need, as Serequeberhan (1994) argues, to grasp the distinctive particularity of the African situation. Memory therefore plays a critical role in defining and shaping priorities in African philosophical discourse. This is the case with an interest in indigenous traditions and philosophies. In this book I have argued that the question of indigenous Shona philosophy has more to do with a retrieval and revitalisation of an intellectual heritage from the past in search of identity. It is equally important that at a time when postcolonial Africa is seeking to ensure that Africa plays a significant role in the production, validation and distribution of knowledge, special attention be given to the reconstruction of indigenous philosophies. However, interest in African traditions should not only be viewed as an attempt to recover and revitalise crucial ideas and philosophies from the past but it should also be seen as an attempt to reaffirm and vindicate African rationality. Reclaiming the past is itself an act of liberation. The historical and political horizons out of which philosophy in Africa originates, calls on us to place special significance on the African archive. The future of Africa does not lie in 'becoming, in thought, speech and habit, like [our] erstwhile colonisers' (Owomoyela 1987:93). My aim in articulating the thoughts of the indigenous Shona was to contribute towards the creation of a body of literature which would constitute the basis for continuous philosophical reflection and other important cross-cultural conceptual considerations. Human beings are the only animals with a distinct interest in understanding their past and in reclaiming their identity. For reasons largely to do with history, the endeavour to understand the African past decolonises the mind as much as it inspires it to higher goals. Every articulation of the African intellectual heritage remains important as a means to question epistemic hegemony and promote dialogue across cultures.

This work was also driven by the historico-philosophical imperative to tell the story of Africa from the African standpoint. Such a call is fundamentally in tune with what has always obtained in other cultures across the world where different cultures tell their own stories about the world. Without the retrieval and critical articulation of indigenous philosophies and knowledges, the story of Africa would be incomplete. Indigenous traditions of thought and practices must be accorded priority in our endeavour to understand and therefore transform Africa and its relations with the world. Such classical ideas should reclaim their immortality by being made available in written form to future generations, so that they can continue to dialogue, critique and innovate them.

Through this book I also meant to reinforce the need for philosophers around the world to document the philosophies of their indigenous peoples, because that intellectual heritage has potential to contribute towards mediating those forces which threaten human existence. Knowledge of each other's beliefs and traditions is becoming more and more important if we are to have a desirable future together as humanity. Huntington's (1993:49) apt observation that 'for the relevant future, there will be no universal civilisation, but instead a world of different civilisations, each of which will learn to coexist with others' reminds us of the need to direct our attention at understanding each other's traditions in pursuit of universal dialogue. The future of humanity lies in the success of intercultural dialogue. Intercultural dialogue would progress better if all philosophies of the world including those of the indigenous peoples are made available to the rest of humanity. In an era of unprecedented population movements mostly from the crisis ridden Third World to the West, some of it reminiscent of the theory of 'counter-penetration', philosophy has a huge responsibility to help societies understand the

Chapter 8

meaning of life and existence. This is how knowledge of the different traditions and of the assumptions that drive particular modes of human action or inaction becomes fundamental.

References

Abimbola, W. and Hallen, B. 1993. 'Secrecy and objectivity in the methodology and literature of Ifa divination'. In Nooter, M.H. (ed.). *Secrecy: African Art that Conceals and Reveals*. New York: The Museum for African Art, 213–221.

Alderman, D.H. 2008. 'Place naming and interpretation of cultural landscapes'. In Graham, B. and Howard, P. (eds). *The Ashgate Research Companion to Heritage and Identity*. Hampshire: Ashgate, 195–213.

Amadiume, I. 1997. *Re-Inventing Africa: Matriarchy, Religion and Culture*. London: Zed.

Amaladass, A. 2007. 'Aesthetics and religion from the Indian perspective'. In Floistad, G. (ed.). *Contemporary Philosophy: A New Survey, Vol 9, Aesthetics and Philosophy*. Dordrecht: Springer, 67–82.

Anyanwu, K.C. 1981. 'Artistic and aesthetic experience'. In Ruch, E.A. and Anyanwu, K.C. (eds). *African Philosophy: An Introduction to the Main Trends in Contemporary Africa*. Rome: Catholic Book Agency, 270–282

Anyanwu, K. 1987. 'The idea of art in African thought'. In Floistad, G. (ed.). *Contemporary Philosophy: A New Survey, Vol 5*. Dordrecht: Martinus Nijhoff, 235–260.

Appiah, K.A. 1992. *In My Father's House*. Oxford: Oxford University Press.

Asad. T. 1992. 'Conscripts of Western civilization'. In Gailey C.W. (ed.) *Dialectical Anthropology: Essays in Honour of Stanley Diamond*. Gainesville: University Press of Florida

Asante, M.K. 2003. 'The Afrocentric idea'. In Mazama, A. (ed.). *The Afrocentric Paradigm*, Asmara: Africa World Press, 36–53.

Ashforth, A. 2002. *Witchcraft, Violence, and Democracy in South Africa*. Chicago: University of Chicago Press.

References

Asouzu, I. 1998. 'Science and African metaphysics: A search for direction'. *Proceedings of the Twentieth Congress of Philosophy, Vol. 12.* Available at: www.bu.edu/wcp/Papers/Afri/AfriAsou.htm (Accessed 18 October 2011).

Awolabi, K.A. 2001. 'The quest for a method in African philosophy: A defense of the hermeneutic-narrative approach, *The Philosophical Forum*, 32(2), 147–163.

Ba, H.A. 1981. 'The living tradition'. In Ki-Zerbo, J. (ed.). *UNESCO General History of Africa Volume 1.* UNESCO: University of California Press, 166–205.

Bailey, M.D. 2003. *Historical Dictionary of Witchcraft.* Oxford: Scarecrow Press.

Banchetti-Robino, M.P. and Headley, C.R. (eds). 2006. *Shifting the Geography of Reason: Gender, Science and Religion.* Newcastle: Cambridge Scholar Press.

Baron, N.S. 1981. *Speech, Writing, and Sign: A Functional View of Linguistic Representation.* Bloomington: Indiana University Press.

Bartlett, L. 1999. 'Zimbabwe-AIDS: Cremation a burning issue in Zimbabwe as AIDS toll rises'. *Agence France-Presse.* Available at: http://www.freerepublic.com/focus/news/819957/replies?c=1 (Accessed 22 June 2013).

Beach, D.N. 1980. *The Shona and Zimbabwe 900–1850. An Outline of Shona History.* London: Heinemann.

Beach, D.N. 1984. *Zimbabwe before 1900.* Gweru: Mambo Press.

Bell, R. 1989. 'Narrative in African philosophy'. *Philosophy,* 64(249), 363–379.

Bell, R. 2002. *Understanding African Philosophy: A Cross-cultural Approach to Classical and Contemporary Issues.* London: Routledge.

Bellman, B.L. 1984. *The Language of Secrecy: Symbols and Metaphors in Poro Ritual.* New Brunswick: Rutgers University Press.

Benedict, R. 1946. *The Chrysanthemum and the Sword: Patterns of Japanese Culture.* Boston: Houghton Mifflin.

Bennett, J. (ed.)., 'Hume: An Enquiry Concerning Human Understanding', *Early Modern Texts* Available at: http://www.earlymoderntexts.com/assets/pdfs/hume1748.pdf (Accessed 14 May 2014).

Bernal, M. 1987. *Black Athena: The Afroasiatic Roots of Classical Civilization, Vol 1.* London: Free Association.

Bernasconi, R. 1997. 'African philosophy's challenge to continental philosophy'. In Eze, E.C. (ed.). *Postcolonial African Philosophy: A Critical Reader*. Cambridge: Blackwell, 183–196.

Bernstein, R.J. 1988. 'Metaphysics, critique, and utopia'. *The Review of Metaphysics*, 42(2), 255–273.

Bewaji, J.A.I. 2003. *Beauty and Culture: Perspectives in Black Aesthetics*. Ibadan: Spectrum.

Bond, G.C. and Ciekawy, D.M. 2001. 'Introduction: Contested domains in dialogues of "witchcraft"'. In Bond, G.C. and Ciekawy, D.M. (eds). *Witchcraft Dialogues: Anthropological and Philosophical Exchanges*. Ohio: Ohio University Centre for International Studies, 1–38.

Bourdillon, M. 1976. *The Shona Peoples: An Ethnology of the Contemporary Shona, with Special Reference to their Religion*. Gweru: Mambo Press.

Bourdillon, M. 1987. *The Shona Peoples: An Ethnography of the Contemporary Shona with Special Reference to their Religion*. Gweru: Mambo Press.

Brutt-Griffler, J. 2002. *World English: A Study of its Development*. Clevedon: Multilingual Matters Press.

Bucher, H. 1980. *Spirits and Power: An Analysis of Shona Cosmology*. Cape Town: Oxford University Press.

Bujo, B. 1998. *The Ethical Dimension of Community: The African Model and the Dialogue between North and South*. Nairobi: Paulines.

Bullock, C. 1927. *The Mashona: The Indigenous Natives of Southern Rhodesia*. Cape Town: Juta.

Burtt, E.A. 1945. 'What is metaphysics?' *The Philosophical Review*, 54(6), 533–557.

Chakrabarty, D. 2000. *Provincialising Europe: Postcolonial Thought and Historical Difference*. Princeton: Princeton University Press.

Chatterjee, P. 1997. *Our Modernity*. Dakar: CODESRIA.

Chavunduka, G. 1978. *Traditional Healers and the Shona Patient*. Gwelo: Mambo Press.

Chavunduka, G. 1980. 'Witchcraft and the law in Zimbabwe'. *Zambezia*, 8(2), 129–147.

Chavunduka, G. 1994. *Traditional Medicine in Modern Zimbabwe*. Harare: University of Zimbabwe Publications.

Chigwedere, A.S. 1985. *The Karanga Empire*. Harare: Books for Africa.

Chike, J. 2013. *Listening to Ourselves: A Multilingual Anthology of African Philosophy*. Albany, NY: State University of New York Press.

References

Chimhundu, H. 1992. 'Early missionaries and the ethnolinguistic factor in the "invention of tribalism" in Zimbabwe. *Journal of African History*, 33(1), 87–109.

Chimuka, A.T. 2008. '*Kugara hunzwana*: Conceptions of social cohesion in African culture'. *Council for Research in Values and Philosophy*. Available at: http://www.crvp.org/book/Series02/II-12/front.htm (Accessed 10 February 2012).

Chung, F. and Kaarsholm, P. 2006. *Re-living The Second Chimurenga: Memories from Zimbabwe's Liberation Struggle.* Uppsala: Nordic Africa Institute.

Colson, E. 1997. 'Places of power and shrines of the land'. *Paideuma*, 43, 47–57.

Crawford, J.R. 1967. *Witchcraft and Sorcery in Rhodesia.* London: Oxford University Press.

Creighton, M.R. 1990. 'Revisiting shame and guilt cultures: A forty-year pilgrimage'. *Ethos*, 18(3), 279–307.

D'Israel, I. (1766–1848). 'Curiosities of Literature. The philosophy of proverbs'. *Spamula*. Available at: http://www.spamula.net/col/archives/2006/02/the_philosophy.html (Accessed 13 May 2014).

Daneel, M.L. 1970. *The God of Matopo Hills: An Essay on the Mwari Cult in Rhodesia.* Leiden: Afrika Studiecentrum.

Deacon, M. 2002. 'The status of Father Tempels and ethnophilosophy in the discourse of African Philosophy'. In Coetzee, P. H. and Roux, A.P.J. (eds). *Philosophy from Africa: A Text with Readings.* Oxford: Oxford University Press, 97–111.

Derrida, J. 1967. *Of Grammatology*, trans. by Spivak, G.C. Baltimore: John Hopkins University.

Des Fontaine, F. 1974. Rhodesian African Art (1857–1974). Unpublished Masters Dissertation, University of Rhodes. Available at: http://contentpro.seals.ac.za/iii/cpro (Accessed September 2015).

Dewey, J.W. 1986. 'Shona male and female artistry'. *African Arts*, 19(3), 64–67.

Diagne, S.B. 2011. *African Art as Philosophy: Senghor, Bergson and the Idea of Negritude*, trans. by Jeffers, C. New York: Seagull.

Dilthey, W. 1986. 'The understanding of other persons and their life–expressions'. In Mueller-Vollmer, K. (ed.). *The Hermeneutics Reader.* London: Basil Blackwell, 152–164.

Diop, A.C. 1974. *The African Origin of Civilisation: Myth or Reality.* Westport: Lawrence Hill.

Diringer, D. 1978. 'Introduction Writing'. In Winckler, P.A. (ed.). *Reader in the History of Books and Printing*. Englewood: Information Handling Services, 64–71.

Doke, M.I. 1931. *A Comparative Study in Shona Phonetics*. Johannesburg: University of Witwatersrand Press.

Dussel, E. 2009. 'The new age in the history of philosophy'. *Philosophy and Social Criticism*, 35(5), 499–516.

Dussel, E. 2013. 'Agenda for a South–South philosophical dialogue'. *Human Architecture: Journal of the Sociology of Self-Knowledge*, 11(1), 3–18.

Dutton, D. 2006. A naturalist definition of art. *The Journal of Aesthetics and Art Criticism*, 64(3), 367–377.

Dziemidok, B. 2002. 'Aesthetics'. In Outhwaite, W. (ed.). *The Blackwell Dictionary of Modern Social Thought*. Blackwell Reference Online. Available at: http://www.blackwellreference.com/subscriber/tocnode (Accessed 10 April 2012).

Dzobo, N.K. 1992. 'African symbols and proverbs as sources of knowledge and truth'. In Wiredu, K. and Gyekye, K. (eds). *Person and Community: Ghanaian Philosophical Studies 1*. Washington DC: Council for Research in Values and Philosophy, 85–98.

Eze, E.C. 1997. 'Introduction: Philosophy and the (post)colonial'. In Eze, E. C. (ed.) *Postcolonial African Philosophy: A Critical Reader*. London: Blackwell, 1–21.

Eze, E.C. 1998. 'The problem of knowledge in "divination": The example of Ifa'. In Eze, E.C. (ed.). *African Philosophy: An Anthology*. Oxford: Blackwell, 173–175.

Fagan, B.M. 1984. 'The Zambezi and Limpopo basins: 1100–1500'. In Niane, D. T. (ed.). *UNESCO General History of Africa, Vol 4*, Paris: UNESCO, 525–550.

Feierman, S. 1999. 'Colonisers, scholars and the creation of invisible histories'. In Bonnell, V.E. and Hunt, L. (eds), *Beyond the Cultural Turn: New Directions in the Study of Culture and Society*. Berkeley: University of California Press, 181–216.

Feyerabend, P. 2011. *The Tyranny of Science*. Cambridge: Polity.

Floistad, G. 2007. 'Introduction'. In Floistad, G. (ed.). *Contemporary Philosophy: A New Survey, Vol. 9, Aesthetics and Philosophy*. Dordrecht: Springer, 1–23.

Fortune, G. 1973. 'Who was Mwari?' *Rhodesian History: The Journal of the Central African Historical Association*, 4, 1–20.

References

Foucault, M. 1979. *Discipline and Punish: The Birth of the Prison*, trans. by Sheridan, A. New York: Random House.

Fricker, M. 2007. *Epistemic Injustice: Power and the Ethics of Knowing.* Oxford: Oxford University Press.

Gardner, P. 2010. *Hermeneutics, History and Memory.* London: Routledge.

Garlake, P.S. 1973. *Great Zimbabwe.* London: Thames and Hudson.

Gbadegesin, S. 2002. 'Eniyan: The Yoruba concept of a person'. In Coetzee, P.H. and Roux, A.P.J. (eds). *Philosophy from Africa: A Text with Readings.* Oxford: Oxford University Press, 175–191.

Gelfand, M. 1959. *Shona Ritual.* Cape Town: Juta.

Gelfand, M. 1973. *The Genuine Shona: Survival Values of an African Culture.* Gweru: Mambo Press.

Giddens, A. 1999. Reith Lecture 3 'Tradition'. *BBC*. Available at: http://news.bbc.co.uk/hi/english/static/events/reith-99 (Accessed 19 May 2014).

Gieryn, T.F. 1999. *Cultural Boundaries Of Science: Credibility On The Line.* Chicago: University of Chicago Press.

Goddard, H.R. (1882–1945). 'US physicist and rocket engineer'. *NASA*. Available at: http://www.nasa.gov/centers/goddard/about/history/dr_goddard.html (Accessed 20 November 2015).

Goldman, A.I. 1999. *Knowledge in a Social World.* Oxford: Clarendon Press.

Gordon, L.R. 2005. 'From the President of the Caribbean Philosophical Association'. *Caribbean Studies*, 33(2), xv–xxii.

Gordon, L.R. 2011. 'Shifting the geography of reason in an age of disciplinary decadence'. *Transmodernity: Journal of Peripheral Cultural Production of the Luso-Hispanic World*, 1(2), 95–103.

Gracia, J.J.E. 1992. *Philosophy and its History: Issues in Philosophical Historiography.* New York: State University of New York.

Graw, K. 2009. 'Beyond expertise: Reflections on specialist agency and the autonomy of the divinatory ritual process'. *Africa: The Journal of the International African Institute*, 79(1), 92–109.

Grosfoguel, R. 2011. 'Decolonising post-colonial studies and paradigms of political economy: Transmodernity, decolonial thinking, and global coloniality'. *Transmodernity: Journal of Peripheral Cultural Production of the Luso-Hispanic World*, 1(1), 1–38.

Gross, D. 1992. *The Past in Ruins: Tradition and the Critique of Modernity.* Massachusetts: University of Massachusetts Press.

Guiley, R.E. 2009. *The Encyclopedia of Demons and Demonology.* New York: Facts on File.

Gyekye, K. 1987. *An Essay on African Philosophical Thought: The Akan Conceptual scheme*. Cambridge: Cambridge University Press.

Gyekye, K. 1996. *African Cultural Values: An Introduction*. Accra: Sankofa.

Gyekye, K. 1997. *Tradition and Modernity: Philosophical Reflections on the African Experience*. Oxford: Oxford University Press.

Gyekye, K. 2000. *Beyond Cultures: Perceiving a Common Humanity*. Accra: Ghana Academy of Arts and Sciences.

Gyekye, K. 2010. 'African ethics'. *Stanford Encyclopedia of Philosophy*. Available at: http://www.science.uva.nl/~seop/archives/spr2011/entries/african-ethics/ (Accessed 14 May 2014).

Hales, S.D. 2001. 'Evidence and the afterlife'. *Philosophia*, 28(1–4), 335–346.

Hallen, B. and Sodipo, J.O. 1997. *Knowledge, Belief and Witchcraft: Analytic Experiments in African Philosophy*. Stanford: Stanford University Press.

Hallen, B. 2002. *A Short History of African Philosophy*. Indiana: Indiana University Press.

Hallen, B. 2006. *African Philosophy: The Analytic Approach*. Asmara: Africa World Press.

Hamlyn, D.W. 1984. *Metaphysics*. Cambridge: Cambridge University Press.

Hamutyinei, M.A. and Plangger, A.B. 1974. *Tsumo–Shumo: Shona Proverbial Lore and Wisdom*. Gwelo: Mambo Press.

Hare, J. 2010. 'Religion and Morality'. *Stanford Encyclopedia of Philosophy*. Available at: http://plato.stanford.edu/entries/religion-morality/ (Accessed 14 May 2014).

Healy, P. 2000. 'Self-other relations and the rationality of cultures'. *Philosophy and Social Criticism*, 26(26), 61–83.

Hegel, G.F.W. 1956. *History of Philosophy*. New York: Dover.

Helms, M.W. 1988. *Ulysses' Sail: An Ethnographic Odyssey of Power, Knowledge and Geographical Distance*. New Jersey: Princeton University Press.

Hingley, R. 2009. 'Esoteric knowledge? Ancient bronze artefacts from Iron Age contexts'. *Proceedings of The Prehistoric Society*, 75, 143–165.

Hobsbawm, E. and Ranger, T. 1983. *The Invention of Tradition*. Cambridge University Press.

Horton, R. 1998. 'African traditional thought and western science'. In Eze, E.C. (ed.). *African Philosophy: An Anthology*. Oxford: Blackwell, 181–192.

Hountondji, P. 1983. *African Philosophy: Myth And Reality*. Indianapolis: Indiana University Press.

References

Hountondji, P. 1989. 'Occidentalism, elitism: Answer to two critiques', trans. by Chanda, J.K. *Quest: An African Journal of Philosophy*, 3(2), 3–29.

Hountondji, P. 2002. 'Knowledge Appropriation in a Postcolonial Context'. In Hoppers, C.O. (ed.). *Indigenous Knowledge and the Integration of Knowledge Systems: Towards a Philosophy of Articulation.* Claremont: New Africa, 23–38.

Hubbard, P. 2009. 'The Zimbabwe birds: Interpretation and symbolism'. *Honeyguide: Journal of Birdlife Zimbabwe*, 55(2), 109–116.

Huffman, T.N. 1981. 'Snakes and birds: Expressive space at Great Zimbabwe'. *African Studies*, 40(2), 131–150.

Huffman, T.N. 1985. 'The soapstone birds from Great Zimbabwe'. *African Arts*, 18(3), 68–100.

Huffman, T.N. 1996. *Snakes and Crocodiles: Power and Symbolism in Ancient Zimbabwe.* Johannesburg: Witwatersrand University Press.

Hume, D. 1748. 'An Enquiry Concerning Human Understanding'. In Bennett, J. (ed.). *Early Modern Texts.* Available at: http://www.earlymoderntexts.com/assets/pdfs/hume1748.pdf (Accessed 14 May 2014).

Hume, D. (1758). 'Essays and Treatises on Several Subjects Vol 1'. *David Hume.* Available at: http://www.davidhume.org/texts/etss.html. (Accessed 14 February 2013).

Huntington, S. 1993. 'The clash of civilizations?' *Foreign Affairs*, 72(3), 22–49.

James, G.M.J. 1954. *Stolen Legacy: Greek Philosophy is Stolen Egyptian Philosophy.* Washington: African American Images.

Kadiattu, K. 1998. *African Identities: Race, Nation and Culture in Ethnography, Pan-Africanism and Black Literatures.* London: Routledge.

Kant, I. 1997. 'On the different races of man'. In Eze, E.C. (ed.). *Race and the Enlightenment: A Reader.* Oxford: Blackwell, 38–64.

Kaphagawani, D.N. 1991. 'Bantu nomenclature and African philosophy'. In Oruka, H.O. (ed.). *Sage Philosophy: Indigenous Thinkers and Modern Debate on African Philosophy.* Nairobi: ACTS, 179–196.

Kaphagawani, D.N. and Malherbe, J.G. 2002. 'African epistemology'. In Coetzee, P.H. and Roux, A.P.J. (eds). *Philosophy from Africa: A Text with Readings.* Oxford: Oxford University Press, 219–229.

Kauffman, R. 1969. 'Some aspects of aesthetics in the Shona music of Rhodesia'. *Ethnomusicology*, 13(3), 507–511.

Kebede, M. 2004. *Africa's Quest for a Philosophy of Decolonization.* Amsterdam: Rodopi.

Keita, L. 1984. 'The African philosophical tradition'. In Wright, R.A. (ed.). *Philosophy: An Introduction.* Lanham: University Press of America, 57–76.

Keita, L. 1991. 'The search for a method in contemporary African philosophy'. In Oruka, O.H. (ed.). *Sage Philosophy: Indigenous Thinkers and Modern Debate on African Philosophy.* Nairobi: ACTS Press, 197–214.

Kimmerle, H. 1997a. 'The philosophical text in the African oral tradition: The opposition of oral and literate and the politics of difference'. *Intercultural Philosophy and Art.* Available at: http://www.galerie-inter.de/kimmerle/kimmerle3.htm (Accessed 20 April 2012).

Kimmerle, H. 1997b. 'Proverbs as a source of African philosophy: A methodological consideration'. In Saayman, W. (ed.). *Embracing the Baobab Tree: The African Proverb in the 21st Century.* Pretoria: Unisa Press, 58–71.

Ki-Zerbo, J. 1981. 'African prehistoric art'. In Ki-Zerbo, J. (ed.). *UNESCO General History of Africa Volume 1.* Berkeley: University of California Press, 656–686.

Kopytoff, I. 1971. 'Ancestors as elders in Africa'. *Centre for Social Anthropology and Computing.* Available at: http://lucy.ukc.ac.uk/era/ancestors/kopytoff.html (Accessed 31March 2014).

Kriel, A. 1971. *An African Horizon.* Cape Town: Permanent.

Kudadjie, J.N. 1997. 'Are African proverbs an ambiguous source of wisdom for living? A case study of Ga and Dangme proverbs'. In Saayman, W. (ed.). *Embracing the Baobab Tree: The African Proverb in the 21st Century.* Pretoria: Unisa Press, 177–192.

Kuper, H. 1955. *The Shona and Ndebele of Southern Rhodesia.* London: International African Institute.

La Gama, A. 2000. 'Art and oracle: Spirit voices of Africa'. *African Arts*, 33(1), 52–69.

Lan, D. 1985. *Guns and Rain: Guerrillas and Spirit Mediums in Zimbabwe.* Harare: Zimbabwe.

Lauer, H. 2006, 'Rethinking 'tradition vs. modernity': The social construction of the 'HIV/AIDS crisis' in Africa, *Culture Today*, 7(1), 120.

Lawrence, P.K. 1999. 'Enlightenment, modernity and war'. *History of the Human Sciences*, 12(1), 3–25.

Levy-Bruhl, L. 1923. *Primitive Mentality.* Boston: Beacon.

Linne, C. 1735. 'The God-given order of nature'. In Eze, E.C. (ed.). *Race and the Enlightenment: A Reader.* Oxford: Blackwell, 10–14.

Liszka, J.J. 1999. *Moral Competence: An Integral Approach to the Study of Ethics*. New Jersey: Prentice Hall.

Maffie, J. 2000. 'Alternative epistemologies and the value of truth'. *Social Epistemology: A Journal of Knowledge, Culture and Policy*, 14(4), 247–257.

Maffie, J. 2005. 'Ethnoepistemology'. *Internet Encyclopedia of Philosophy*. Available at: http://www.iep.utm.edu/ (Accessed 20 August 2012).

Maffie, J. 2009. '"In the end, we have the Gatlin gun, and they have not": Future prospects of indigenous knowledges'. *Futures*, 41, 53–65.

Makang, J. M. 1997. 'Of the good use of tradition: Keeping the critical perspective in African philosophy'. In Eze, E.C. (ed.). *Postcolonial African Philosophy: A Critical Reader*. London: Blackwell, 324–338.

Maldonado-Torres, N. 2007. 'On the coloniality of being'. *Cultural Studies*, 21(2&3), 240–270.

Mangena, F. 2014. 'Ethno-philosophy is rational: A repy to two famous critics' *Thought and Practice: A Journal of the Philosophical Association of Kenya*, 6(2), 23–38.

Martin, D.S. 2000. 'The burden of the name: Classifications and constructions of identity. The case of the 'Coloureds' in Cape Town (South Africa)'. *African Philosophy*, 13(2), 99–124.

Masolo, D.A. 1994. *African Philosophy In Search of Identity*. Indianapolis: Indiana University Press.

Masolo, D.A. 2000. 'From myth to reality: African philosophy at century end' *Research in African Literatures*, 31(1), 149–172.

Masolo, D.A. 2003. 'Philosophy and indigenous knowledge: An African perspective'. *Africa Today*, 50(2), 21–38.

Matenga, E. 2011. 'The soapstone birds of Great Zimbabwe: Archaeological heritage, religion and politics in postcolonial Zimbabwe and the return of cultural property'. Department of Archaeology and Ancient History, Uppsala University. Unpublished PhD Dissertation. Available at: www.dart-europe.eu/full.php?id=482623 (Accessed 21 April 2014).

Matereke, K. and Mungwini, P. 2012. 'The occult, politics and African modernities: The case of Zimbabwe's Diesel N'anga'. *African Identities*, 10(4), 423–438.

Mazrui, A.A. 1986. *The Africans: A Triple Heritage*. London: BBC.

Mazrui, A.A. and Ajayi, J.F.A. 1993. 'Trends in philosophy and science in Africa'. In Mazrui, A.A. and Wondji, C. (eds), *General History of Africa. Vol. 8: Africa since 1935*. UNESCO. Berkeley: University of California Press, 633–677.

Mbiti, J.S. 1969. *African Religions and Philosophy*. London: Heinemann

M'bow, A.M. 1981. 'Preface'. In Ki-zerbo, J. (ed.). *Unesco General History of Africa Vol 1*, Berkeley: University of California Press, xvii–xxi.

Menkiti, I.A. 2004. 'On the normative conception of a person'. In Wiredu, K. (ed.). *A Companion to African Philosophy*. Oxford: Blackwell, 324–330.

Metz, T. 2007. 'Towards an African moral theory'. *The Journal of Political Philosophy*, 15(3), 321–341.

Meyer, B. 2004. 'Christianity in Africa: From African independent to Pentecostal-charismatic churches'. *Annual Review of Anthropology*, 33, 447–474.

Mieder, W. 2004. *Proverbs: A Handbook*. Westport, C.T: Greenwood.

Mignolo, W.D. 2011. *The Darker Side of Western Modernity: Global Futures, Decolonial Options*. Durham: Duke University Press.

Miller, C.L. 1990. *Theories of Africans: Francophone Literature and Anthropology in Africa*. Chicago: The University of Chicago Press.

Mills, C.W. 1988. 'Alternative epistemologies'. *Social Theory and Practice*, 14(3), 237–263.

Moore, H.L. and Sanders, T. 2001. *Magical Interpretations, Material Realities: Modernity, Witchcraft and the Occult in Postcolonial Africa*. London: Routledge.

Mudenge, S.I.G. 1988. *A Political History of Munhumutapa*. Harare: Zimbabwe Publishing House.

Mudimbe, V.Y. 1983. 'African philosophy as ideological practice: The case of French speaking Africa'. *African Studies Review*, 26(3&4), 133–154.

Mudimbe, V.Y. 1988. *The Invention of Africa*. London: James Carrey.

Mudimbe, V.Y. 1997. *Tales of Faith: Religion as Political Performance in Central Africa*. London: The Athlone Press.

Mungwini, P. 2011a. 'Philosophy and tradition in Africa': Critical reflections on the power and vestiges of colonial nomenclature'. *Thought and Practice: Journal of the Philosophical Association of Kenya*, 3(1), 1–19.

Mungwini, P. 2011b. 'The challenges of revitalizing an indigenous and Afrocentric moral theory in postcolonial education in Zimbabwe'. *Educational Philosophy and Theory*, 43(7), 773–787.

Mungwini, P. 2011c. 'Orality and ordinary language philosophy: Revisiting the intellectual heritage of Africa's indigenous cultures'. *Southern African Journal of Folklore Studies*, 21(2), 1–11.

References

Mungwini, P. 2012. 'Surveillance and cultural panopticism: Situating Foucault in African modernities'. *South African Journal of Philosophy*, 31(2), 340–353.

Mungwini, P. 2013. 'AIDS and the challenge of rethinking sex education in postcolonial Africa: An Afro-philosophical perspective'. In Ramose, M.B. (ed.). *Hegel's Twilight: Liber Amicorum Discipulorumque: Pro Heinz Kimmerle, Amsterdam: Rodopi*. (Studies in Intercultural Philosophy, 23, 193–211).

Mungwini, P. 2014. 'The African renaissance and the quest for epistemic liberation'. *Australasian Review of African Studies*, 35(2), 88–108.

Mungwini, P. 2015. 'Dialogue as the negation of hegemony: An African perspective'. *South African Journal of Philosophy*, 34(4), 395–407.

Murove, M. 2009a. 'Introduction'. In Murove, M. (ed.). *African Ethics: An Anthology of Comparative and Applied Ethics*. Durban: UKZN Press, xiv–xvi.

Murove, M. 2009b. 'An African environmental ethic based on the concepts of *ukama* and *ubuntu*'. In Murove, M. (ed.). *African Ethics: An Anthology of Comparative and Applied Ethics*. UKZN Press, 315–331.

Mutsvairo, S. 1978. 'Oral literature in Zimbabwe: An analytic-interpretive approach'. Unpublished PhD Thesis. Department Of African Studies and Research Programme. Howard University.

Nasseem, S.B. 2002. 'African heritage and contemporary life'. In Coetzee, P.H. and Roux, A.P.J. (eds). *Philosophy from Africa: A Text with Readings*. Oxford: Oxford University Press, 259–271.

Ndlovu-Gatsheni, S.J. 2013. *Coloniality of Power in Postcolonial Africa: Myths of Decolonization*. Dakar: CODESRIA.

Nelson, H.D. 1983. *Zimbabwe a Country Study*. Washington, DC: Foreign Area Studies.

Nkrumah, K. 1964. *Conscienscism: Philosophy and Ideology of De-Colonization and Development with Particular Reference to the African Revolution*. New York: Monthly Review Press.

Nkulu-Nsengha, M. 2002. 'African epistemology'. In Asante, M.K and Mazama, A. (eds). *Encyclopedia of Black Studies*. Available at: http://knowledge.sagepub.com/view/blackstudies/n16.xml. (Accessed 20 April 2014).

Nooter, M.H. 1993. 'Introduction: The aesthetics and politics of things unseen'. In Nooter M.H. (ed.). *Secrecy: African Art That Conceals and Reveals*. New York: The Museum for African Art, 23–39.

Norris, C. nd. 'Derrida and Oralcy: Grammatology revisited'. Available at: http://www2.lingue.unibo.it/acume/acumedvd/Essays%20ACUME/Norris.pdf (Accessed 21 October 2013).

Nyamnjoh, F.B. 2004. 'A relevant education for African development: Some epistemological considerations'. *Africa Development*, 29(1), 161–184.

Obenga, T. 2004. 'Egypt: Ancient history of African philosophy'. In Wiredu, K. (ed.). *A Companion to African Philosophy*. Oxford: Blackwell, 31–49.

Oberheim, E. 2011. 'Editor's introduction'. In Feyerabend, P. *The Tyranny of Science*. Cambridge: Polity Press, vii–xii.

O'Hear, A. 1985. *What Philosophy is: An Introduction to Contemporary Philosophy*. New York: Penguin.

Okere, T. 1983. *African Philosophy: A Historico-Hermeneutical Investigation of the Conditions of its Possibility*. Lanham, MD: University Press of America.

Okere, T. 1996. 'Names as building blocks of an African philosophy'. In Okere, T. (ed.). *Identity and Change: Nigerian Philosophical Studies 1*. Washington, DC: Council for Research in Values and Philosophy, 133–149.

Okere, T. 2003. 'Philosophy and intercultural dialogue'. *Urbaniana University*. http://www.urbaniana.edu/news2004/12_03_04.htm. (Accessed 8 March 2015).

Okere, T. 2005. 'Is there one science, Western science?' *Africa Development*, 30(3), 20–34.

Okpewho, I. 1977. 'Principles of traditional African art'. *The Journal of Aesthetics and Art Criticism*, 35(3), 301–313.

Omoregbe, J. 1990. *Knowing Philosophy: A General Introduction*. Lagos: Joja Press.

Onyewuenyi, I. 2000. 'Traditional African aesthetics: A philosophical perspective'. In Coetzee, P.H. and Roux, A.P.J. (eds). *Philosophy from Africa: A Text with Readings*. Oxford: Oxford University Press, 396–400.

Osuagwu, I.M. 1999. *A Contemporary History of African Philosophy*. Owerri: Amamihe.

Outlaw, L. 1996. *On Race and Philosophy*. New York: Routledge.

Owomoyela, O. 1987. 'Africa and the imperative of philosophy: A skeptical consideration'. *African Studies Review*, 30(1), 79–99.

Palgi, P and Abramovitch, H. 1984. 'Death: A cross-cultural perspective'. *Annual Review of Anthropology*, 13, 385–417.

Palmer, R.E. 1969. *Hermeneutics*. Evanston: Northwestern University Press.

References

Parker, G.W. 1917. 'The African origin of Grecian civilization'. *Journal of Negro History*, 2(3), 334–344

Pearce, C. 1990. '"Tsika", "hunhu" and the moral education of primary school children'. *Zambezia*, 17(2), 145–160.

Pearce, C. 1992. 'African philosophy and the sociological thesis, *Philosophy of the Social Sciences*, 22(4), 440–460.

Peek, P.M. 1991. *African Divination Systems: Ways of Knowing*. Indianapolis: Indiana University Press.

Pikirayi, I. 2006. 'The kingdom, the power and forevermore: Zimbabwe culture in contemporary art and architecture'. *Journal of Southern African Studies*, 23(4), 755–770.

Plant, B.K. 2008. 'Secret, powerful, and the stuff of legends: Revisiting theories of invented tradition'. *The Canadian Journal of Native Studies*, 28(1), 175–194.

Pongweni, A.J. 1983. *What's in a Name? A Case Study of Shona Nomenclature*. Gweru: Mambo Press.

Quine, W.V. 1948. 'On what there is'. *Review of Metaphysics*, 2, 21–38.

Ramose M.B. 1995. 'Specific African thought structures and their possible contribution to world peace'. In Von Heinrich Beck, H. and Schadel, E. (eds). *Kreativer Friede Durch Begegnug Der Weltkulturen*. Berlin: Peter Lang, 227–251.

Ramose, M.B. 1998. 'Foreword'. In Seepe, S. (ed.). *Black Perspective(s) on Tertiary Institutional Transformation*. Johannesburg: Vivlia, iv–vii.

Ramose, M.B. 1999. *African Philosophy through Ubuntu*. Harare: Mond.

Ramose, M.B. 2006. 'Alexis Kagame on the Bantu philosophy of be-ing, Aristotle's categoriae, and de-interpretation'. In Botz-Bornstein. T. and Hengelbrock, J. (eds). *Re-ethnicising the Minds? Cultural Revival in Contemporary Thought*. Amsterdam: Rodopi, 53–61.

Ramose, M.B. 2007. 'But Hans Kelsen was not born in Africa: A reply to Thaddeus Metz'. *South African Journal of Philosophy*, 26(4), 347–355.

Ramose, M.B. 2008. 'Birth, death and truth: An essay in memory of Emmanuel Chukwudi Eze'. *South African Journal of Philosophy*, 27(4), 325–331.

Ramose M.B. 2011. 'African metaphysics: Introductory remarks'. *Advanced African Philosophy Tutorial Letter 501*. Department of Philosophy and Systematic Theology, University of South Africa.

Ranger, T.O. 1974. 'The meaning of Mwari'. *Rhodesian History: The Journal of the Central African Historical Association*, 5, 5–17.

Ranger, T.O. 1985a. 'The invention of tribalism in Zimbabwe'. *Mambo Occasional Papers-Socio-Economic Series No. 19*. Gweru: Mambo Press.

Ranger, T.O. 1985b. *Peasant Consciousness and Guerrilla War in Zimbabwe*. Harare: Zimbabwe.

Ranger, T.O. 1993. 'The invention of tradition revisited: The case of colonial Africa'. In Ranger, T. and Vaughan, O. (eds). *Legitimacy and the State in Twentieth Century Africa: Essays in Honour of A.H.M. Greene*. London: Macmillan, 5–50.

Ranger, T.O. 1999. *Voices from the Rocks: Nature, Culture and History in the Matopos Hills of Zimbabwe*. Harare: Baobab Books.

Ranger, T.O. 2006. 'African religion, witchcraft and liberation war in Zimbabwe'. In Nicolini, B. (ed.). *Studies in Witchcraft, Magic, War and Peace in Africa: Nineteenth and Twentieth Centuries*. Lewiston, NY: Edwin Mellen, 351–378.

Rengger, N.J. 2000. *International Relations, Political Theory and the Problem of Order: Beyond International Relations Theory?* London: Routledge.

Ricoeur P. 1974. *The Conflict of Interpretations: Essays in Hermeneutics*. Evanston: Northwestern University Press.

Roberts, A. 1993. 'Insight, or, not seeing is believing'. In Nooter, M.H. (ed.). *Secrecy: African Art that Conceals and Reveals*. New York: The Museum for African Art, 65–79.

Rukuni, M. 2009. *Leading Afrika*. Johannesburg: Penguin.

Saayman, W. (ed.). 1997. *Embracing the Baobab Tree: The African Proverb in the 21st Century*. Pretoria: Unisa Press.

Samkange, S. and Samkange, T.M. 1980. *Hunhuism or Ubuntuism: A Zimbabwean Indigenous Political Philosophy*. Salisbury: Graham.

Sanders, T. 2003. 'Reconsidering witchcraft: Postcolonial Africa and analytic (un)certainties'. *American Anthropologist*, 105(2), 338–352.

Santos, B.S., Nunes, J.A. and Meneses, M.P. 2007. 'Opening up the canon of knowledge and recognition of difference'. In Santos, B.S. (ed.). *Another Knowledge Is Possible*. London: Verso, xix–lxii.

Schlesinger, G.N. 1981. What is metaphysics? *American Philosophical Quarterly*, 18(3), 229–235.

Senner, W.M. 1989. 'Theories and myths on the origin of writing: A historical overview'. In Senner, W.M. (ed.). *The Origins Of Writing*. Lincoln: University of Nebraska Press, 1–26.

Serequeberhan, T. 1994. *The Hermeneutics of African Philosophy: Horizon and Discourse*. New York: Routledge.

References

Shils, E. 1981. *Tradition*. Chicago: University of Chicago Press.

Silberbauer, G. 1993. 'Ethics in small-scale societies'. In Singer, P. (ed.). *A Companion To Ethics*. Oxford: Wiley Blackwell, 13–28.

Smith, H. 1980. 'Western and comparative perspectives on truth'. *Philosophy East and West*, 30(4), 425–437.

Smith, T.V. and Grene, M. (eds). 1957. *Philosophers Speak For Themselves. Berkeley, Hume, and Kant*. Chicago: University of Chicago Press.

Sogolo, G.S. 2002. 'The concept of cause in African thought'. In Coetzee, P.H. and Roux, A.P.J. (eds). *Philosophy from Africa: A Text with Readings*. Oxford: Oxford University Press, 192–199.

Southern Rhodesia. 1929. *Southern Rhodesia Report of the Director of Native Development for the year 1929*. Salisbury, Southern Rhodesia: Government Printers.

Soyinka, W. 1999. *The Burden of Memory, the Muse of Forgiveness*. Oxford: Oxford University Press.

Spear, T. 2003. 'Neo-traditionalism and the limits of invention in British colonial Africa'. *Journal of African History*, 44, 3–27.

Sumner, C. 1999. 'The proverb and oral society'. *New Political Science*, 21(1), 11–31.

Tabensky, A.P. 2008. 'The postcolonial heart of African philosophy'. *South African Journal of Philosophy*, 27(4), 285–295.

Tatarkiewicz, W. 1971. 'What is art? The problem of definition today'. *British Journal of Aesthetics*, 11(2), 134–153.

Taylor, A. 1981. 'The wisdom of many and the wit of one'. In Mieder, W. & Dundes, A. (eds). *The Wisdom of Many: Essays on the Proverb*. Wisconsin: The University of Wisconsin Press, 3–9.

Tempels, P. 1969. *Bantu Philosophy*. Paris: Presence Africaine.

Ter Haar, G. 2007. 'Introduction: The evil called witchcraft'. In Ter Haar, G. (ed.). *Imagining Evil: Witchcraft Beliefs and Accusations in Contemporary Africa*. Asmara: Africa World Press, 1–30.

Ter Haar, G. and Ellis, S. 2009. 'The occult does not exist: A response to Terence Ranger'. *Africa: The Journal of the International African Institute*, 79(3), 399–412

Thayer-Bacon, B.J. nd. 'Humanity educating philosophy'. Available at: https://www.bu.edu/wcp/Papers/Educ/EducThay.htm (Accessed 03 September 2015).

Trevelyan, G.M. 1949. *An Autobiography And Other Essays*. London: Longman.

Tutu, D. 1999. *No Future Without Forgiveness*. Doubleday: University of Michigan.

Unesco. 1945. 'Constitution of the United Nations' educational, scientific and cultural organization'. UNESCO. Available at: http://portal.unesco.org/en/ev.php (Accessed 12 November 2015).

Unesco. 1995. 'Paris Declaration for Philosophy'. UNESCO. Available at: http://www.unesco.org (Accessed 12 November 2015).

Van Binsbergen, W. 1981. *Religious Change in Zambia: Exploratory Studies*. London: Kegan Paul.

Van Binsbergen, W. (ed.). 2011. *Black Athena Comes Of Age: Towards A Constructive Re-Assessment*. Berlin: Lit Verlarg Munster.

Van Hensbroek, P.B. 2013. 'Beyond crossing borders, beyond intercultural philosophy'. In Ramose M.B. (ed.). *Hegel's Twilight, Studies in Intercultural Philosophy 23*, Amsterdam: Rodopi, 31–41.

Vansina, J. 1990. *Paths in the Rainforests: Toward a History of Political Tradition in Equatorial Africa*. London: James Currey.

Varzi, A.C. 2011. 'On doing ontology without metaphysics'. *Philosophical Perspectives*, 25(1), 407–423.

Vaz, P. and Bruno, F. 2003. 'Types of self-surveillance: From abnormality to individuals "at risk"'. *Surveillance and Society*, 1(3), 272–291.

Wallner, F.G. 2010. 'Intercultural philosophy: The Viennese Programme'. In Allner, F.G., Schmidsberger, F. and Wimmer, F.M. (eds)., *Intercultural Philosophy: New Aspects and Methods*. Frankfurt: Peter Lang, 13–20.

Wanjohi, G.J. 1997. 'The ontology, epistemology, and ethics inherent in proverbs: The case of the Gikuyu'. In Saayman, W. (ed.). *Embracing the Baobab Tree: The African Proverb in the 21st Century*. Pretoria: Unisa Press, 72–83.

Wanjohi, G.J. 2008. *The Wisdom and Philosophy of African Proverbs: The Gikuyu World-View*. Nairobi: Nyaturima.

Wa Thiong'o, N. 2013. 'Tongue and pen: A challenge to philosophers from Africa'. *Journal of African Cultural Studies*, 25(2), 158–163.

Wimmer, F.M. 2002. *Essays on Intercultural Philosophy*. Chennai: Satya Nilayam.

Wimmer, F.M. 2010. 'Is intercultural philosophy a new branch or a new orientation in philosophy?' In Allner, F.G., Schmidsberger, F. and Wimmer, F.M. (eds), *Intercultural Philosophy: New Aspects and Methods*. Frankfurt: Peter Lang, 21–39.

References

Winch, P. 1964. 'Understanding a primitive society'. *American Philosophical Quarterly*, 1(4), 307–324.

Wingo, A.H. 2004. 'The many-layered aesthetics of African art'. In Wiredu, K. (ed.). *A Companion to African Philosophy*. Oxford: Blackwell, 425–432.

Wiredu, K. 1980. *Philosophy and an African Culture*. Cambridge: Cambridge University Press.

Wiredu, K. 1984. 'How not to compare African thought with Western thought'. In Wright, R.A. (ed.). *African Philosophy: An Introduction*. New York: University Press of America, 149–162.

Wiredu, K. 1992. 'The Ghanaian tradition of philosophy'. In Wiredu, K and Gyekye, K. (eds). *Person and Community: Ghanaian Philosophical Studies, Vol.1*. Washington, DC: Council for Research in Values and Philosophy, 1–12.

Wiredu, K. 1995. 'Metaphysics in Africa'. In Kim, J. and Sosa, E. (eds). *A Companion to Metaphysics: Blackwell Reference Online*. Available at: http://www.blackwellreference.com (Accessed 17 September 2015).

Wiredu, K. 1996. *Cultural Universals and Particulars*. Bloomington: Indiana University Press.

Wiredu, K. 1998. 'Toward decolonising African Philosophy and Religion', *African Studies Quarterly*, 1(4), 17–46.

Wiredu, K. 2002a. 'On decolonizing African religions'. In Coetzee, P.H. and Roux, A. P.J. (eds). *Philosophy from Africa: A Text with Readings*. Oxford: Oxford University Press, 20–34.

Wiredu, K. 2002b. 'The moral foundations of an African culture'. In Coetzee, P.H. and Roux, A.P.J. (eds). *Philosophy from Africa: A Text with Readings*. Oxford: Oxford University Press, 287–296.

Wiredu, K. 2009. 'An oral philosophy of personhood: Comments on philosophy and orality'. *Research in African Literatures*, 40(1), 8–18.

Wiredu, K. 2010. 'African religions from a philosophical point of view'. In Taliafero, C., Draper, P. and Quinn, P.L. (eds). *A Companion to Philosophy of Religion*. Oxford: Blackwell, 34–43.

Yai, O. 1977. 'Theory and practice in African philosophy: The poverty of speculative philosophy'. *Second Order: An African Journal of Philosophy*, 6(2), 3–20.

Yankah, K. 1984. 'Do proverbs contradict?' *Folklore Forum*, 17, 2–19.

Zeleza, P.T. 2006. 'The inventions of African identities and languages: The discursive and developmental implications'. In Arasanyin, O.F. and Pemberton, M.A. (eds). *Selected Proceedings of the 36th Annual Conference on African Linguistics*, Somerville, MA: Cascadilla Proceedings Project, 14–26.

Index

A

Abimbola, W. 124
aesthetics *see* philosophy
Africa
    naming 55
    pre-colonial 28, 30, 35, 37–38,
        49–50, 60–63, 66, 884, 116, 143,
        158
    postcolonial 18–19, 24, 27–30,
        35, 47, 58–59, 84, 88–89, 107,
        115, 144, 162, 184
African
    archive 3, 60, 116, 185
    culture 32, 35, 39, 62, 89–90, 110,
        164–165, 174
    intellectual heritage 3, 9–10,
        27–32, 185
    metaphysics 70, 74–76, 100, 109,
        133
    modernity 88, 110, 162
    nationalists 56
    philosophers 8–10, 12–13, 15–16,
        18, 24–25, 28, 38, 45–46, 75,
        100, 103, 139, 142, 165, 184
    Renaissance 90
    traditional heritage 15–16, 22–23,
        25, 27, 31, 33, 38, 158, 169–170,
        174–175
Afrocentrism 30, 56, 143
agency 61–62
Akan people 9, 14, 80, 95, 122, 131
Alderman, D.H. 57

analytic philosophy *see* philosophy
ancestors 84–86, 178
Anderson, Benedict 63
anthropology and anthropologists 3,
    6, 33–34, 62, 65, 100–103, 109, 115,
    130, 142, 147, 182
Anyanwu, K.C. 171–172
Appiah, Kwame Anthony 15, 50–51
appropriation 6, 9, 74, 80, 88, 165
Aquinas, Thomas 92
arche-ecriture *see* writing
archive *see* Africa
architecture 80, 147, 168, 175, 179
Aristotle (384–322 BC) 11, 17, 69, 74,
    112, 146
art and artists 6, 24, 164, 167, 169–
    170, 175–176, 182–183
Asante, M.K. 30
Asouzu, Innocent 109
axiology 21
Azikiwe, Mnandi 17

B

Bailey, M.D. 101–104
Beach, D.N. 50–51, 53–54, 83
beauty 165–166, 172–174
be-ing 16, 42, 61, 76–77, 134, 140,
    145, 164
Bell, Richard 34–35, 86, 164, 170
Benedict, Ruth 63, 147
Bernal, M. 28–29
Bernstein, R.J. 68–69, 72–73

Bewaji, J.A.I. 165–167, 181–182
Bourdillon, M. 52–53, 105
brotherhood 90, 151
Brutt-Griffler, J. 52–53
Bullock, C. 53, 80–81
burials and burial sites 99–100, 110

C

carvings 37, 169, 176–178
causality 69, 91–94, 101
cave art *see* rock art
ceremonies 76, 97, 120, 168, 174, 176, 182
Chakrabarty, D. 4
character 44, 96, 121, 130, 138–140, 145–149, 156, 168, 172–174
Chatterjee, P. 87
Chavunduka, Gordon 99, 102–103, 105, 110
chiefs and chieftains 52, 64, 82–83, 120, 178, 182
Chigwedere, Aeneas 50, 56
Chimhundu, H. 51–52, 56
chinobhuruka chinomhara 108
chinokura chichirwa mwana wengwe wemunhu anodzidza murairo 155
chinonzi munhu hunhu 144
Chiri pamumwe chiri padanda 155
chirungu (Western values) 91
chisingaperi chinoshura 160
chiShona see Shona
chivanhu (beliefs) 86–90, 98, 100–102, 105, 106, 107, 115, 121, 124, 128, 132, 135, 164, 169, 170, 174, 175, 180, 182
chokwadi (truth) 86–91, 101, 110
Christianity 78–80, 91, 102–103, 106, 109, 124, 132–133, 154, 180, 182
churches 23, 106, 111, 133
clans 83, 96, 120, 140, 181
classification 12–14, 16, 52–53, 63, 69, 166
colonial administration 19, 61, 63, 102
colonialism 9, 18–19, 26, 30, 54, 56, 58, 61–62, 67, 91, 116, 157–159
communication 31, 76, 85, 90, 93, 112, 117, 151, 181

conduct 6, 22, 41, 90, 138–139, 148–149, 162
correspondence theory of truth *see* truth
cosmology 67, 72–78, 101–102, 105, 118, 120, 128, 136, 171, 175, 182
Council for Research in Values and Philosophy 2, 7
cremation 97, 99, 110
criminal justice 152
critical school *see* philosophy
critical self-reflection 22
crocodiles 177–178, 182
cultural school *see* philosophy
culture *see* Africa
customs 6, 38, 55, 60–63, 66, 86, 89–90, 139, 151–156, 160

D

dance and dancers 168, 172
Daneel, M.L. 78–80
Deacon, M. 13–16
death 76, 85–86, 91–92, 95–101, 105, 110, 134, 150, 155, 158–159, 178
decoloniality 18–20, 47, 59, 136
decoration 168, 179
Derrida, Jacques 24, 35–36, 47
dhimba kushaya besu usati inyana 108
dialogue 2, 10, 34–35, 42, 65, 84, 88, 161–163, 169, 185
dindingwe rinonaka richakweva rimwe kana rokweviwa roti mavara angu azara ivhu 156
Diop, A.C. 3, 28
disputes 11, 20, 34, 71, 150, 166
D'Israeli, I. 40, 45, 47
diversity 1, 18, 24–25, 68, 167
divination and diviners 34, 90, 108, 127–129, 132–133, 135–137, 168, 176–180, 182
Doke, Clemmons 52–53, 56
drawings *see* rock art
Dziemidok, Bohdan 166, 183
Dzivaguru (the great pool) 79–80

E

education 33, 100, 126, 144–149, 155, 160, 162

Index

Egypt 3, 28, 30
elders 34, 41–42, 44–45, 48, 61, 82–86, 90, 120, 126, 129, 140, 151–153, 158–160, 173
empiricism 25, 77, 98, 122
   see also philosophy
epistemology 21, 33, 46–47, 91, 115–120, 126–127, 134, 140, 170
   ethnoepistemology 6, 114–115
esoteric knowledge 121, 124–126, 128, 175
ethics 109, 134, 138–139, 141, 146, 151, 157–160, 162, 171
   see also philosophy
ethnoepistemology 6, 114–115
ethnophilosophy *see* philosophy
ethnoscience 47, 115
eurocentricism 5, 9, 25, 30, 56, 58
European modernity 18–19, 86–87
extrahuman beings 76
Eze, E.C. 18, 27, 47, 136

F

Fanon, Franz 17
feminist philosophy 24, 118
fertility 78–79, 90, 168
Feyerabend, Paul 23–24, 47, 133
figurative language 49, 97
Floistad, G. 170–171
folktales 27
Fontaine, Des 79, 168
forefathers 46, 151, 159, 169
forests 159
Foucault, Michel 24, 110, 147, 149, 162
Fricker, M. 19–20

G

Gardner, P. 31
gaze 51, 56, 148–149
gender 79, 115, 159
Ghana 5, 9, 80, 95, 122, 162
Giddens, Anthony 65, 67
Goddard, Robert 1, 7
Goldman, A.I. 112
Great Zimbabwe complex *see* Zimbabwe

Gross, D. 88
Guiley, R. 103–104
guilt culture *see* shame culture
Guyu kutsvukira kunze mukati muzere makonye 173
Gyekye, K. 9, 39–41, 49, 65–66, 138–140, 146, 157, 162, 172, 180

H

Hamlyn, D.W. 69–70, 72
hakata (bones/dice) 128, 178
hana (heart) 96–97
healers and healing 34, 54, 90, 99, 127, 159, 176
hegemonic culture 2, 25–26, 29–30, 61, 63, 114, 117, 161, 163, 185
Heraclitus (535–475 BC) 39, 160
hermeneutics 24, 31–32
   see also philosophy
historico-philosophical 112, 185
honesty 122, 152
Hountondji, P. 10–11, 15, 21–22, 46
Hume, David 70, 72
hunhu 90–91, 110, 140, 143–146 *see also* ubuntu
hunhuism 8, 143–144
hunters and hunting 121, 159, 179
Huntington, S. 20, 185
hybridation 88

I

ibwa inoroverwa pachinyiro 146
identity 15, 34–35, 49–50, 54–59, 62–66, 82, 88–90, 95–97, 171, 180, 184–185
ideology 2, 12, 15–19, 24, 27, 57, 109, 116–117, 143–144, 180
idioms 27, 49
illiteracy 33, 37
imagination 6, 27, 37, 60, 63, 81, 164, 167, 170, 175, 182–183
immortality 4, 58, 95, 149, 185
imperialism 21, 54, 87, 115
indigenous cultures 12, 22, 27, 49, 53, 55, 58–60, 102, 112–113, 132, 138–139, 161, 164, 180, 185
Ini ndiri muroyi ndapikwa 104

intellectual traditions 3–4
intelligibilities 49, 66, 94, 129, 132, 171
interpretation 32, 36, 38, 41, 49, 68, 139, 142, 147, 154, 168, 170
invisible beings 76, 82, 85–86, 91, 99, 108, 121, 123, 128, 136, 151, 158, 171, 181
Islam 80, 102
iva munhu pavanhu 144

J

Jesus Christ 91, 131

K

Kadiattu, K. 33
Kagame, Alexis 14, 16–17
Kant, Immanuel 24, 39, 72–73, 98, 141
Karanga 51–53, 55
Kaunda, Kenneth 17
Kauffman, R. 166, 174
Kebede, M. 25–26, 32
Keita, L. 11, 33
Kimmerle, H. 39, 154
kings and kingship 82–84, 120, 178, 180
Ki-Zerbo, J. 37, 117, 120 167, 184
knowledge-belief-practice 121
knowledge claims 114, 119, 123, 134, 136
knowledges 113–115, 132, 136, 185
Kolakowski, Leszek 73
Kopytoff, I. 85–86
Kramer, Heinrich 101
Kriel, A. 43, 44, 51
Kudadjie, J.N. 41
kudyidzana (use of resources by all and for all) 154
kugamuchirana (tolerance and acceptance) 154
kugara hunzwana (mutual co-existence) 154
kugarisana nevamwe (living well with others) 153
kugarisana savanhu (living like true human beings) 152
kunaka (beauty) 172–173
Kunaka hakudyiwi 173
kunzwa (to hear) 172
kunzwana (living well together) 152, 154
kuona (to see) 172
kureva nemazvo (report as it is) 121
kuromba (magic/witchcraft) 83
Kusaziva kwakafana nekufa 134
kusimudza hapwa (exposing one's armpit) 152
kutaura nomumutsetse (report in a straight line) 121
kutsiura (correct) 146
kutsva kwendebvu varume tinodzimurana 156
Kuva munhu muvanhu 144–145
kuvimbika (being one who can be trusted) 152–153
kuwadzana (living well together) 152
kuyanana (peaceful co-existence) 154

L

land 50, 82–84, 100, 120, 157, 161
landscape 33, 57, 73, 84, 86, 88, 116, 170
language 5, 16, 31–34, 36–38, 44, 49–55, 64, 75, 80–81, 89, 110, 134, 154, 181
    Nguni languages 53, 144
laws and legislation 100, 107, 109, 155, 160, 171
liberation and revolution 17, 19, 25–26, 29, 47, 84, 115–116, 158, 179, 184
linguistics 29, 37, 39, 49, 52–54, 80–81
literacy 33, 35–36
libraries 69
living dead 76–77, 81–82, 84–85, 90, 97, 99–100, 148, 151, 160
local 4, 8, 51, 55, 107, 114–115
logic 5, 19, 39, 66, 74, 99, 103, 115, 124, 132–133, 135, 142, 170, 174–175

logical positivism 23, 70–72
    see also philosophy
logico-scientific reason 23

M

madzinza (kinship) 52
magic 50, 83–84, 90, 94, 101–108, 111, 119, 121, 126–128, 131
magicians 83, 90, 104
magicomedicinal practice 102
Makang, J.M. 48, 162
Maldonaldo-Torres, N. 19–20
Malinowski, Bronislaw 103
Mangena, F. 15
Mapungubwe 3, 9
Martin, D.S. 57–58
Masolo, D.A.
Masrui, A.A. #34, 49, 88
Matopos 78
Mazano moto anogokwa kune vamwe 134
Mbire 56
Mbiti, J.S. 81, 97–98
mbudzi kudya mufenje hufana nyina 145
medicine 47, 76, 90, 96–97, 102–103, 119, 121, 126, 171, 178
metaphor 41, 49, 131, 157
metaphysics 69
    see also African metaphysics, Shona metaphysics
methodology 5, 11–12, 23–25, 31, 36, 39, 117, 124–127, 131, 147
Metz, Thaddeus 141–142
mhepo (winds) 91–92
mhondoro (tribal spirits) 83, 85
Mieder, W. 44–45
Mignolo, W.D. 19–21
Miller, C.L. 33–34
miracle/s 98, 132
missionaries 14, 52, 61–62, 80, 102–103, 130
modernity *see* African modernity, European modernity

monopolies 100, 116–117
morality 6, 90, 122
    see also Shona morality
morphology 166
Mudenge, S.I.G. 50, 54
Mudimbe, V. 11, 21–22, 34, 88, 157–158
mudzimu (spirits of the ancestors) 83
mukadzi munaku akasaba anoroya 173
munhu asina nyadzi haasi munhu 146–147
munhu munhu nevanhu 141
munhu vanhu 144
Mungwaru haati chandareva ndicho asi benzi ndichandagwinyira 135
muroyi munhu kubaiwa anochemawo 154
Murove, M. 139, 157
music 47, 115, 168–169, 175
Musikavanhu (God) 42, 79–80
muti (medicine) 106
Mutsvairo, Solomon 44, 56
muviri (physical body) 95, 97
Mwari 78–82, 84–85, 90, 109–110, 180–182
    shrine 81, 180
mweya (soul/spirit) 95, 97
mwoyo momunhu ndiye munhu kwete chiso 173
mysticism 25, 85, 101, 106, 135, 170, 175
mythology 6, 127, 164, 170–171, 174, 176–178, 180–181
myths 31–32, 38–39, 50, 169–170, 174–176, 182

N

naming 16, 55–59, 89
Ndakachiravira ndini 123
Ndinochiziva nomunhuhwi wacho 123
Ndakatochibata nemaokoko angu awa 123
Ndinotaura zvandanzwa 123
Ndinotaura zvandawona 123

ndiri kutaura chokwadi changu 122
ndizvo chaizvo 121
Ndlovu-Gatsheni, S.J. 20
negritude 89–90 143
Nguni languages *see* language
njuzu (mermaid) 178, 182
Nkrumah, Kwame 4–5, 17–18, 143
Nyadenga (Possessor of the skies)
nyadzi (shame) 79–80
Nyerere, Julius 5, 17, 43, 143

O

occult 83, 94, 100–101, 105–107, 110, 133, 174
O'Hear, Anthony 68–69
Okere, T. 2, 31–32, 57–58, 114, 116
Okpewho, 169–170
Omoregbe, J. 100–101
ontology 42–43, 69–70, 73–77, 81–82, 85–87, 107–108, 120–124, 128, 140–141, 171–172, 181
onto-triadic being 81
Onyewuenyi, I. 165
orality 33, 36, 38, 110
Oromo 9
Oruka, Odera Henry 12–13, 16, 22, 30
Osuagwu, I.M. 16–18
Outlaw, L. 21–22

P

panopticism 110, 147, 149, 162
paradigms 13, 124, 131–132
paranormal 124, 128
Parker, G.W. 28
particularism 23, 25–26
  see also universalism
personhood 95, 142, 144–145, 147, 149, 159–160
petroglyphs *see* rock art
philosophy
  see also aesthetics, empiricism, epistemology, ethics, hermeneutics
  aesthetics 6, 46, 109, 134, 164–183
  African 5–6, 9–21, 24–35, 40, 46–49, 70, 77, 81, 136, 139–140, 164, 184
  analytic 11, 16, 19, 24–26, 38, 128
  contemporary 1–2, 12–14, 18, 29–30, 35, 62, 100, 102, 170
  continental 11, 25–26, 30
  critical school 16–19
  cultural school 14, 16, 18–19
  ethnophilosophy 10–16, 21–24, 26, 46–47, 116
  indigenous Shona 3–6, 8–47, 68–111, 138–163, 184
  intercultural philosophy 2, 133, 162, 185
  nationalistic 12, 24
  philosophical enquiry 1, 11, 22–23, 117
  political philosophy 17–18, 143
  professional philosophy 12–14, 16–18, 21, 40
  Rwandese 16
  sage philosophy 9, 24, 30–31, 42, 116, 182
  transformative 1, 3, 14, 31, 158, 161, 174, 185
  Western European 14, 21, 24–25, 35, 39, 49, 71, 118, 130, 141–142
pictography 37
Pikirayi, I. 56–57
plurality *see* diversity
poets 27, 38, 168
positivism 70–73, 81, 94, 129, 131
postcoloniality 18–19, 24, 27–28, 30, 47, 58–59, 88–89, 115, 144, 184
postmodernity 26, 39
power 19–20, 55–58, 61, 66–67, 82–84, 93, 103, 106–107, 111, 115, 121–122, 127–128, 176–177, 180, 182
primitive societies 20, 23, 27, 34, 36, 88–89, 100–101, 107
propositions 39, 56, 66, 72, 130–131

proto-writing *see* writing
proverbs 5, 27, 32, 38–47, 108, 133–135, 143–146, 153–157, 160, 173–174
pseudo-science 119
psychology 166

Q

Quine, W.V. 11, 69–70

R

race and racism 29–30, 50, 58, 61, 63
Ramose, M.B. 5, 16–17, 57–58, 76–78, 81, 98, 112–113, 117, 136, 140–141, 158, 162
Randall-MacIver, David 50
Ranger, Terence 51, 60–64, 78, 84, 102, 104–105
rarama somunhu kwete semhuka 144
rationality 1, 15–17, 23–26, 71, 78, 92, 95–97, 112, 119, 127, 135, 159, 162, 165
regulation 66, 90, 105–106, 126, 147–149, 159, 162
reincarnation 124
religions 3, 50, 63, 74, 79–83, 90, 102–103, 109–110, 124, 162, 171, 175, 181–182
Rengger, N.J. 87–88
revealed knowledge 128–129, 132–133
Rhodes, Cecil John 59, 179
Ricoeur, Paul 24, 32
riddles 27, 154
rituals 27, 76, 82, 84–85, 99, 106–107, 126, 168, 170, 176
rock art 37, 169
role reversal 153
ropa (blood) 95–96
rudzi (lineage) 95
rules 6, 22, 37, 90, 103, 138–139, 155–156
ruzivo (knowledge) 120–121

S

sacred 84–85, 126, 158, 171, 174, 177–178, 180–182

sage philosophy *see* philosophy
Samkange, S. and T.M. 8–9, 143–144
science 1, 22–26, 47, 63, 71–73, 94, 98, 100, 106–107, 118–119, 125, 129–133, 165
scientism 11, 46, 141
Schlesinger, G.N. 71
scriptocentric fallacy 27, 33
sculpture 168, 175, 181–182
secrecy 34, 105, 108, 124–127, 152
self-surveillance 148
Senghor, Léopold Sédar 143, 171
senses 71, 75, 122–123, 131, 135, 165, 172
settlers 82
sexuality 107, 149, 162
shame culture 147–150, 162
Shona
   see also philosophy
   aesthetics 6, 164–183
   epistemology 120–124
   expressions, maxims, proverbs 38, 41–43, 45, 91, 97, 141, 144–145, 173
   history 50–56, 84
   indigenous philosophy 2, 5, 8, 10, 27, 32, 59, 66, 143, 160, 184–185
   language 49, 51, 53–55, 59, 64, 81, 97, 110, 134
   metaphysics 6, 69, 74, 78, 85, 91, 107, 109, 127
   morality 6, 96, 138–139, 141, 143–145, 147, 155–157, 159–162
   name/ing 56–59
   uprisings 82
shrines 56, 78, 81, 84–85, 180
Socrates (469–399 BC) 34–35
Sogolo, G.S. 92–93
Sophists 26, 37, 71
sorcery 90, 94, 101–104
   see also witches
souls 95, 98–99, 117
Spear, T. 61, 64–66
spirits and spiritual beings 75–77,

80–85, 90–94, 97–101, 126, 151, 158–159, 176–179, 181–182
suicide 150
Sumner, Claude 9, 42, 45, 154
supernatural 75–76, 83, 92, 101–103, 127, 135, 158, 180, 182
superstition 113, 124, 135
Supreme Being 79–80, 83, 95
symbolism 30, 32, 37, 41, 58, 63, 82, 85, 90, 94, 100, 111, 168–170, 175–182

T

taboos 148, 151, 159
tales 27, 38–39
Tatarkiewicz, W. 166–167
Tempels, Father P. 14, 21, 29, 171
Ter Haar, G. 107, 110
territory *see* land
truth 12, 24, 28–34, 112, 119, 121–122, 129–132, 136–137, 142
  correspondence theory of truth 121, 131
stereotyping 10

U

ubuntu 9, 140–146, 158, 160–161
  see also hunhu
umuntu ngumuntu ngabantu 141
Unesco 2, 5, 7, 13, 64, 184
universality 1, 12–13, 23, 25–27, 40, 53, 101–106, 109, 112–117, 132, 138, 162, 167, 185
  see also particularism
uprising *see* Shona
uroyi (harm) 104
usaona imbwa kuchenama ukati inokusekerera 108

utilitarianism 40, 141

V

vabereki (parents) 154
vadzimu (spirits of the ancestors) 182
vakuru vakati (the elders said) 41–43
value theory 166

Van Binsbergen, W. 28–29, 84
Van Hensbroek, P.B. 1, 116–117
vana (children) 154
vanhu (people) 52, 86, 144
Vansina, J. 59, 66, 83–84
village palaver 34, 150

W

Wa Thiong'o, Ngũgĩ 37
Wanjohi, G.J. 39
Western philosophy *see* philosophy
Wimmer, F.M. 1, 39–40, 117–118
Wiredu, K. 5, 9, 21, 26, 38, 49, 74–78, 80, 95, 122, 131, 138, 140, 145, 160
wisdom 6, 40–43, 46, 48, 74, 120, 127, 135, 138, 162, 170
wise sayings 27, 41
Wokumusoro (the One above) 79–80
worldviews 15, 23, 32, 54–55, 75–76, 86, 90–91, 94, 119, 123, 132, 168, 181
writing 5, 22, 32–33, 35–38, 58–59, 91, 158, 160, 175–176

Y

Yai, O. 46
Yankah, K. 44
Yoruba 9, 14, 96

Z

Zeleza, P.T. 55, 60
Zimbabwe 8, 37, 50, 53–59, 84, 89, 106, 110, 143
  Great Zimbabwe complex 3, 9, 30, 50, 52, 56, 85, 168, 176–181
  Zimbabwe bird 175–182
Zimbabwe Traditional Healers Association 99
zuva igore rinovira rava nemarevo mavi nemauya 108
zvidawo (totems) 82
zvomene 121